IMAGES
of America

THE HISTORIC MANZANITA SPEEDWAY IN PHOENIX

On the Cover: The Super Late Models are lined up in perfect order on the half-mile track as they approach the green flag at the 2008 Winter Super Late Model Championships at Manzanita Speedway in Phoenix, Arizona. (Courtesy of Don Iverson.)

IMAGES
of America

THE HISTORIC MANZANITA SPEEDWAY IN PHOENIX

Larry Upton, Judy McDonald,
and the Stock Car Racing Association

ARCADIA
PUBLISHING

ISBN 978-0-7385-8517-8

Published by Arcadia Publishing
Charleston, South Carolina

Printed in the United States of America

Library of Congress Control Number: 2011940763

For all general information, please contact Arcadia Publishing:
Telephone 843-853-2070
Fax 843-853-0044
E-mail sales@arcadiapublishing.com
For customer service and orders:
Toll-Free 1-888-313-2665

Visit us on the Internet at www.arcadiapublishing.com

This book is dedicated to Don Appley and Phil Hertel, two men whose passion for Manzanita Speedway and its place in Arizona racing culture has proved limitless.

Contents

ACKNOWLEDGMENTS

This book has been made possible through the generosity of two men in particular, James A. Fargo and Don Iverson, both of whom served as official track photographers at Manzanita Speedway and made their collections of photographs available to the authors. Of important note, LaVerne Doyle and Ted Bloomquist were instrumental in providing images and stories that brought the early days of Manzanita Speedway to life.

In addition, we thank Joe Atkinson (president of the Stock Car Racing Association), Margaret and Winston Brown Jr., Linda and Larry Price, Don Costa, Mike Lubanovich, Jane and Justin Upton, Robert Husted, Kenny Gill, Don Appley, Troy Mangano, Shawna Funk, Crystal Hemphill, Katherine Aragon, Mary and Mike McCullough, Stacy Mecl, Danny Pearson, Bobby Erdman, Clay Cady, Phil Hertel, Windy McDonald, Bonnie Stevens, Steve Alford, John Patterson, and Jody Henderson. Finally, we salute the members of the Stock Car Racing Association for their perseverance in promoting stock-car racing in Phoenix for over 42 consecutive years, continuing even beyond the life of Manzanita Speedway. In conclusion, we must recognize the thousands of Manzy race-car drivers who have entertained fans in Phoenix, Arizona, covering a span of 58 years.

Lastly, we salute our editor. Only authors know the value of an editor, and we are especially grateful to our editor, Stacia Bannerman, for her cheerful and constant encouragement, which moved the project to a successful conclusion.

Several titles are used frequently throughout this book. For easier reading, the following abbreviations have been substituted for the Arizona Jalopy Racing Association (AJRA), Stock Car Racing Association (SCRA), United States Auto Club (USAC), and Manzanita Speedway (Manzy).

INTRODUCTION

Swilling's Mill, founded in 1868, was located in the northern reaches of the Sonoran Desert near the Salt River in Central Arizona. The tiny settlement had little going for it other than the irrigation canals left behind by the ancient Hohokam people, who had vanished after 1,000 years of civilization in the area, most likely because of periodic droughts and floods.

Shortly after its founding, Swilling's Mill changed its name to Phoenix in recognition of its rise from the ruins of the Hohokam civilization. Nestled in a broad valley surrounded by craggy mountains, the valley was ideal for farming, with the help of the remains of the Hohokam irrigation system. Although farming was the foundation of the local economy, Phoenix leadership has always found ways to promote the community. After some years of boosting by the early settlers, the area eventually became known for the five Cs: cattle, cotton, citrus, copper, and climate.

World War II changed the face and character of Phoenix, as military bases popped up here and in other parts of Arizona. This exposure led to the migration of thousands of new inhabitants after the war, especially with the introduction of the evaporative cooler and air conditioning. Nevertheless, in 1951, Phoenix remained a small farming and cow town, far from its position today as the sixth largest city in the United States and a sports mecca that features the Phoenix Suns, Phoenix Mercury, Arizona Cardinals, Arizona Diamondbacks, Phoenix Coyotes, and NASCAR's Phoenix International Raceway. Professional baseball continues to expand its spring-training operation in Phoenix with the Cactus League, which now boasts 15 teams.

Long before the stick-and-ball sports took center stage in Phoenix, racing, the most ancient of sports, dominated the scene. Automobile racing made its debut at the Arizona State Fairgrounds in 1909, which became the center of the racing world in Phoenix for many years. Later, small dirt racetracks emerged all over Phoenix to accommodate the growing popularity of the sport: South Mountain Speedway, near the entrance to South Mountain Park; Jordan Speedway at Sixteenth Street and Camelback Road; Riverside Park Speedway, which included a popular swimming pool and dance hall, located at Central Avenue just north of the Salt River; Disabled American Veterans Speedway at Sixteenth Street and Camelback Road; Roosevelt Field at Seventeenth Avenue and Roosevelt; Phoenix Midget Speedway at Seventeenth Avenue and Garfield Street; and Phoenix Speedway at Sixty-second Street and Thomas Road. There may have been more.

In the early days of stock-car racing after World War II, the dirt tracks that popped up across America were humble affairs without the fancy trimmings of today's elaborate stock-car venues. The tracks in Phoenix were no exception, consisting primarily of a quarter-, third- or half-mile circle track scratched out of the desert, a water truck, wooden-plank grandstands, and a promoter.

Manzanita Park was a dog racetrack located at Thirty-fifth Avenue and Broadway Road, operated by Rudy Everett and Lawrence Meskimen. Financial results of racing dogs had not met expectations, so they were open to the entreaty of Jack Holloway, the president of the AJRA, when he approached the two partners about creating a permanent home for stock-car racers. The truth was, however, that the stock-car drivers, who had been racing at South Mountain

Speedway, had a couple of beefs with that track's promoter. One, the drivers had their own secret people-counters and believed that the promoter was shorting them on their percentage of the front gate by under-reporting attendance, and two, the drivers were put out with the special treatment accorded Art Bisch, South Mountain's big draw, who later became a big-time racer in the most famous motorsports event in the United States, the Indianapolis 500. Once Everett and Meskimen were convinced that there was money in stock-car racing, Holloway further set the hook by prevailing upon the drivers, particularly several men who worked for Arizona Sand & Rock Co., to pitch in with labor and equipment and help Everett and Meskimen convert the dog operation to a quarter-mile oval track. Ted Bloomquist, a young up-and-coming driver at the time, gave the credit to Holloway, saying that "without the leadership of Jack Holloway, a Hollywood stuntman, there would never have been a Manzanita Speedway."

Finally, on the hot night of August 25, 1951, Everett and Meskimen opened the revamped Manzanita Park as a quarter-mile jalopy track in front of a raucous, standing-room-only crowd of 3,923 fans. The two partners had found the mystical Lost Dutchman Gold Mine; only it was not in the Superstition Mountains—it was located at Thirty-fifth Avenue and Broadway Road in Phoenix! Manzanita was on its way to dominating stock-car racing in Arizona.

That first night, Roe Mounts raced himself and his 1933 Ford coupe into the Arizona record books by winning the first feature race at Manzanita Park. It is said that Mounts never won another race in his career. The first championship of 1951 was won by Avery Doyle, who, in typical stock-car fashion, was handy with both the wheel and his fists. Beginning in 1952, Doyle had a running feud with fellow driver Pete Haumont, finally leading to his temporary suspension from the track. The next week Doyle raced at South Mountain Speedway, exchanged blows with Art Bisch, a track favorite, and was suspended from that track. Wimps do not race, and in the early days, drivers enforced their own laws. If someone tangled with a driver, the driver tended to hit back; that principle still exists today.

Over its 58-year history, Manzy has been under the control of only a few men beginning with Rudy Everett and Lawrence Meskimen. Keith Hall, who bought the track in 1965, had the biggest influence in the rise of Manzy from its modest beginnings to its transformation into one of the top dirt tracks in the United States. In 2004, Joe and Millie Kimbro of California assumed ownership of the track, selling it to Mel Martin of Phoenix in 2007. After Martin reportedly invested over $300,000 into improving the track, he sold it in 2009 to Southwest Industrial Rigging of Phoenix, which closed the track on April 12, 2009, demolished the racing facilities, and converted it to a storage area for heavy industrial and construction equipment. Prior to its closing, Manzanita Speedway was the longest-operating sports venue in Arizona.

Track announcers have played a major role in Manzy's success beginning with Bill Close in the inaugural season of 1951. Close was an announcer with KOY radio in Phoenix, later becoming an anchorman with KOOL TV for many years. In 1957, Manzy corralled its most famous announcer, "Windy" McDonald, a young 23-year-old from Madill, Oklahoma. McDonald did not stop talking until the track closed in 2009, and finished up his Manzy career with a three-volume history of racing in Arizona.

KPHO TV televised the first stock-car race in Arizona from Manzanita Park on December 21, 1952, which was won by Bill Cheesbourg, who went on to race in the Indianapolis 500. Not to be outdone, the Powder Puff female racers shared the television spotlight, with Vernie Haumont taking top honors.

In 1954, Everett and Meskimen added a half-mile track to their facility, leaving the jalopy cars on the short track while the faster, modified stock cars moved to the larger track. The addition of the faster track and cars eventually led to periodic visits from NASCAR's Grand National stock cars. NASCAR made its debut on Manzy's half-mile track on August 10, 1963.

The Phoenix-racing world changed when Manzanita Park opened on March 11, 1966 as Manzanita Speedway, under the ownership of Keith Hall, a young, aggressive promoter and former sprint-car driver. Hall invested heavily in the track; some say he paid more than its real value, adding a new press box, concessions, a paved concourse, and additional grandstands. Ultimately, Hall increased the racing divisions from three at the time of his purchase to nine. Hall's showman antics drew top racing talent from all over the country, with such drivers as Bill Cheesbourg, Parnelli Jones, Roger McCluskey, Mario Andretti, Gary Bettenhausen, and Al Unser Jr., who, at age 14, was so small in stature that he used telephone books as a booster seat. Also, the legend, A.J. Foyt, raced at Manzy one time; of course, he won the race. Hall's promotional skills helped pave the way for numerous Manzy drivers to rise to the national spotlight in racing, the most recent being NASCAR's J.J. Yeley.

Perhaps Hall's most successful promotion was his creation of the Western United States Championships in October 1968. This was a three-day event with an unheard of $10,000 purse, drawing 86 sprint-car drivers from all over the country. Later, Hall changed the name of the race to the Western World Championships, which joined the Knoxville Nationals in Iowa and the Pacific Coast at Ascot Park in California as one of the jewels in the sprint-car world's "Triple Crown." The national sprint-car champion was crowned at the last race of the season in November of each year at Manzanita Speedway.

Associations of race-car drivers come and go, often lasting as long as a snowflake in the desert. Anyone who has been around the sport knows that race-car drivers are an independent, sometimes ornery lot; Bobby Taylor, a SCRA Hall-of-Famer stock-car driver, explained their temperament best when he said "Race-car drivers don't have any friends," the result being that their racing organizations generally fall apart over innumerable disputes about how to run things. Manzy, however, spawned one exception: the Stock Car Racing Association, which was founded in 1969 and still exists to this day. It is featured in chapter four of this book.

So, finally, here we are. Manzanita Speedway is a ghost. There is no sign, absolutely nothing to indicate that the "world ended" for thousands of race fans and drivers on April 12, 2009, when, for the last time, the fire and thunder of race cars rumbled across Manzanita Speedway's 33 acres. The spirit was siphoned from these fans and drivers, like a last drop of gas from a dry engine. Manzy's fans and drivers are now the "walking dead." Another era in Phoenix's history is gone. Mel Martin, who appeared to be the savior of Manzanita Speedway when he bought it in 2007, is now a pariah, as many fans and drivers feel themselves betrayed by the sale of the track to an outside commercial enterprise. The anger and frustration has been so intense that the Arizona Motorsports Hall of Fame has expelled Martin from its ranks and demanded his induction plaque be returned. From the perspective of those closest to the action at Manzy, this is a fire that will not go out until this generation of fans and drivers goes the way of historic Manzanita Speedway.

One

THE EARLY YEARS

There was real concern on the part of Rudy Everett and Larry Meskimen of Manzanita Park and their rival, Dr. Vaughn McGuire of South Mountain Speedway, about Phoenix's capacity to support competing jalopy-racing cards as Manzanita Park approached its opening on August 25, 1951. South Mountain Speedway, the older circuit, had typically drawn crowds exceeding 4,000 on Saturday nights during the racing season. The question was, would either track make money by competing against one another and splitting the gate? As it turned out, everyone was happy, as McGuire's South Mountain track drew 4,500 fans to watch Bill Cheesbourg and Art Bisch dominate the night's events. There were signs of trouble, however, in spite of the large crowd: only 35 jalopies competed, while Manzanita Park drew a car count of 52. The loss of the Arizona Jalopy Racing Association and its drivers would, in time, spell the doom of South Mountain Speedway.

At the same time, Manzanita Park was opening to a standing-room-only crowd of 3,923. Admission was $1 for adults and 50¢ for children. In the next day's *Arizona Republic* newspaper, the promoters were promising to eliminate the delays of their first venture and make better preparations to handle the unexpectedly large crowd. At the end, 58 years later, the promoters were still working on the project.

In the words of Ted Bloomquist, a 19-year-old hot-shoe who raced his 1934 Ford that first night: "Everything was a blur to me. All I remember is that it was hot; I won my heat race, but cracked up in the main event and did not finish. I don't even remember the crowd." By the second week, the promoters had added a special event with Jack Holloway, president of the AJRA and Hollywood stuntman, riding the hood of a car racing through a wall of fire. By the third week, the best clay in Arizona had been added to the track, creating a faster racing surface. After three weeks of operations, Everett and Meskimen were advertising in the *Arizona Republic* that their track was "the fastest 1/4-mile track in Arizona and easy to get to—no traffic problems." That was before Phoenix became the sixth largest city in the United States. At the end, Manzanita Speedway sat isolated on a 33-acre county island, surrounded by the continually encroaching suburbs of Phoenix.

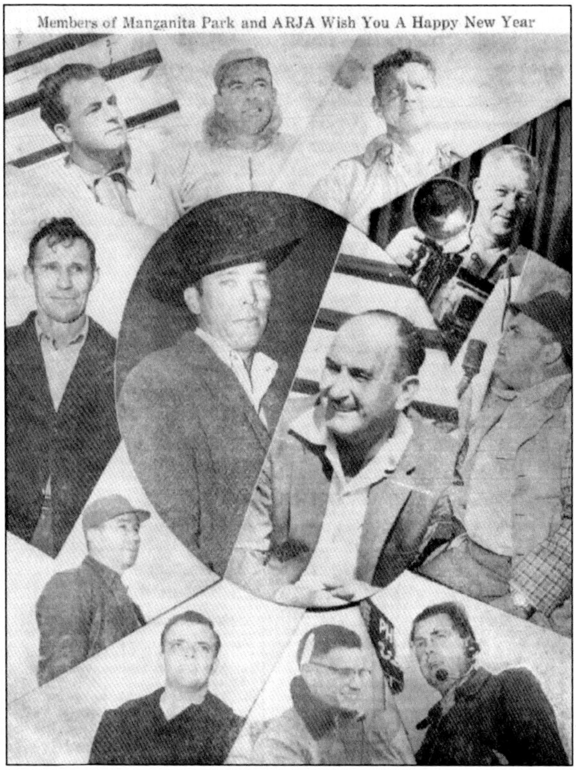

This collage from an early racing program shows, clockwise from top left, George Husky, general manager; Karl Connolly, first vice president of the AJRA; Curley Milner, secretary-treasurer of the AJRA; Andy McGahee, photographer; Tuck Vinson, announcer; Jim Day, pit steward; Bob Brooks, timer; Dick Moseley, flagman; Joe Bailey, second vice president of the AJRA; and Lawrence Meskimen, co-owner. Pictured in the center are Larry Miller, president of the AJRA (left), and R.C. Rudy Everett, co-owner. (Courtesy of LaVerne Doyle.)

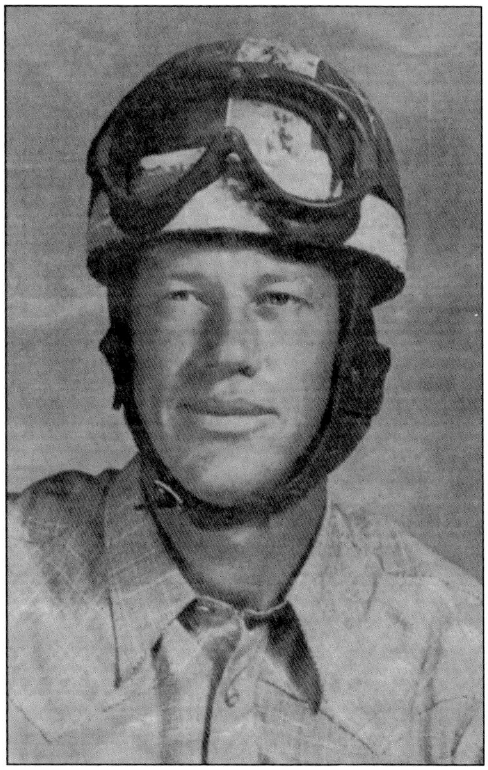

Jack Holloway, president of the AJRA in 1951, has been credited by many people with being the catalyst that led to the creation of Manzanita Park, later Manzanita Speedway. He was also a stuntman who did all kinds of dangerous stunts, such as blowing up his car with dynamite and standing on the hood of a car as it raced through a wall of fire, to build Manzy's attendance. (Courtesy of LaVerne Doyle.)

Avery Doyle, in the police officer's hat, banters with a real Phoenix police officer, who is wearing Doyle's racing helmet. Doyle, along with Gene Gunn, a friend and fellow racer, worked with Jack Holloway in convincing Rudy Everett and Larry Meskimen to reopen their defunct dog track as a quarter-mile dirt oval and home to the AJRA. (Courtesy of LaVerne Doyle.)

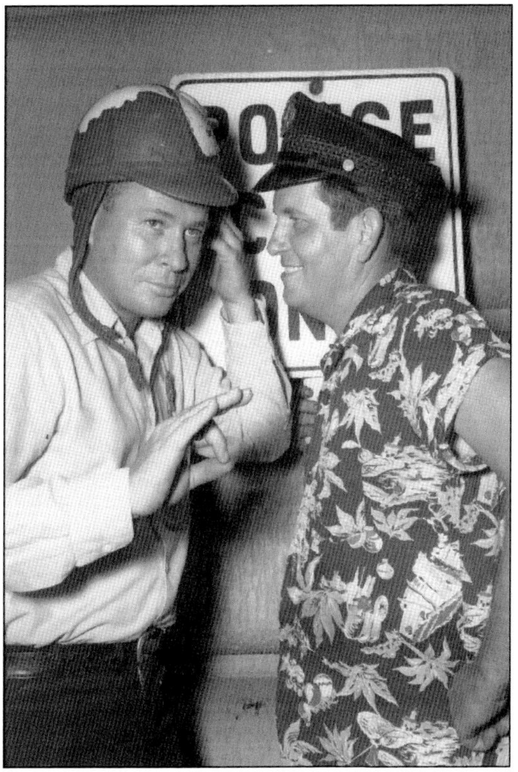

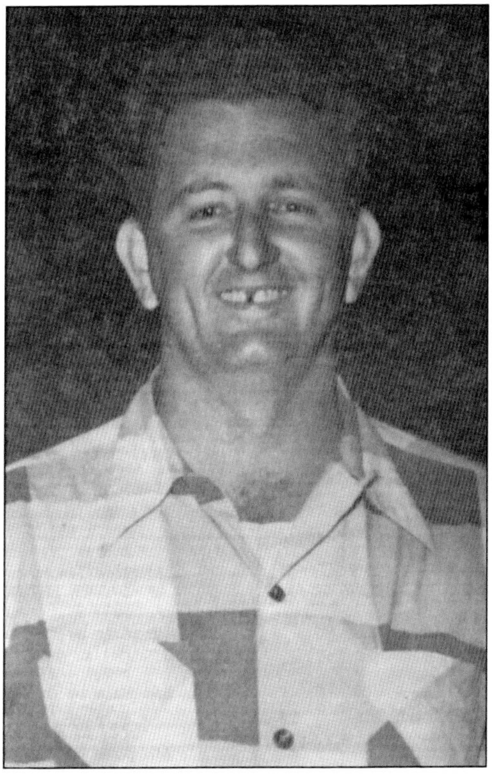

Gene Gunn, one of the men credited with convincing Rudy Everett and Larry Meskimen to convert their dog track to a jalopy track, was 26 years old in 1951 and had been racing jalopies since 1946. In addition, he was a top roadster racer and held several records throughout Arizona. (Courtesy of LaVerne Doyle.)

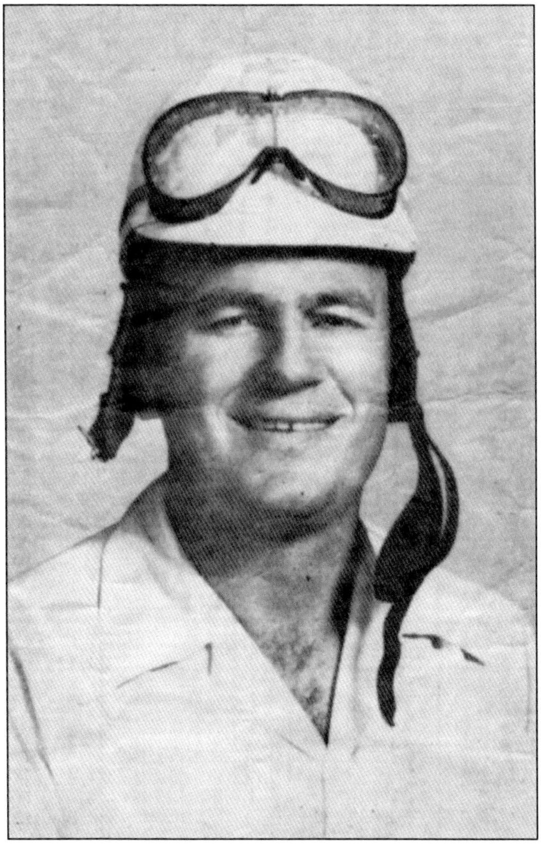

Romaine Dwight Mounts Sr., also known as Roe Mounts, raced his No. 38 jalopy, a 1933 Ford, into history on August 25, 1951, by winning the first main event ever run at Manzanita Park in front of an overflow crowd of 3,923 fans. According to legend, this was the only main event win of Mounts's career. The *Arizona Republic* reported that 48 of the 52 cars did not finish the race as the track's dirt surface broke up. Below are the remains of Mounts's No. 38 jalopy, junked out and abandoned in an alley. Don Appley found the old car, recognized its historical value, and took this photograph. (Left, courtesy of LaVerne Doyle; below, courtesy of Don Appley.)

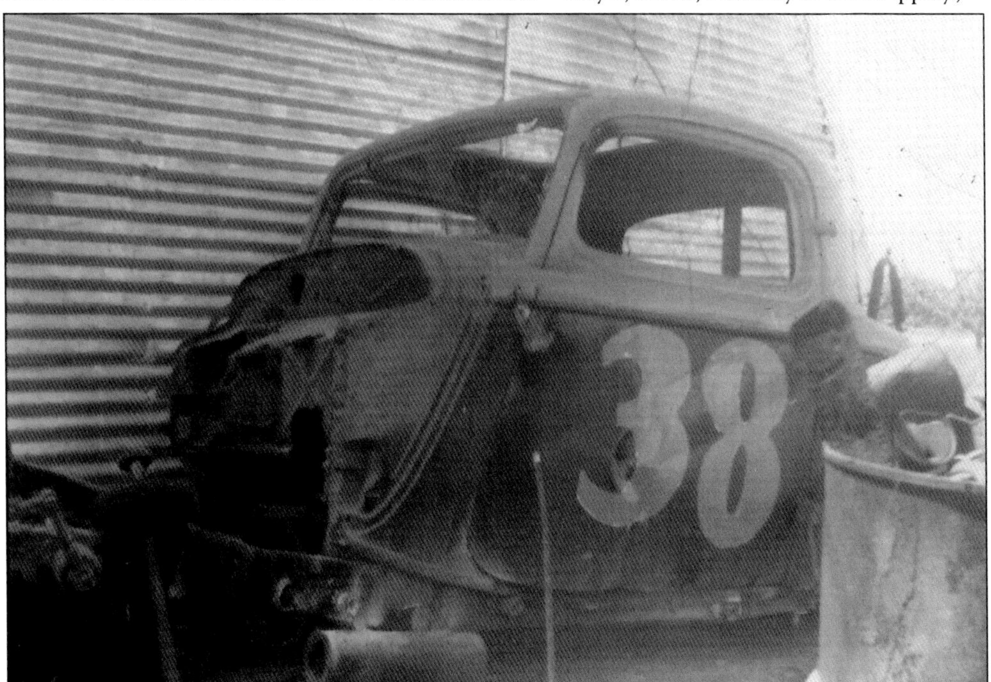

This is a 1951 racing program for Manzanita Park featuring Bill Close on the cover. Close was the sports editor for KOY radio in Phoenix and had been hired in November 1951 as the track announcer. Later, Close moved to KOOL TV in Phoenix, where he was the anchor for the evening news for many years, becoming a fixture in local television. (Courtesy of LaVerne Doyle.)

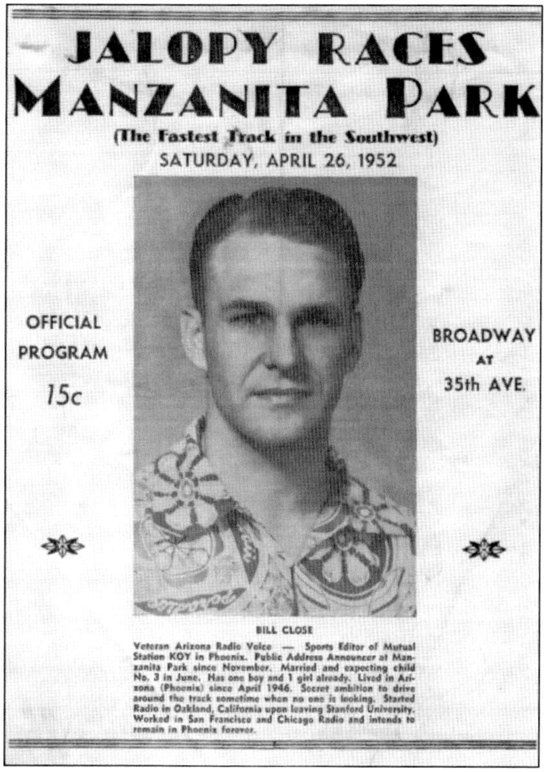

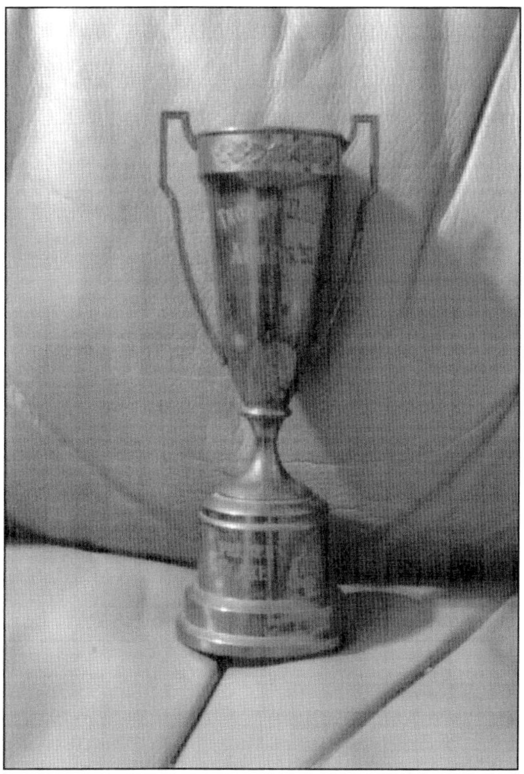

This was the first trophy ever awarded at Manzanita Park. Avery Doyle won the trophy dash and received the small cup, which has the following inscription: "Trophy Dash 8/25/51 Presented by Blakely Oil." (Courtesy of LaVerne Doyle.)

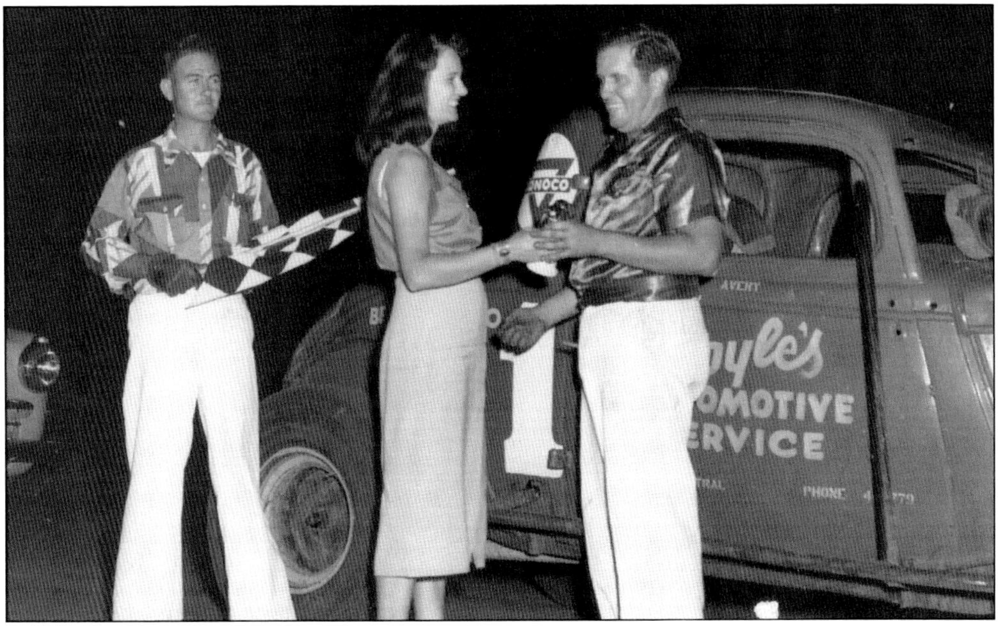

Avery Doyle, seen receiving the winner's trophy, was the champion of the inaugural 1951 season. During his run to the top of the standings that year, Doyle won 18 main events and 16 trophy dashes. In addition, although they did not count in the standings, he won one main event at South Mountain Speedway and one win on the one-mile track at the Arizona State Fairgrounds. (Courtesy of LaVerne Doyle.)

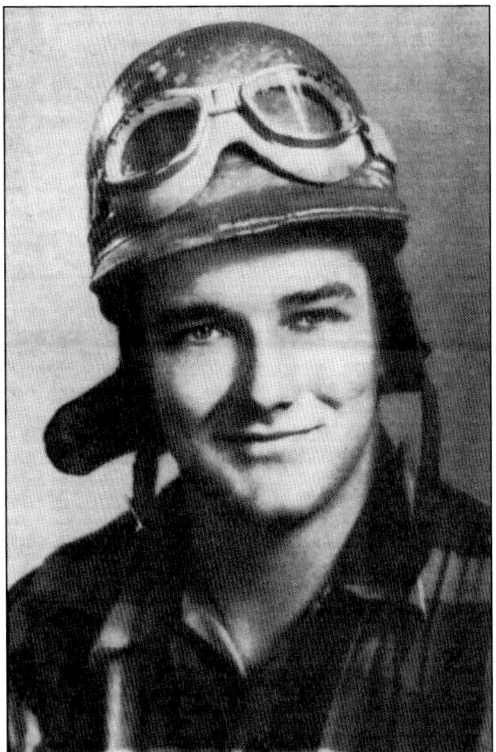

Don Davis began racing at Manzanita Park at age 18 in 1951. He won the AJRA Championship in 1953 and captured the California Racing Association title in 1960, which led to a ride in the Indianapolis 500 in 1961. In 1962, he finished fourth. Davis's amazing career ended later that year on August 8, 1962, when he died in a sprint-car crash at New Bremen, Ohio. (Courtesy of LaVerne Doyle.)

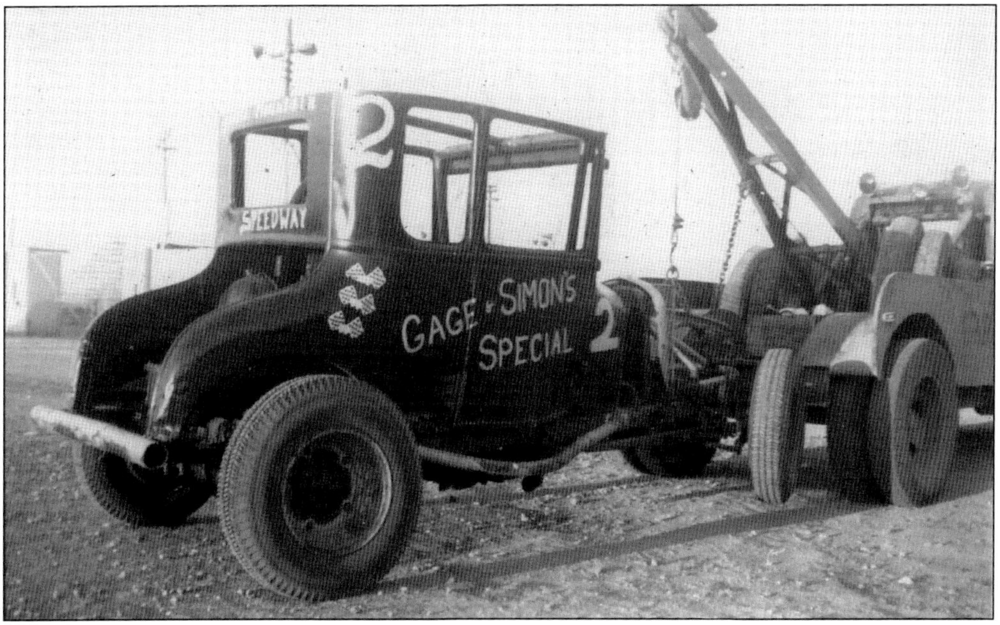

Shown above is car No. 2, the jalopy driven by Art Bisch, the track favorite at South Mountain Speedway, whose special status led the AJRA to petition the owners of Manzanita Park to convert the defunct dog track to a jalopy track. Below, Bisch sits in his No. 2 midget Pittman race car. Bisch could race any type of car, qualifying for his first Indianapolis 500 on Memorial Day 1958. A little over a month later, on July 4, 1958, Bisch was killed in a crash at Lakewood Speedway in Atlanta. Bisch was enshrined in the Arizona Motorsports Hall of Fame in 1987. (Both, courtesy of Don Appley.)

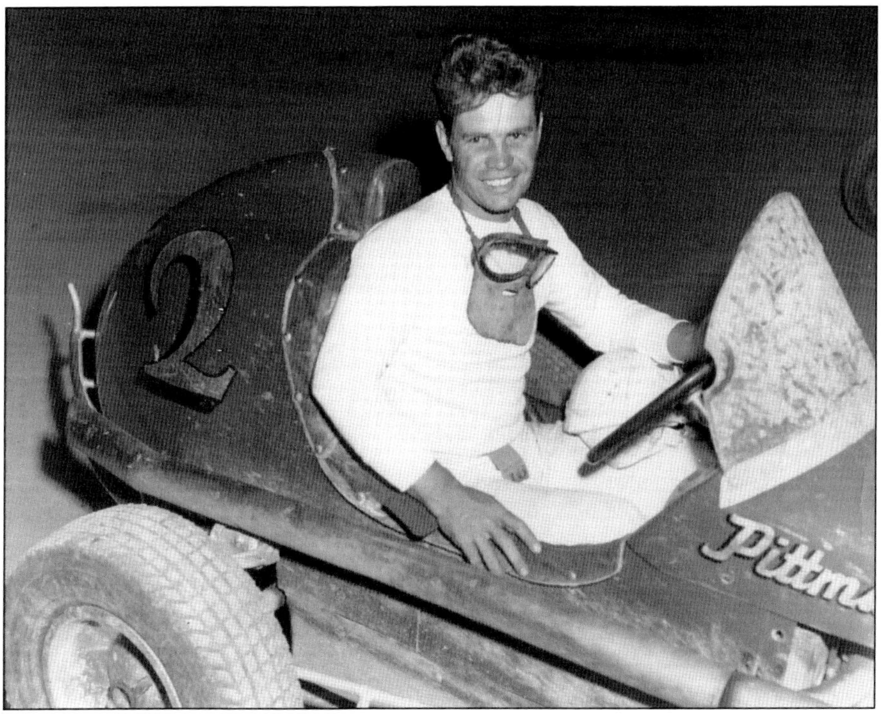

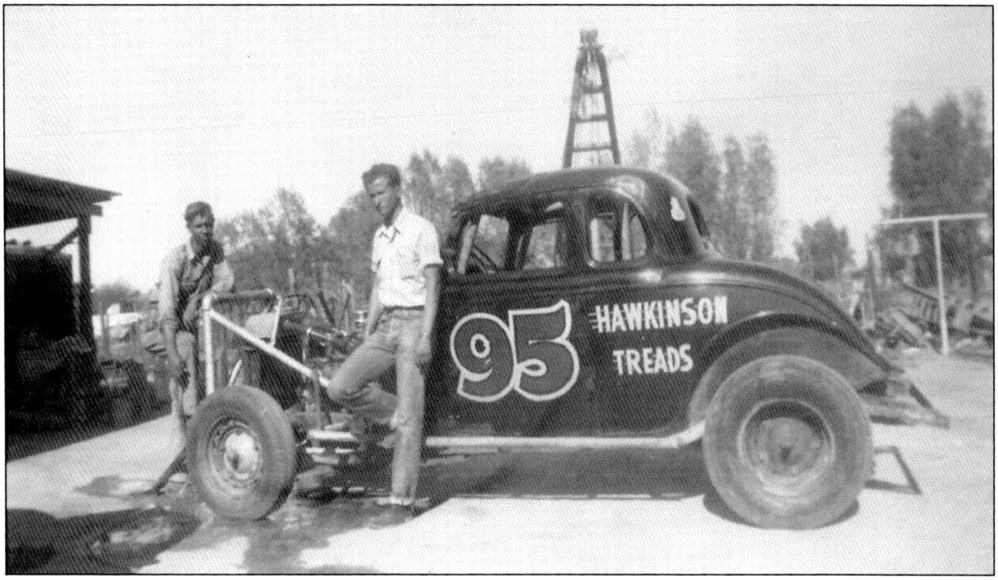

On the left stands Ted Bloomquist with pit crewman Billy Bonds and No. 95, a 1934 Ford powered by a 1948 Ford flathead V8 engine. According to Bloomquist, "Cars had to appear stock, but anything under the hood was okay, but cheating was the name of the game!" (Courtesy of Ted Bloomquist.)

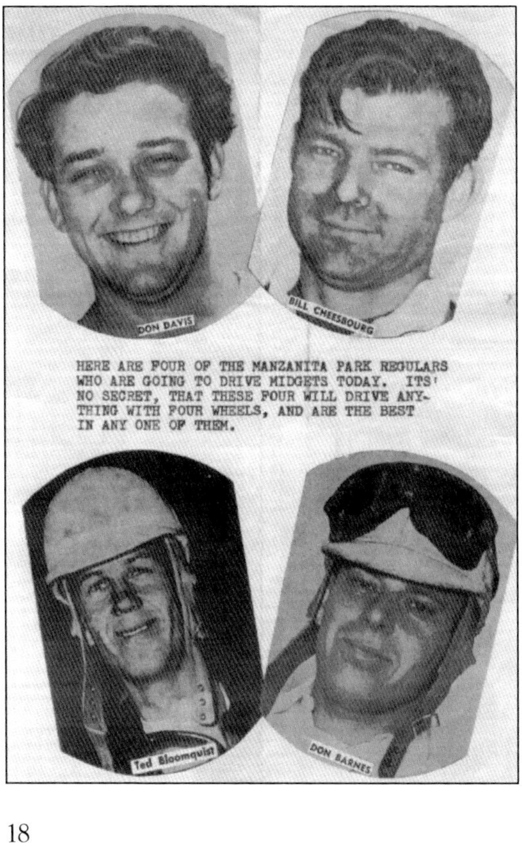

Pictured clockwise from top left are Don Davis, Bill Cheesbourg, Don Barnes, and Ted Bloomquist in an early Manzanita Park program announcing their appearance in a midget race. All four of these men were top competitors in the jalopy ranks. Bloomquist once said of Cheesbourg, "He was a full-time racer and hard to beat, and he would not hesitate to put you in the wall to win." (Courtesy of Ted Bloomquist.)

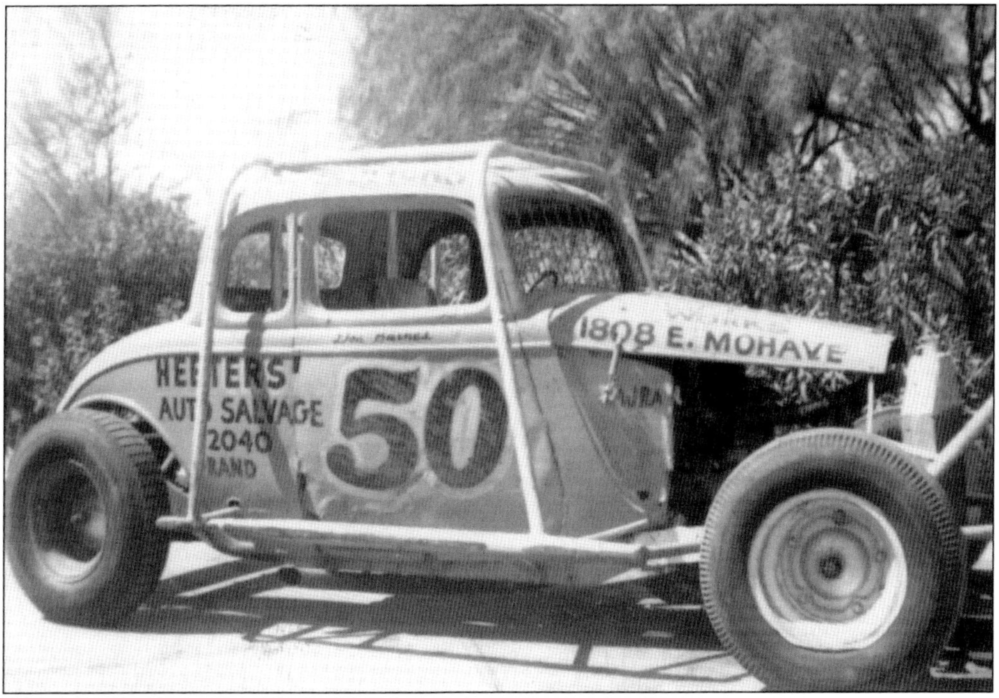

Above is the jalopy driven by Don Barnes, who began racing at Manzanita Park in 1951 at age 23. He was an employee of the Santa Fe Railroad. Arizona native Duke Billie, who was 20 years old when Manzanita Park opened in 1951, is shown below. Both Barnes and Billie were top jalopy drivers in Manzanita Park's early years. (Both, courtesy of Don Appley.)

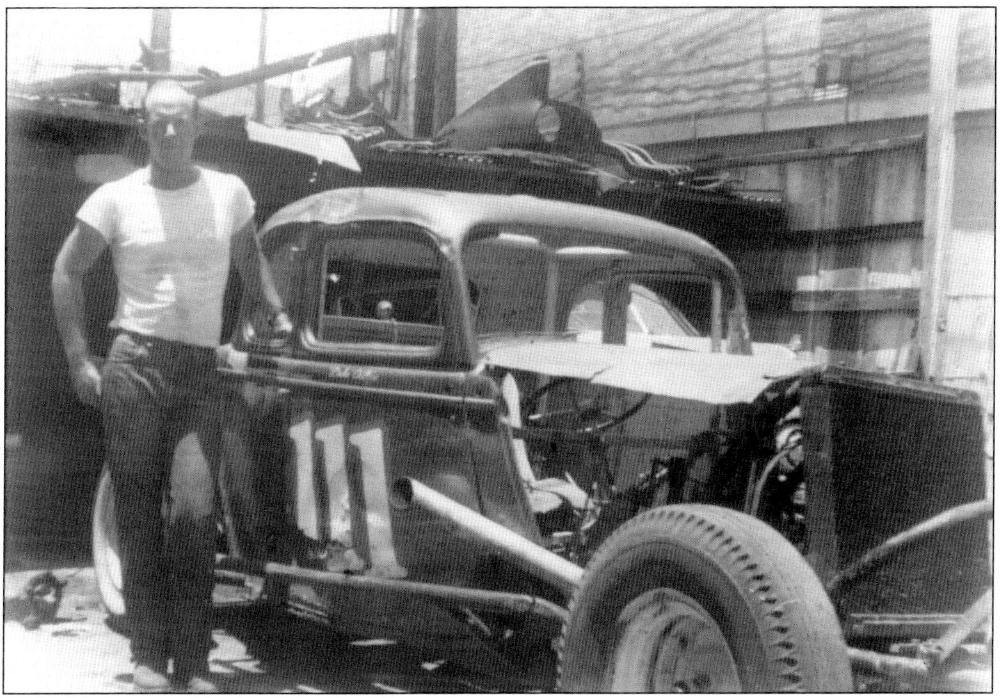

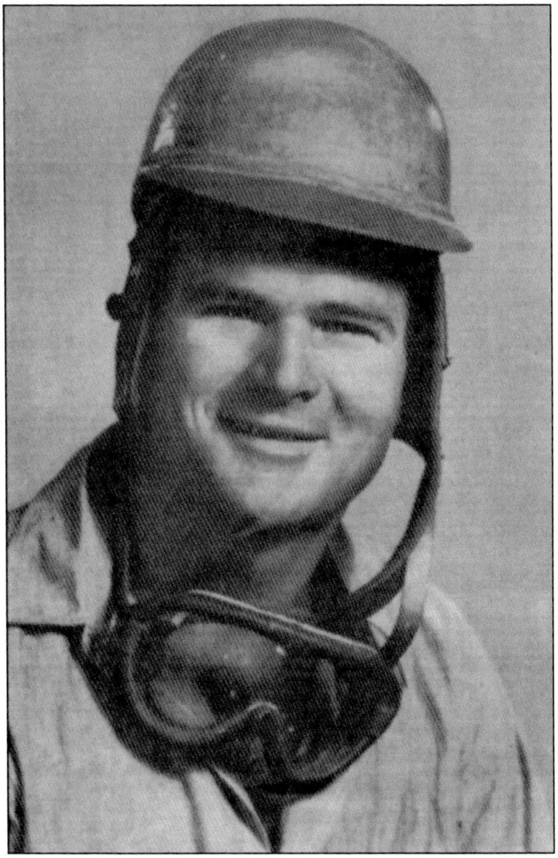

At left is Roy Creach, a hotshot motorcycle rider and jalopy driver who won the 1952 AJRA Championship. It was Creach's motorcycle racing and stunt skills that landed him a position as a Maricopa County deputy sheriff in the motorcycle division in 1953, which ended his racing career. Creach told the *Payson Roundup* in a 1999 interview that the sheriff thought "it was OK to get shot, but they didn't want me to get hurt racing." Below is the jalopy he drove to victory lane. (Left, courtesy of LaVerne Doyle; below, courtesy of Don Appley.)

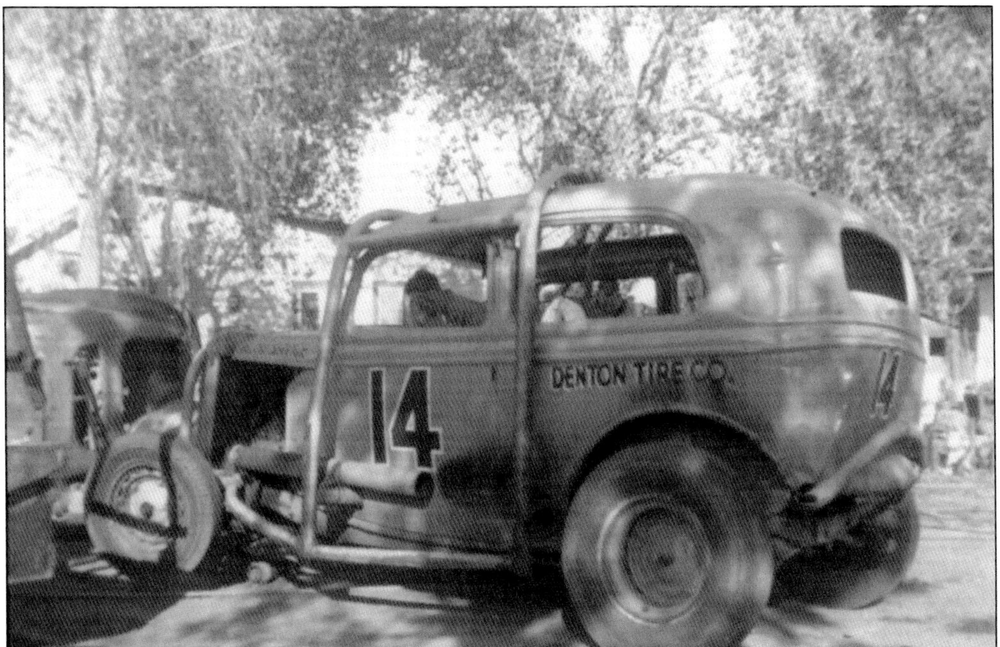

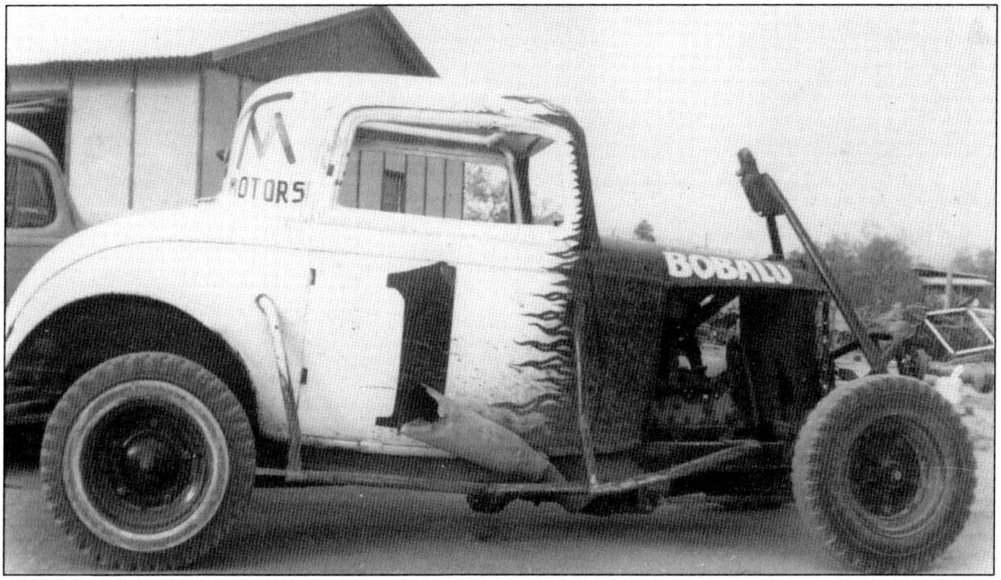

This is Bill Cheesbourg's jalopy, which he named "Bobalu." Cheesbourg was from Tucson but raced at South Mountain Speedway through 1951. When Cheesbourg began racing at Manzy in 1952, the local pilots began a campaign to "Stop Bill Cheesbourg." He capped his career with six runs at the Indianapolis 500 and three Grand Prix's. Cheesbourg was an inductee into both the Arizona Motorsports Hall of Fame and the Pima County Sports Hall of Fame. (Courtesy of Don Appley.)

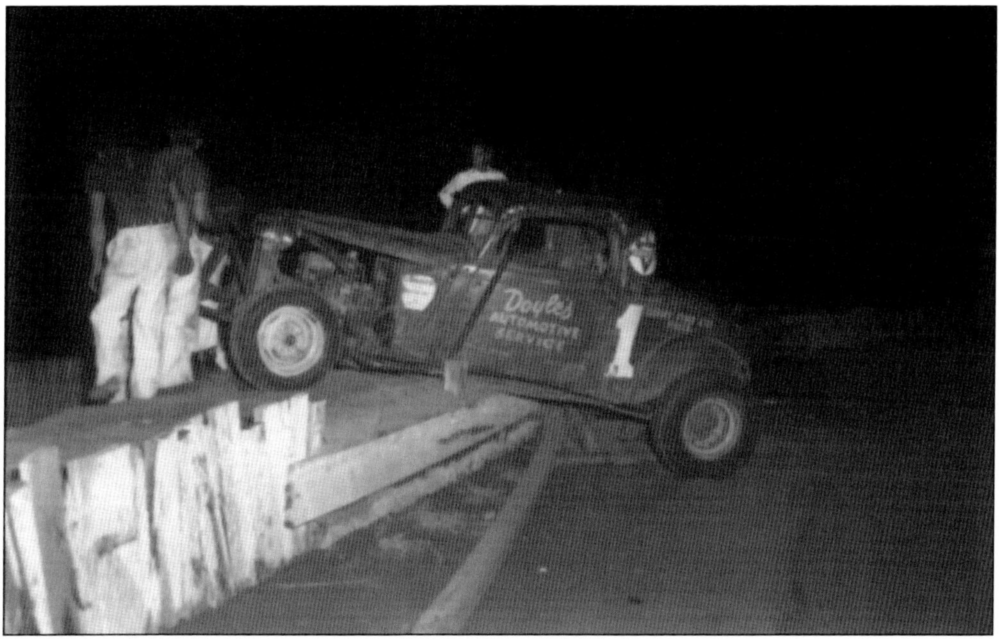

The winner of an AJRA championship was entitled to use No. 1 in the year following a championship. Avery Doyle did not fare well in 1952 with No. 1 on his car. Not only did Doyle have trouble with his car, he was also suspended for two weeks, which almost guarantees that a driver will not win the championship. He anxiously returned No. 35 to his car the following year. (Courtesy of LaVerne Doyle.)

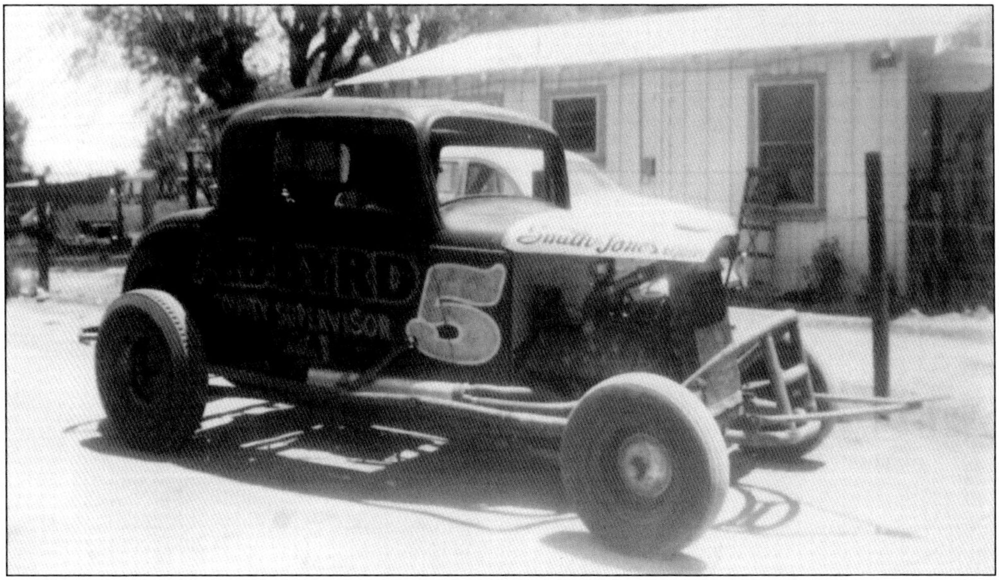

This A.B. Byrd 1932 Ford coupe was powered by a bored and stroked Ford flathead V8. It was owned and driven by Ted Bloomquist. During an early 1952 race, Bloomquist was the fastest qualifier, won the trophy dash, a heat race, and the main event. He won a total of $35 but had to pay $3 for his pit pass. Below is the same 1932 Ford coupe, which has been renumbered as No. 15 to celebrate the first flight of the supersonic X-15 experimental aircraft. (Both, courtesy of Ted Bloomquist.)

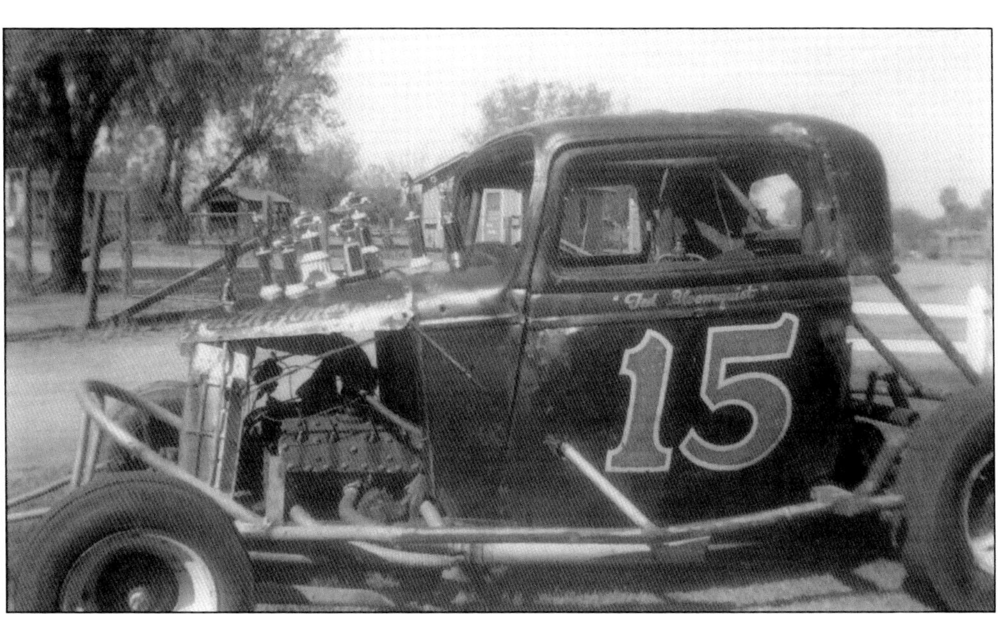

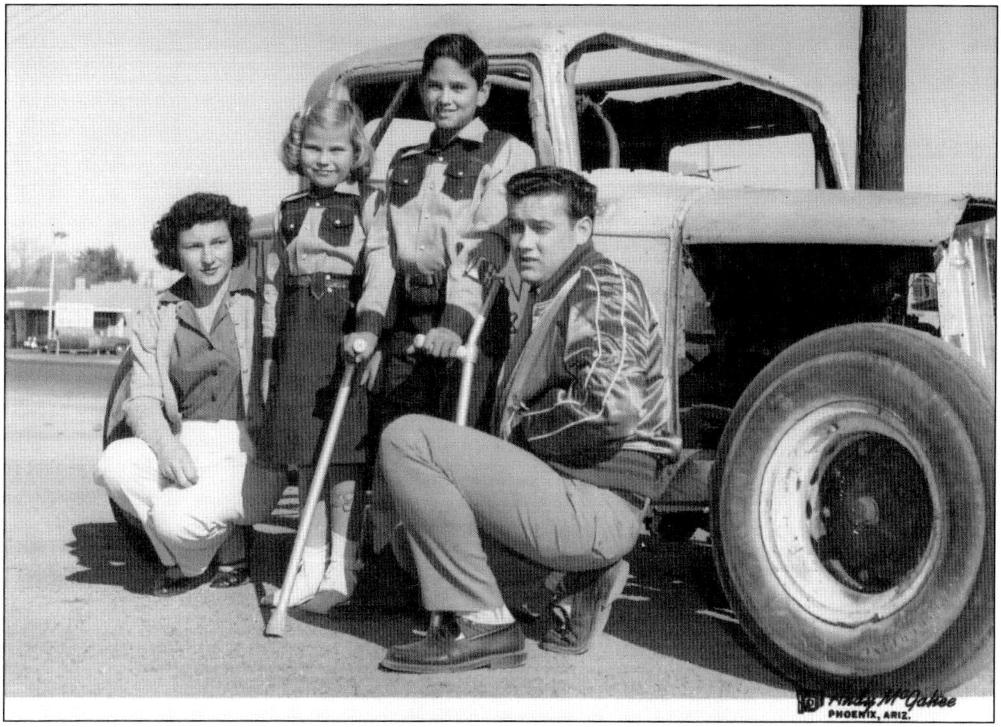

The promoter and AJRA were heavily involved in the Phoenix community. Obviously, there was an angle to be played that included drawing fans to the track, but the track and drivers made a solid contribution to various community organizations. The above photograph shows, from left to right, Powder Puff racer LaVerne Doyle, two unidentified youngsters representing the March of Dimes, and Manzanita hotshot Donnie Davis. The 1952 photograph below shows the defending champion's jalopy, No. 1, surrounded by members of the Phoenix Police Department. Avery Doyle, the champ, stands in the middle behind the car wearing the Hawaiian shirt. (Both, courtesy of LaVerne Doyle.)

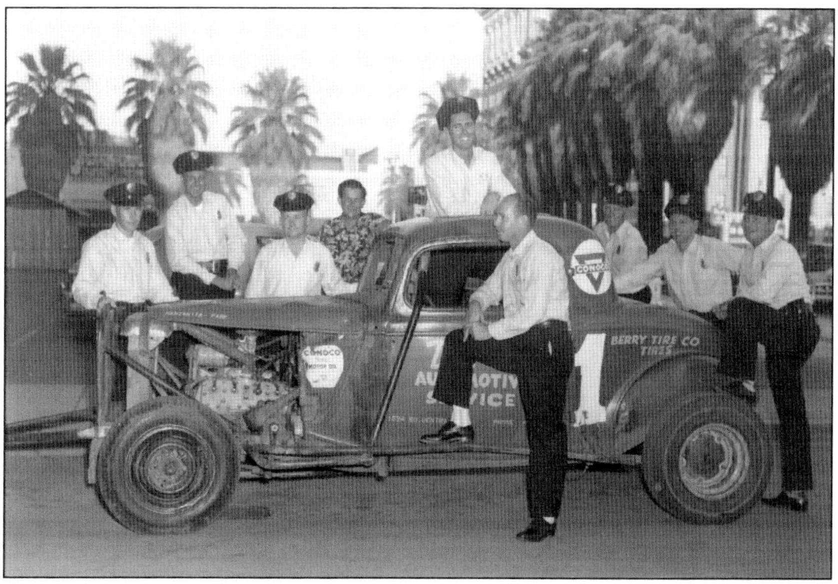

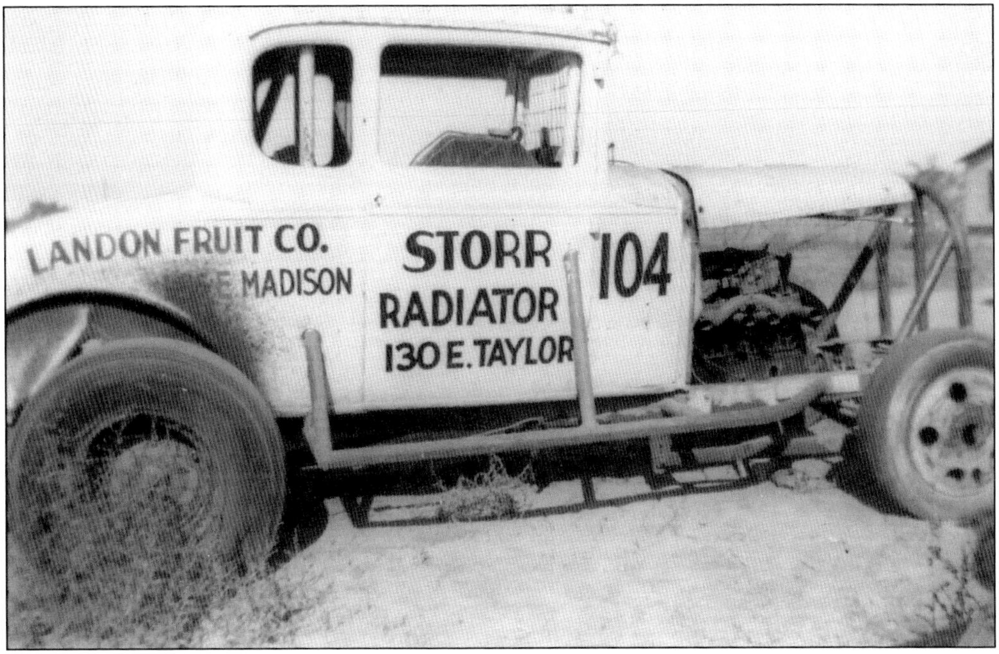

Above is No. 104, a jalopy driven by several drivers, including Bob Buchan and his wife, Norma. Storrs Radiator was located at 130 East Taylor Street in Phoenix, property now occupied by an Arizona State University dormitory. Below is the jalopy owned by Leonard Davenport and driven by Clem McCorkle. (Both, courtesy of Don Appley.)

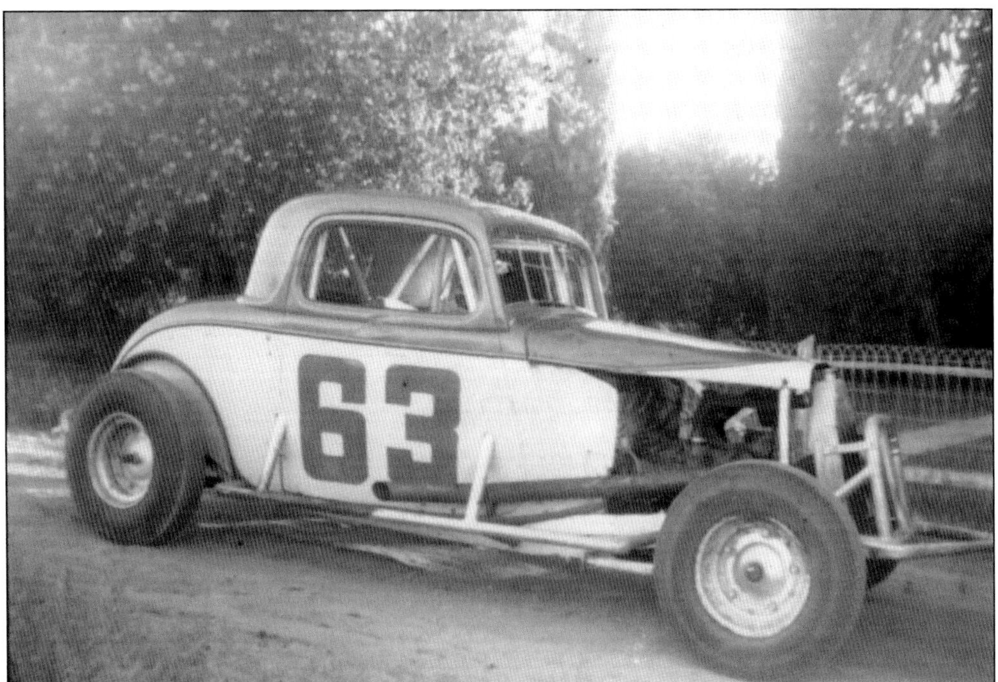

Pierre Henry Haumont, known as Pete, raced at Manzanita Park starting on opening day, driving No. 82. Haumont's most famous incident occurred in 1952 when he and Avery Doyle tangled on the track. Doyle was standing next to his disabled car when Pete charged up and gave Doyle a shove. According to LaVerne Doyle, "Well, Avery wasn't going to stand for that," so Doyle, the defending champion, ended up suspended by the AJRA. (Courtesy of LaVerne Doyle.)

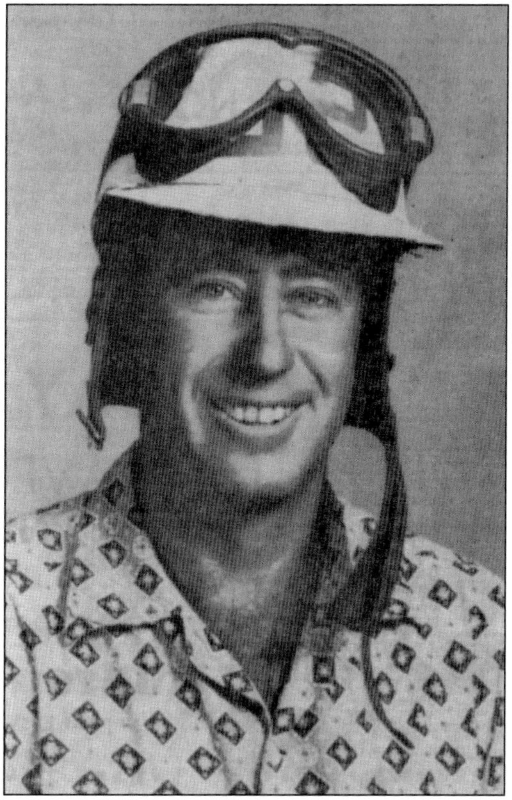

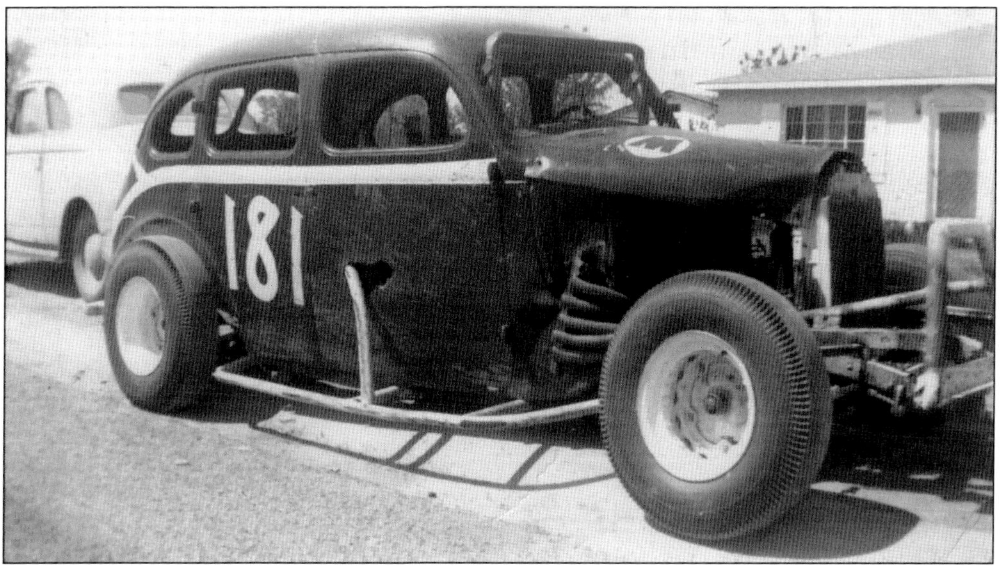

No. 181 is a 1938 Plymouth sedan with a Chrysler six-cylinder engine modified with a racing cam, pistons, and DeSoto crankshaft. The car was co-owned by former Phoenix Union High School buddies John Lamb and Don Bratt. Although Lamb and Bratt took turns driving the car, publicly, the driver was Bratt. This was because Lamb was married, and his wife had laid down the law, saying "choose me or choose the car!" She always believed that Lamb was the pit man. (Courtesy of Don Appley.)

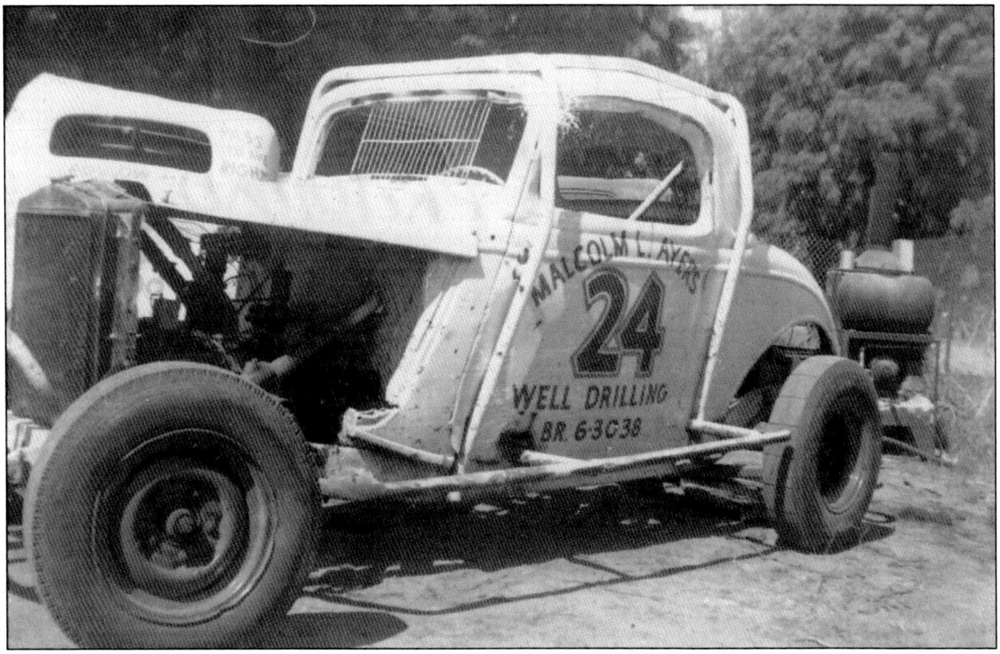

This jalopy was raced in 1951–1952 by Steve Pritchard, the first driver killed in action at Manzanita Park on July 28, 1956. Pritchard had won the race and slowed to take the checkered flag. The second-place car roared past the finish line at top speed, clipping the back of Pritchard's car and causing him to roll over just beyond the finish line. (Courtesy of Don Appley.)

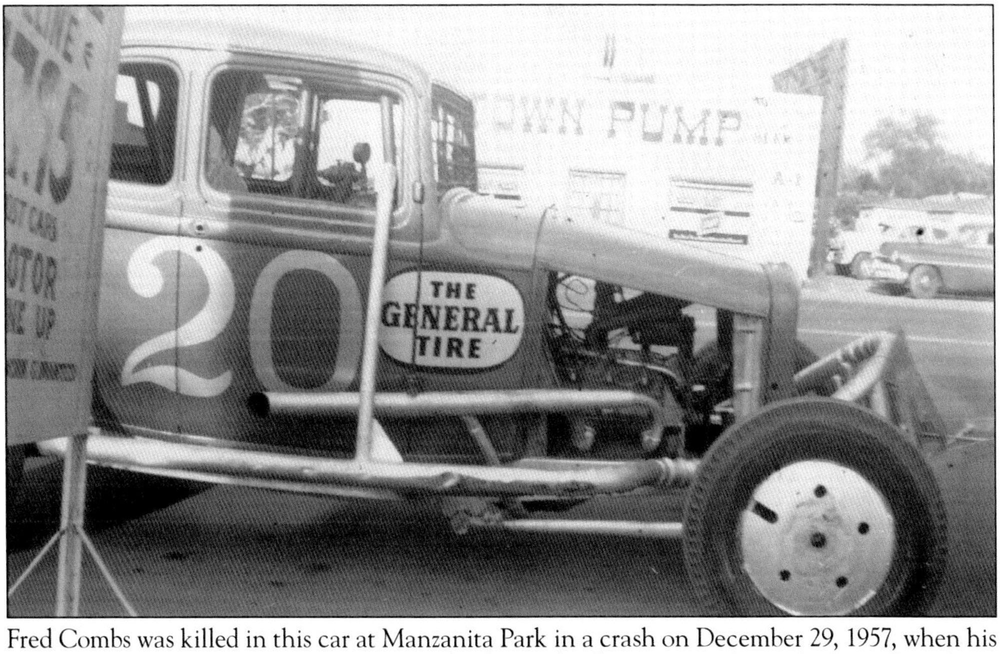

Fred Combs was killed in this car at Manzanita Park in a crash on December 29, 1957, when his seat belt broke and he was ejected. Note the front wheel covers. In the early days of stock-car racing, drivers lost lots of valve stems when tires would rub together during track action. Drivers began to weld plow disks to the wheel, covering the valve stems. Combs is a member of the Arizona Motorsports Hall of Fame. (Courtesy of Don Appley.)

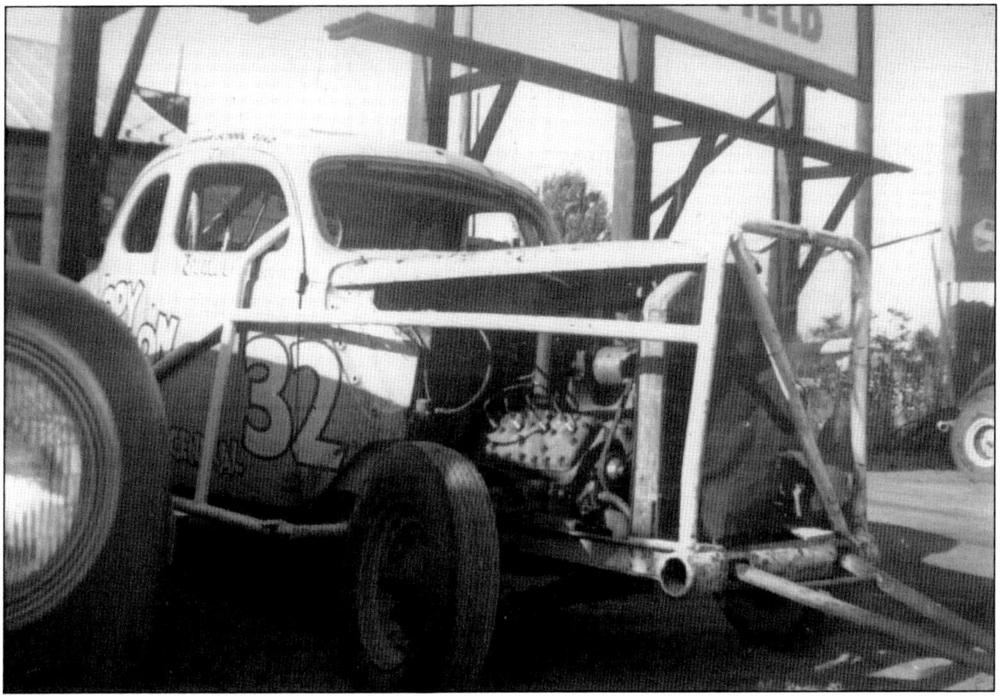

Shown above is No. 32, Jack Pritchard's Ford jalopy. No. 33, pictured below, was Len Pritchard's jalopy. The entire Pritchard family, including the women, were involved in jalopy racing at Manzanita Park. Most family members lived in the South Mountain area of Phoenix. (Both, courtesy of Don Appley.)

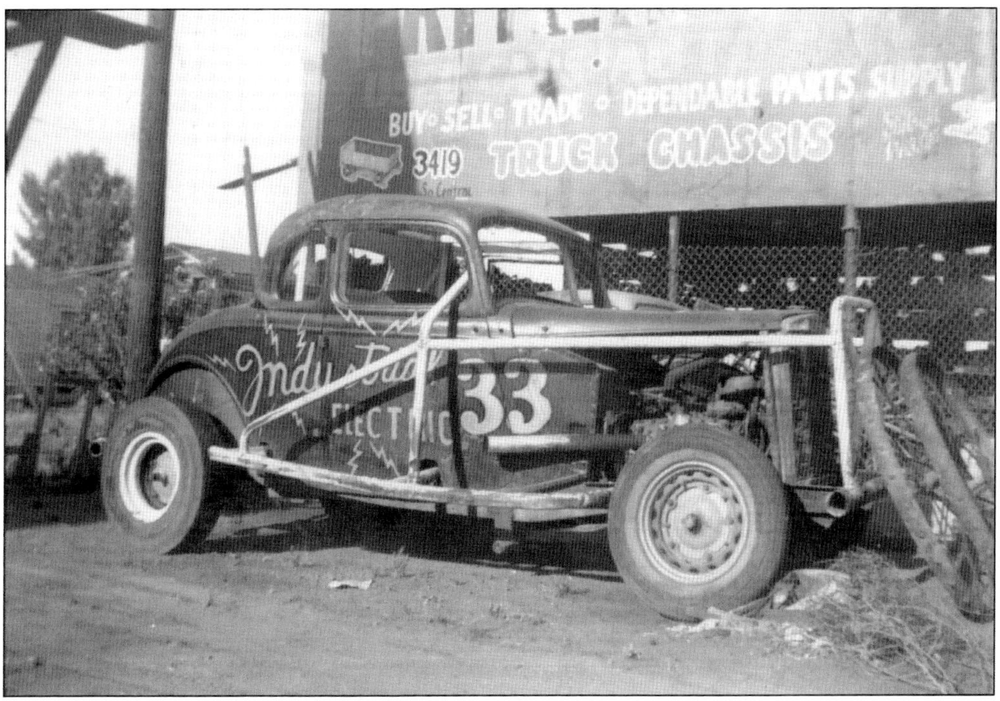

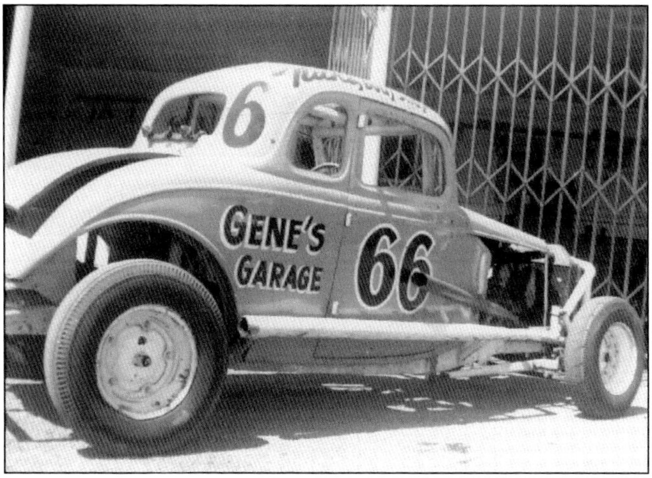

Mel Larson, who vaulted from Manzanita Park to the NASCAR world, drove jalopy No. 66. Though he was successful on the track, Larson's real talent was in public relations. He became a corporate vice president of the Circus Circus Hotel-Casino in Las Vegas and was later instrumental in the development of Las Vegas Motor Speedway. He is a member of the Arizona Motorsports Hall of Fame. (Courtesy of Don Appley.)

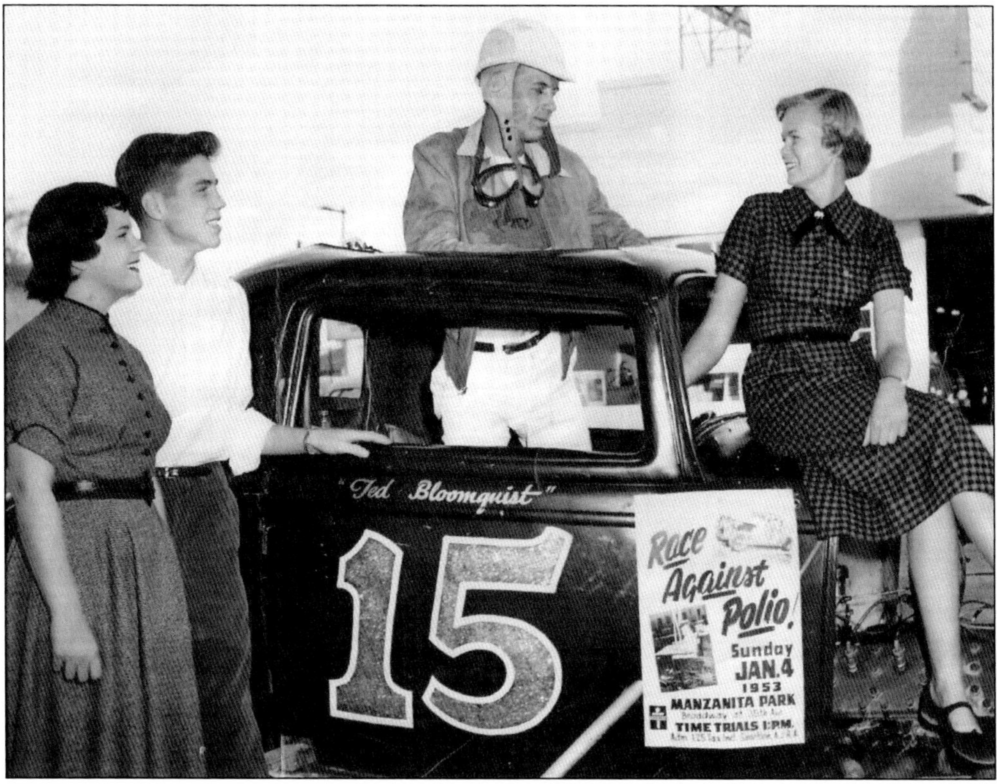

Pictured here are, from left to right, Bessie Poulos; LeRoy Blake; Ted Bloomquist (the driver of No. 15), and Dorothy Nyland. Bloomquist, as well as the other jalopy drivers and the owners of Manzanita Park, Rudy Everett and Lawrence Meskimen, were major backers of the March of Dimes effort to beat polio. This benefit race was held on January 4, 1953, with all proceeds and drivers' purses donated to the March of Dimes. (Courtesy of Ted Bloomquist.)

Shown at right is Don Appley at age 16 in 1956. Below is Appley's first race car, a 1937 Ford. Appley bought it and convinced another racer who was having his car towed to the track to let him hook on behind by a rope. Heading south on Central Avenue, Appley abruptly put his car in gear to try to start it; the car bucked, and the rope broke, leaving him in the middle of Phoenix with no head or tail lights. Finally arriving at the track, Appley convinced the pit steward that he was 21 years old and was told to tag the field. The old car, which he had never tested, overheated immediately. The flagman permitted several parade laps, but Don could not catch up with the field, so the green flag flew; Don was lapped on the first lap of the race. He almost decided to quit on the spot but persevered and eventually became a competitor. (Both, courtesy of Don Appley.)

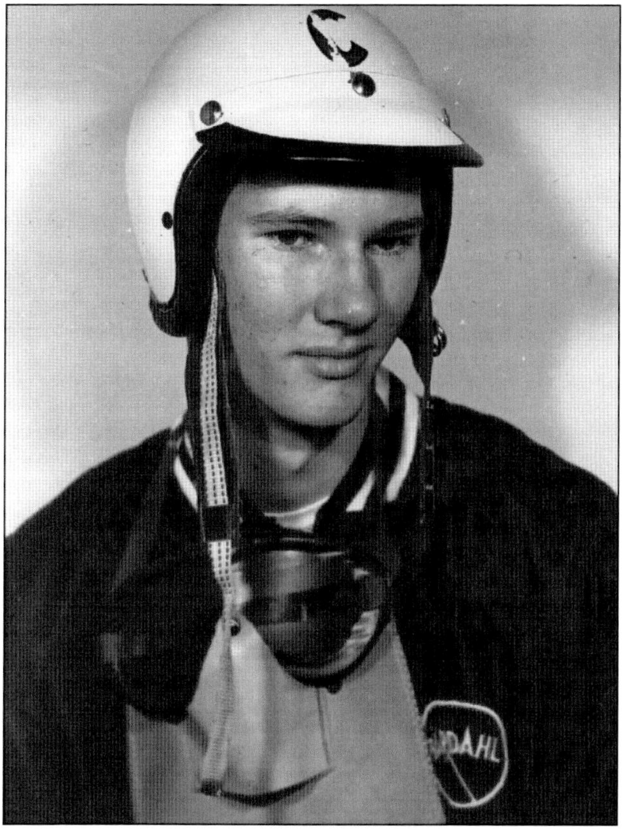

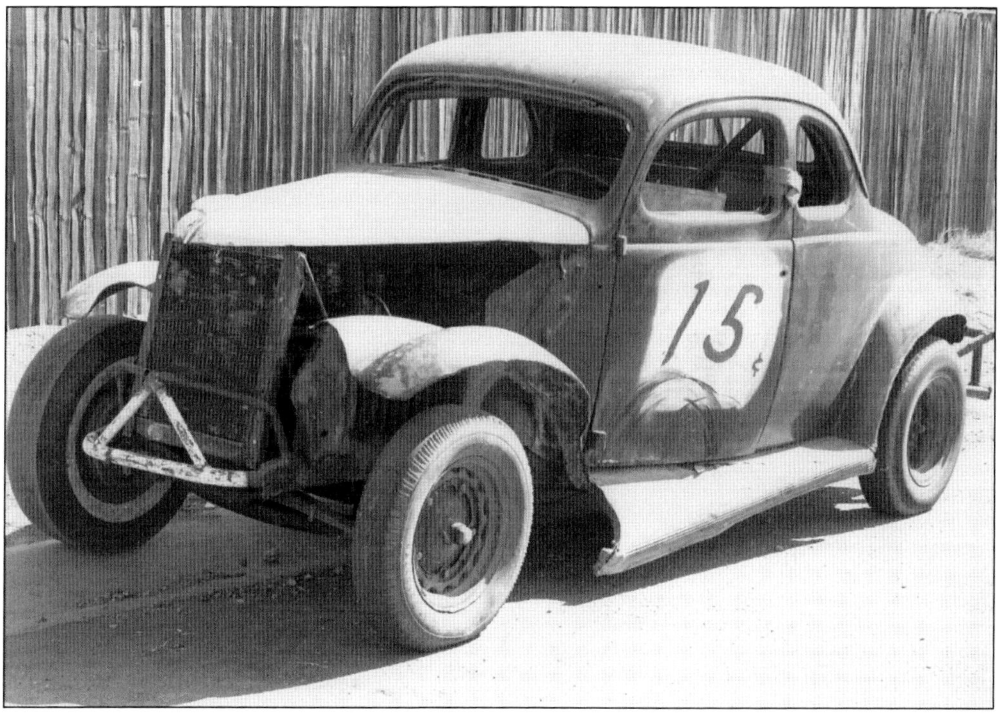

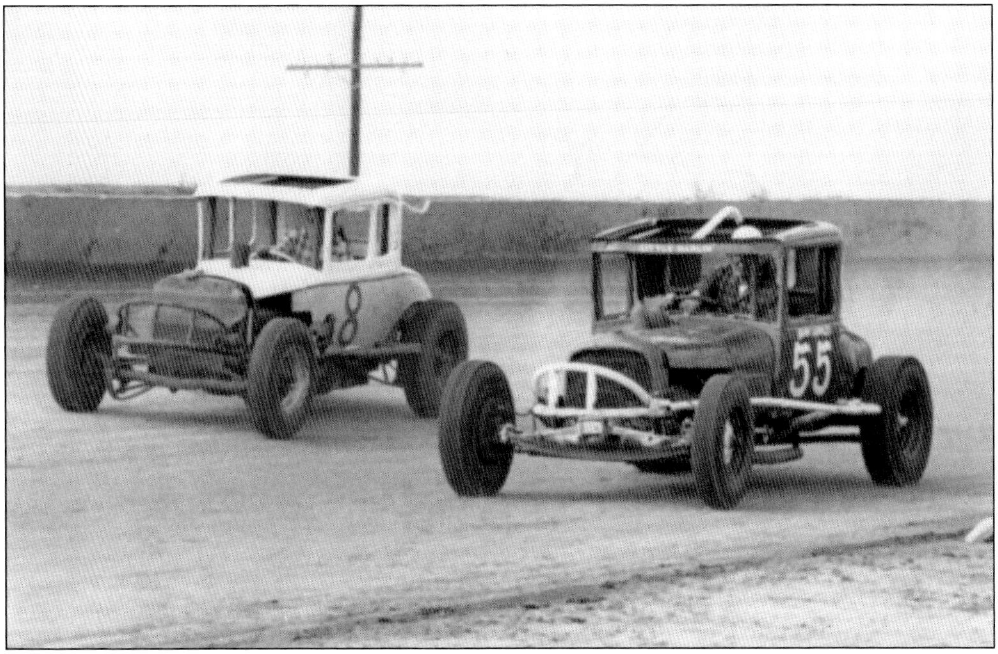

On the left above is Jim Hockley in No. 8 with Don Appley in No. 55 racing modified stocks on the half-mile track in 1960. Loud, fast cars have always been a part of Appley's life. While attending Grand Canyon College in Phoenix, Appley reputedly had the loudest mufflers in Phoenix on his 1955 Ford. Arriving at the religious college one day, a professor came running out to the parking lot and angrily informed Don that he had been expelled because his loud car did not fit the decorum of the school. Appley was not disappointed. Below, Appley races his No. 73 modified stock in a 1959 race at Manzanita Park. (Both, courtesy of Don Appley.)

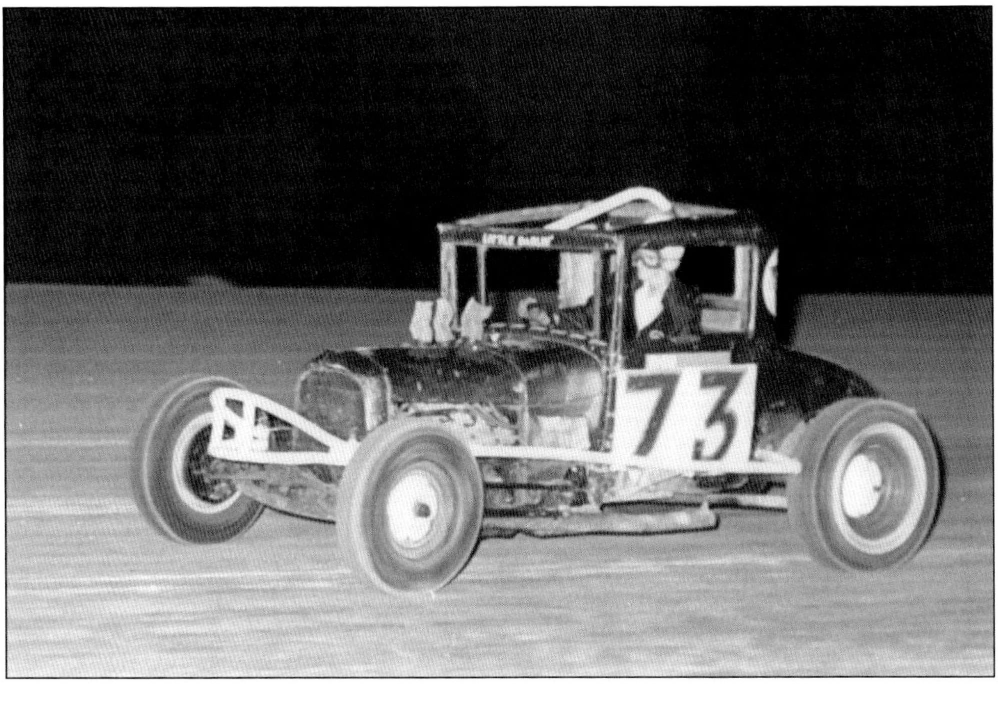

Al Carter, the superintendent of plant and equipment at Arizona Sand & Rock Co., was the owner of No. 82, which was driven by Pete Haumont. Carter served as president of the AJRA in 1952. (Courtesy of LaVerne Doyle.)

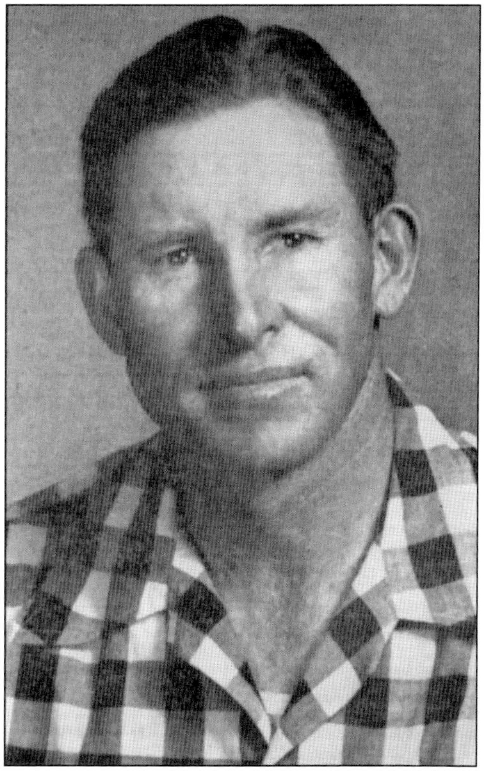

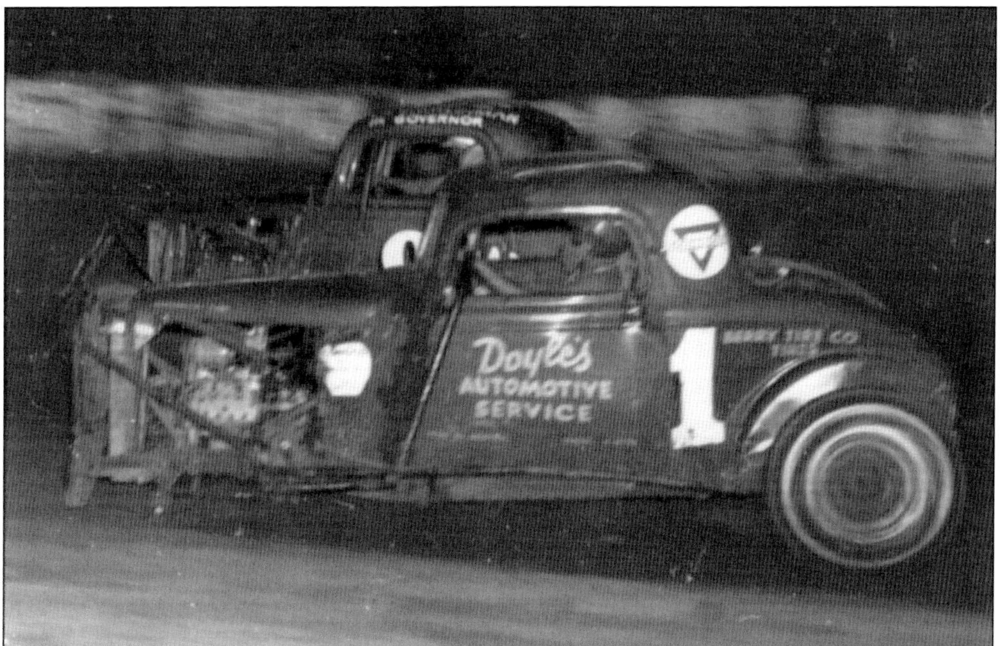

Avery Doyle was one of the fiercest competitors at Manzanita Park, as illustrated in this photograph. Doyle has lost a wheel but continues to race. Ted Bloomquist, the big noise at Manzanita Park by 1953, recalled Avery Doyle as "a real scrapper and a good friend." (Courtesy of LaVerne Doyle.)

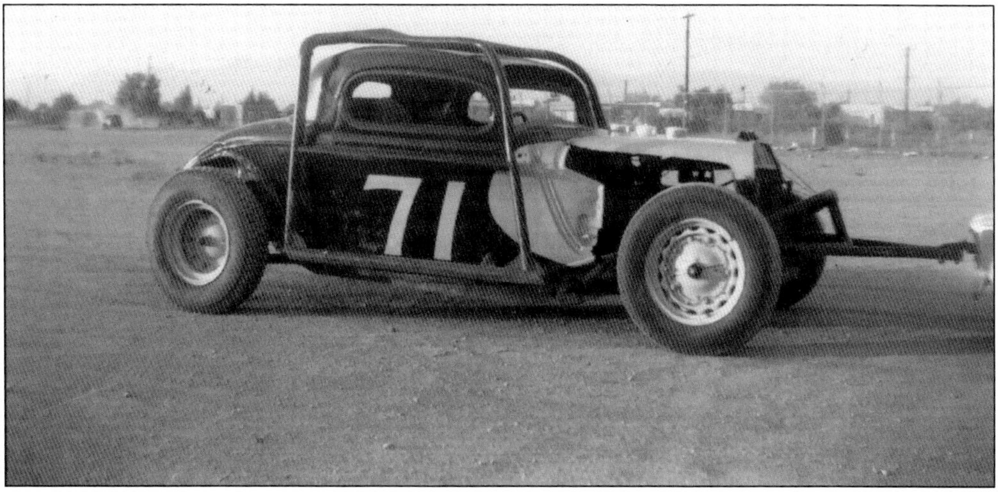

This 1934 Ford jalopy was driven by Henry "Hank" Arnold of Tucson. Arnold was a regular winner at Manzanita Park, and one of the most popular drivers who ever raced there. He always sported a big smile and warm personality. Hank was also a prolific car builder and built the famous sprint car "Twister." Arnold's friends and fans were inconsolable when he was killed in a sprint-car race at Manzy on June 17, 1967. (Courtesy of Don Appley.)

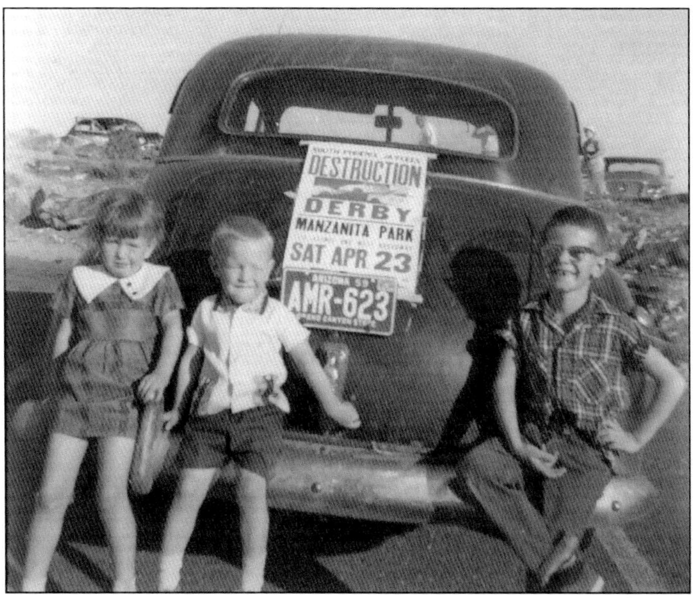

At left is Linda McCubrey, age four, along with her brothers Grovenor McCubrey (center), age three, and Gary Hunsaker (right), age seven, sitting on the back bumper of their father Grovenor "Big Mac" McCubrey Sr.'s car, which has a sign taped to it advertising a "Destruction Derby" at Manzanita Park on April 23, 1959. By the time Manzy closed in 2009, Linda McCubrey Price had become the winningest female driver in Manzy history. (Courtesy of Linda Price.)

Two

Manzanita Speedway's Days of Glory

Those who have been around Manzy for any length of time count the years from 1965 into the 1980s as the glory days of the track. Essentially, this period began when Keith Hall purchased the track and extended through the 1980s when he actively controlled track operations. By all accounts, Hall was a superb, creative promoter during this era.

Ultimately, Hall built Manzy into one of the most famous dirt tracks in the United States. At the end, it was the only track in the United States situated near the center of a major metropolitan area. Aside from that, what many locals forgot, and many never knew, was that Manzanita Speedway was the scene of some of the best automobile racing in America.

When one goes back through the names of the greats who have raced at Manzy, one sees, among others, A.J. Foyt, Mario Andretti, Gary Bettenhausen, Bill Cheesbourg, Hank Arnold, Roger McCluskey, Ron Shuman, Billy Boat, J.J. Yeley, and Al Unser Jr. In addition, there is a long list of drivers who never moved beyond the local scene who were great, like Terry Belcher Sr., the all-time winning driver at Manzy; Anthony Madrid; Jeremy Sherman; Lealand McSpadden; and Gene Brown, among many others.

If one looks at the names of the champions, the list is very small in comparison to the number of drivers who raced at Manzy over its 58-year history. Considering there were numerous divisions of cars and thousands of racers at Manzy, only a few hundred champions were crowned in all those years. In other words, it was a unique experience to win a single race, but rare to win a championship. The ability to win at Manzanita Speedway placed a driver amongst unrivaled company; the competition was that good.

But beyond all that, Hall differentiated Manzy from most other tracks in the United States when he introduced the first Western United States Championship race in 1968. Eventually, the race became the Western World Championships, a national sprint-car contest that spanned several days, paid out a huge purse, became one jewel in the Triple Crown of sprint-car racing, and best of all, was the last sprint-car race of the year at which the national champion was crowned. Hall's brainchild was an awesome achievement; a Hollywood scriptwriter could not have done it better.

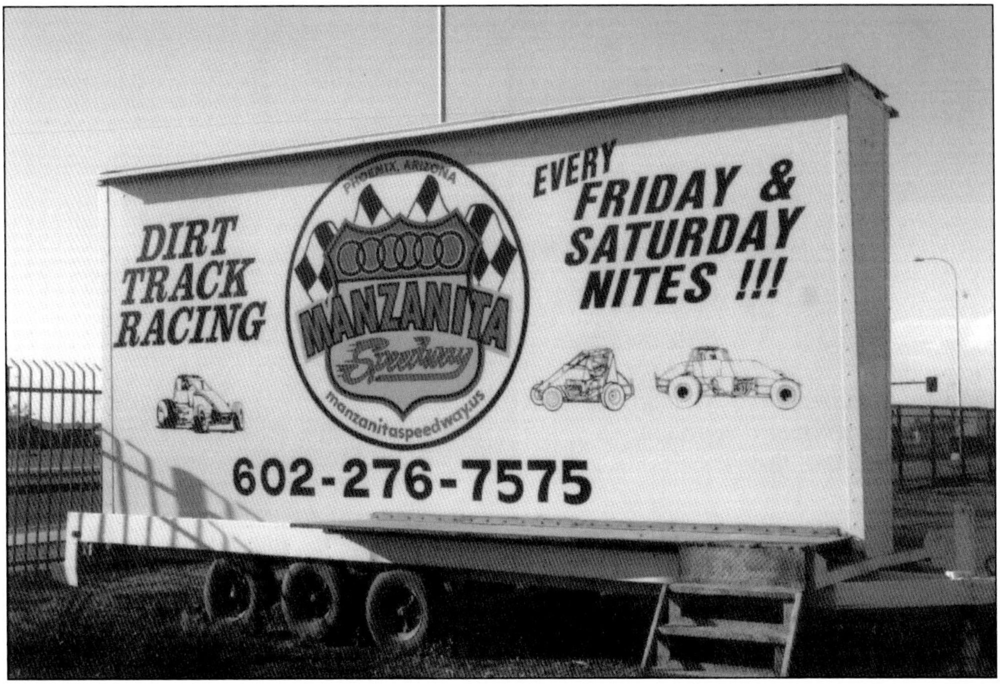

Since the days of Keith Hall, this mobile sign has been used to advertise Manzanita Speedway at locations around the track. At times, the sign was moved to the track for use as a platform for the introduction of drivers and guests. (Courtesy of James A. Fargo.)

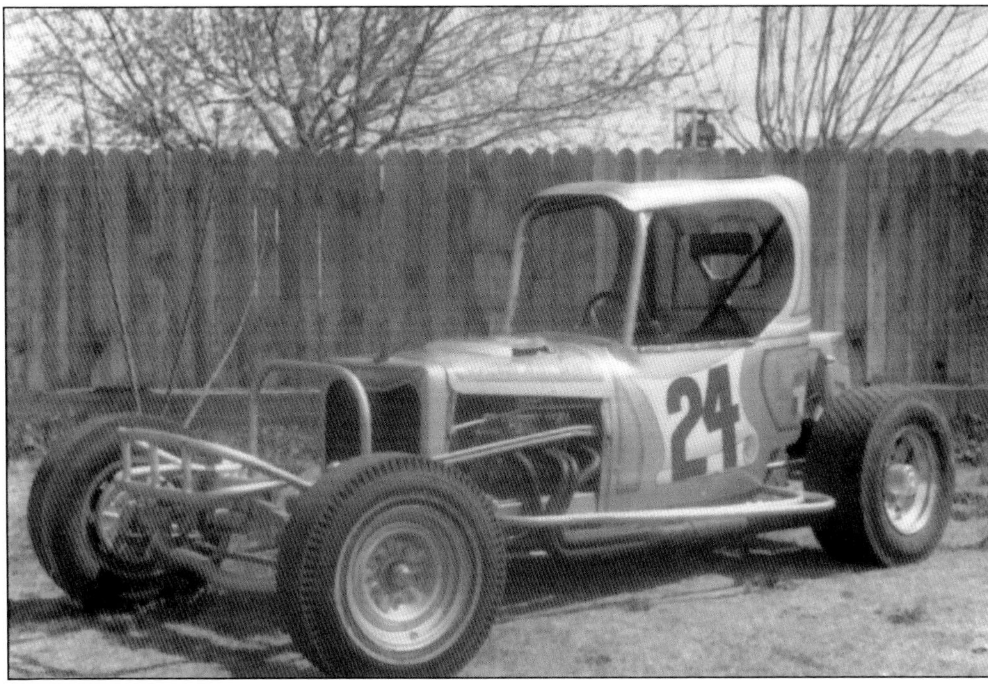

This super modified race car, No. 24, gives some indication of the diversity of race cars that have raced at Manzy over its 58-year history. This short-track car was owned and built by Les Miller, owner of Low Budget Engines in Phoenix. (Courtesy of Winston Brown Jr.)

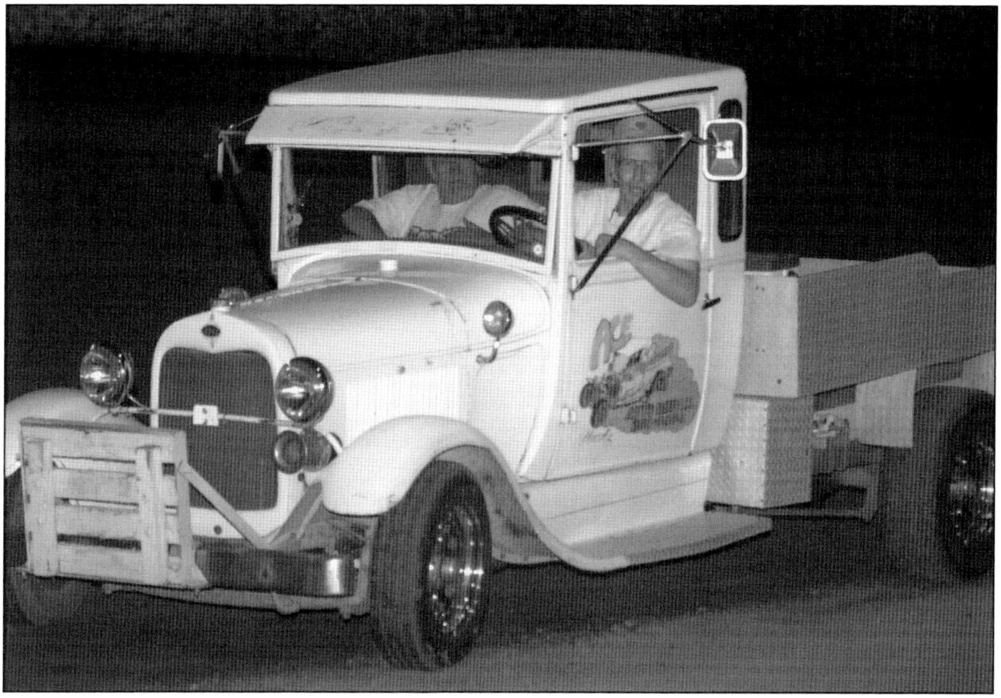

Dick Sellers, owner of Ace Auto Repair in Phoenix, shows off his restored 1929 Ford flatbed tow truck, which he used to push sprint cars for many years. The truck was restored in 1986 and used to push the famous Twister race car. Sellers's involvement at Manzy dated to 1972. He built a super modified car, which Dave Culp drove in the Western World Championships in 1974, the only super modified in the race. (Courtesy of Don Iverson.)

This midget car was driven by Ted Bloomquist in the early 1950s. The car was plagued with mechanical problems and never won a race. In Bloomquist's own words, "The car drove rough; it was like driving a watermelon!" Ted was the last president of the Arizona Midget Owners and Drivers Association. (Courtesy of Ted Bloomquist.)

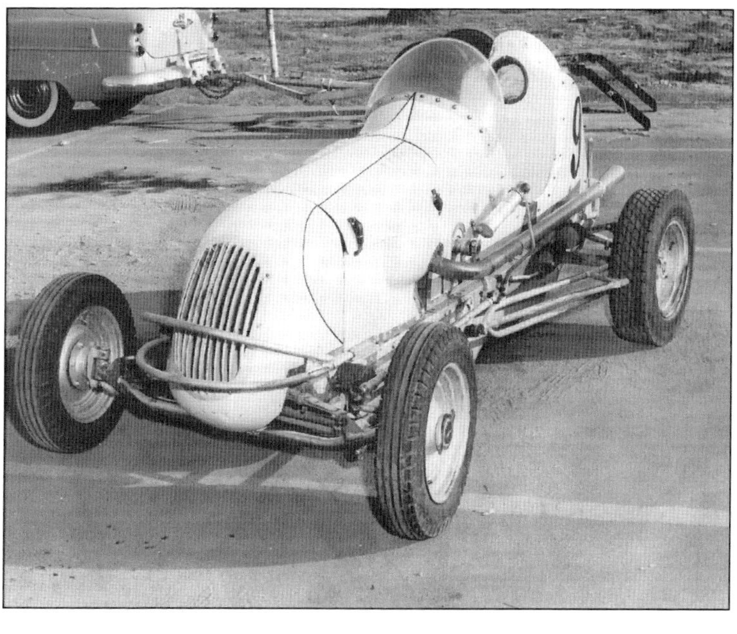

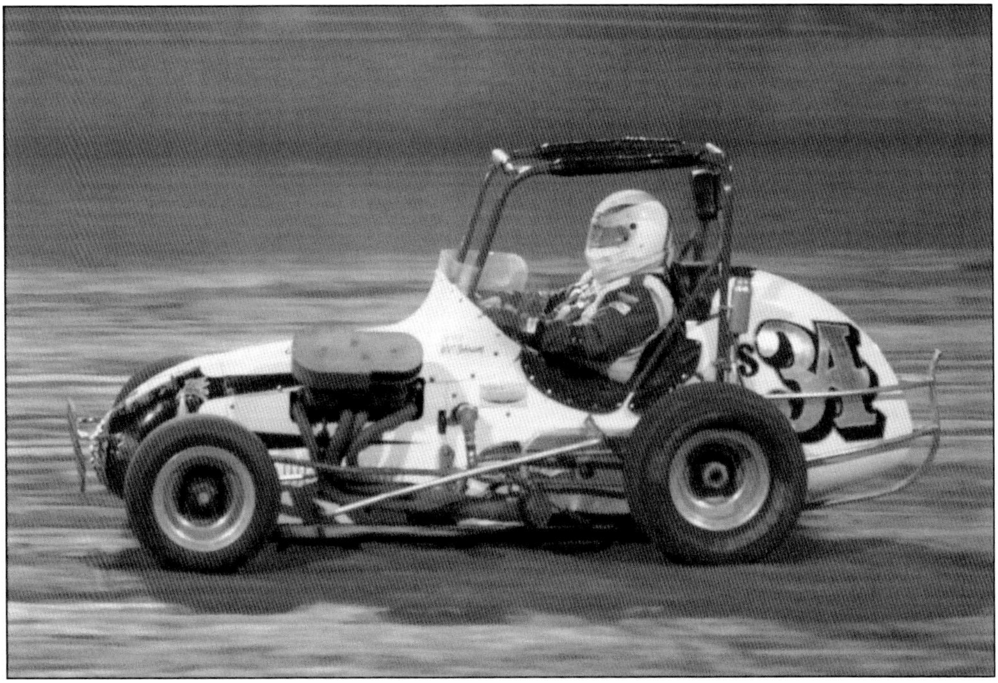

In recent years, Manzy hosted an annual vintage car night in which racers with restored sprint cars and super modifieds returned to compete on the "track that action built." Above, Mike Schrum demonstrates his vintage race car, while below, Roberta Arnold is the guest of honor at Hank Arnold Night on June 16, 2007. Hank Arnold died at Manzy in a sprint-car crash on June 17, 1967. (Both, courtesy of Don Iverson.)

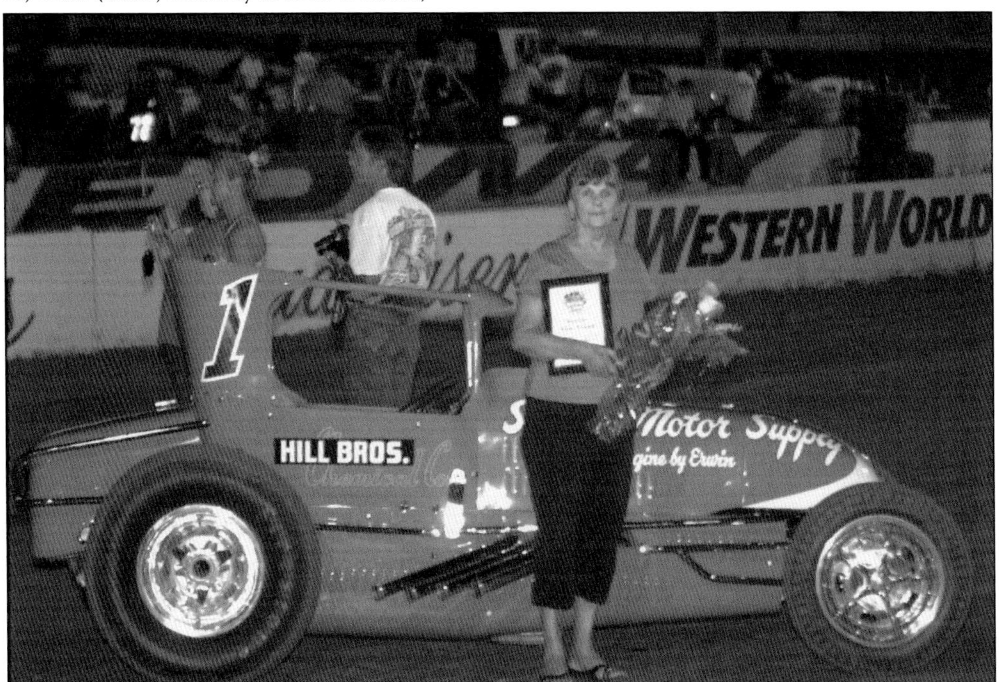

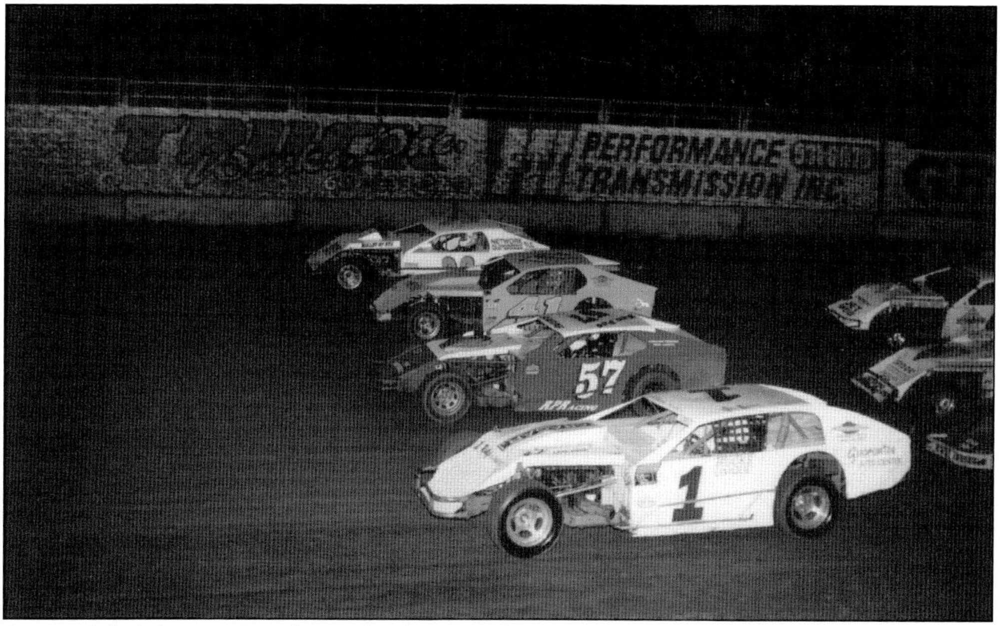

Dirt modifieds line up four abreast for the start of a main event on April 22, 2000. Dirt modifieds may be the most popular type of race cars in the country. They are generally built on a standard car frame with custom-built flat bodies attached. Manzy raced two types of dirt modifieds: dirt modifieds with liberal engine rules, and sport mods, which used a basic factory stock engine. (Courtesy of James A. Fargo.)

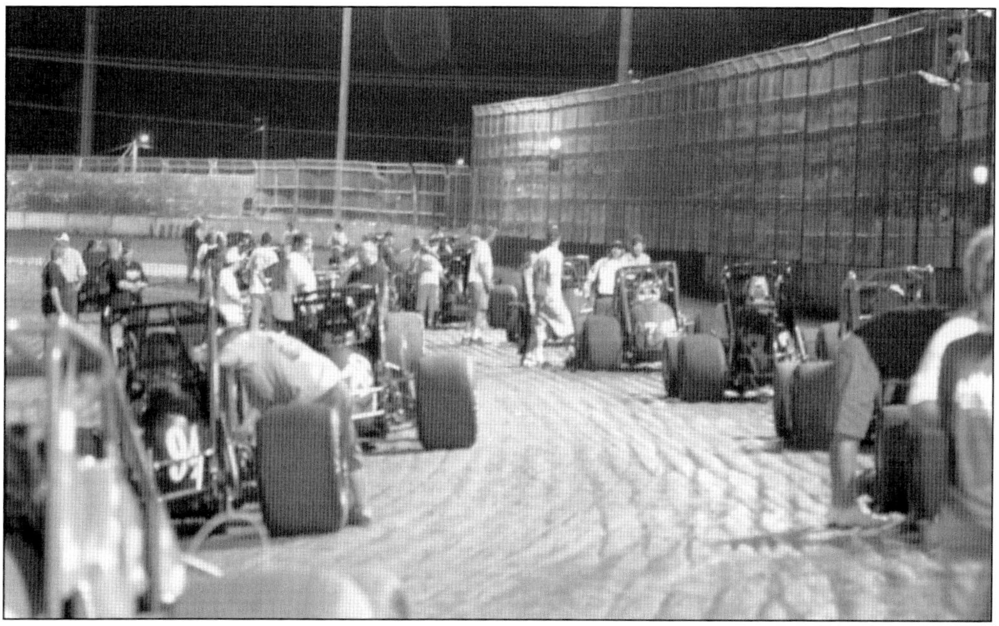
Drivers and crews begin to set up the USAC sprint cars on the starting grid at Manzy for the Western World Championships in November 2007. Although this appears to be a relaxed scene, it is anything but serene. At this point, the tension is building in every driver in anticipation of the big event. Notice the grooves in the track, the result of working the track with a plow. (Courtesy of Don Iverson.)

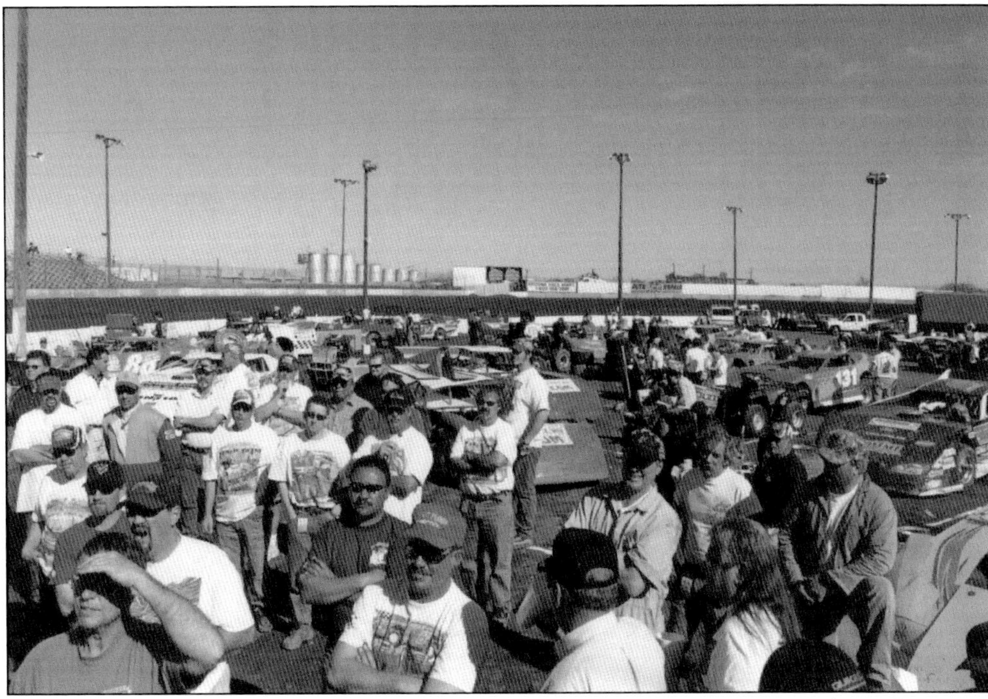

Manzy sponsored many special events during a typical season. In recent years, it hosted a Winter Super Late Model Championship race. Late models are the top cars in stock-car racing and put on an exciting show with their heavier chassis and high-powered engines. Pictured above is the drivers' meeting, which was held prior to the race to instruct the drivers and pit crews of particular rules that would govern the event. Below is the cover photograph, which shows the late models going into turn three on the parade lap on January 19, 2008. (Both, courtesy of Don Iverson.)

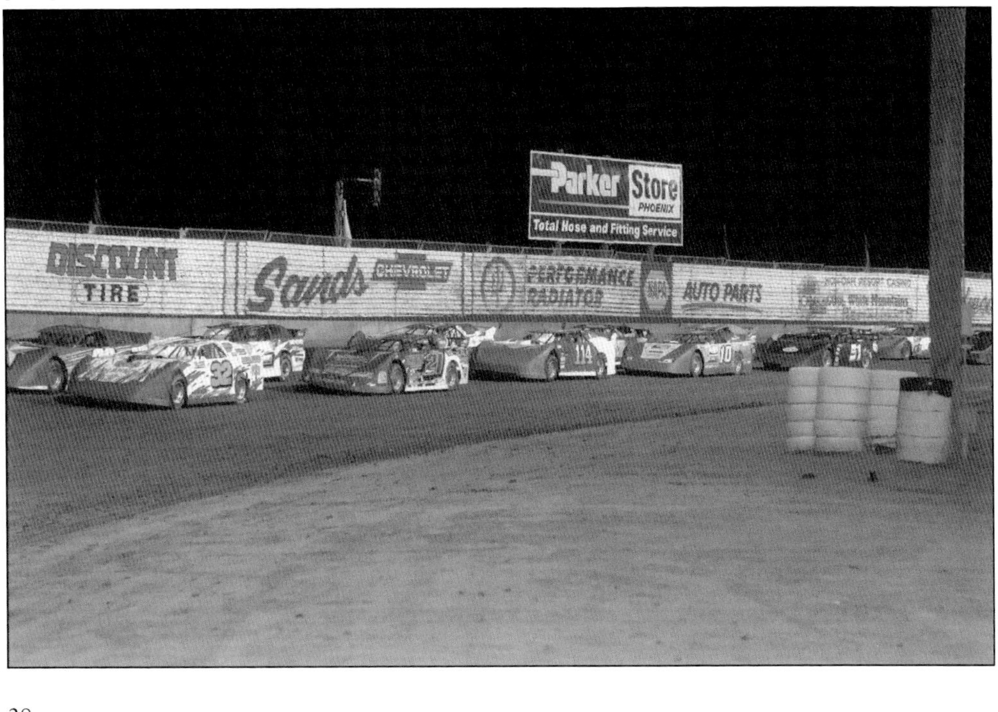

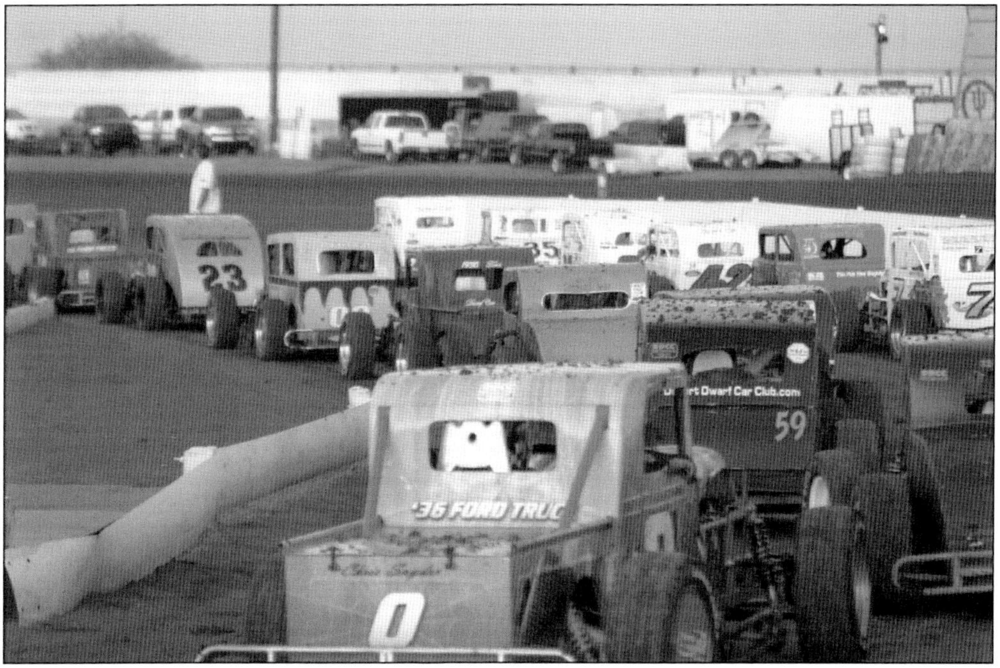

The Desert Dwarf Car Club is positioned for action at Manzy in 2007. Dwarf cars have gained in popularity in Phoenix over the past 20 years, primarily because they remind fans of the "good old days" of jalopy racing. The cars are 5/8 replicas of 1928–1948 American-made automobiles powered by motorcycle engines. (Courtesy of Don Iverson.)

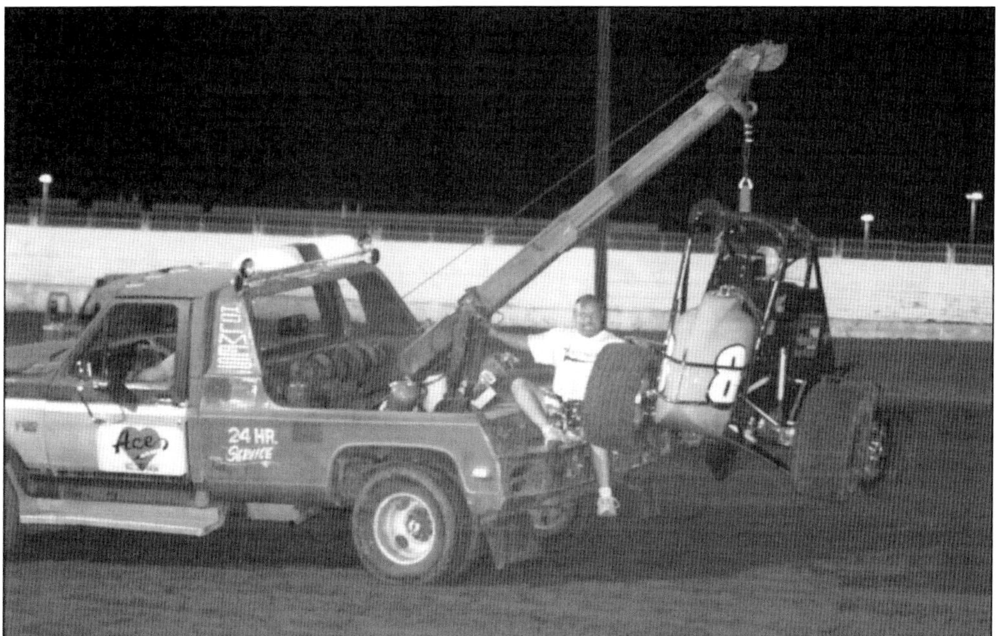

Dick Sellers's Ace Auto Repair tow truck has a midget on the hook. This gives an idea of the size of these race cars. Sellers was a fixture at Manzy from 1972, working the wrecker and operating as a push truck to get the sprint cars off the starting grid. (Courtesy of Don Iverson.)

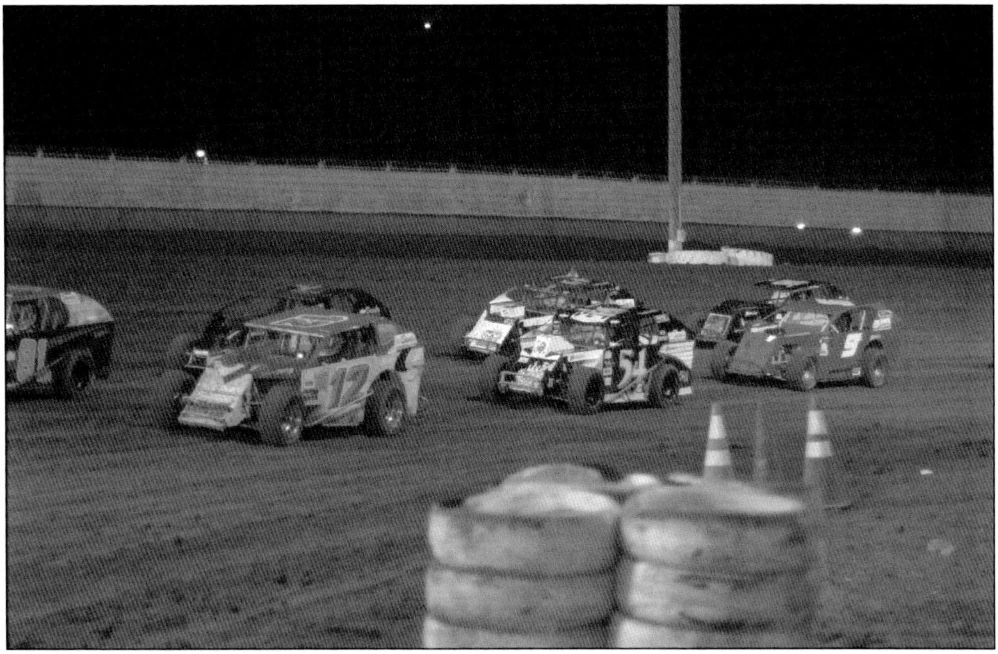

The mod lites were a recent phenomenon at Manzy. Because of the modest cost to buy or build a mod lite, they caught on quickly. Essentially built on the principle of a dwarf car with a motorcycle engine, the cars are lightweight, nimble, and fast. Participants claim it is an exciting class of car at a reasonable cost. (Courtesy of Don Iverson.)

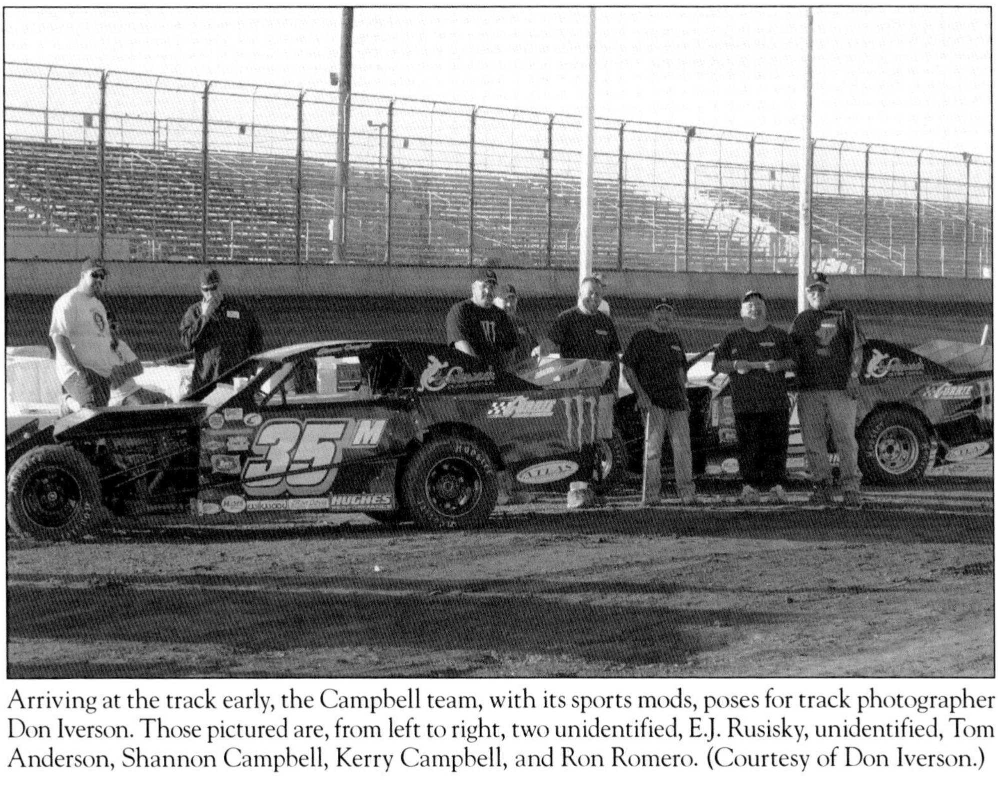

Arriving at the track early, the Campbell team, with its sports mods, poses for track photographer Don Iverson. Those pictured are, from left to right, two unidentified, E.J. Rusisky, unidentified, Tom Anderson, Shannon Campbell, Kerry Campbell, and Ron Romero. (Courtesy of Don Iverson.)

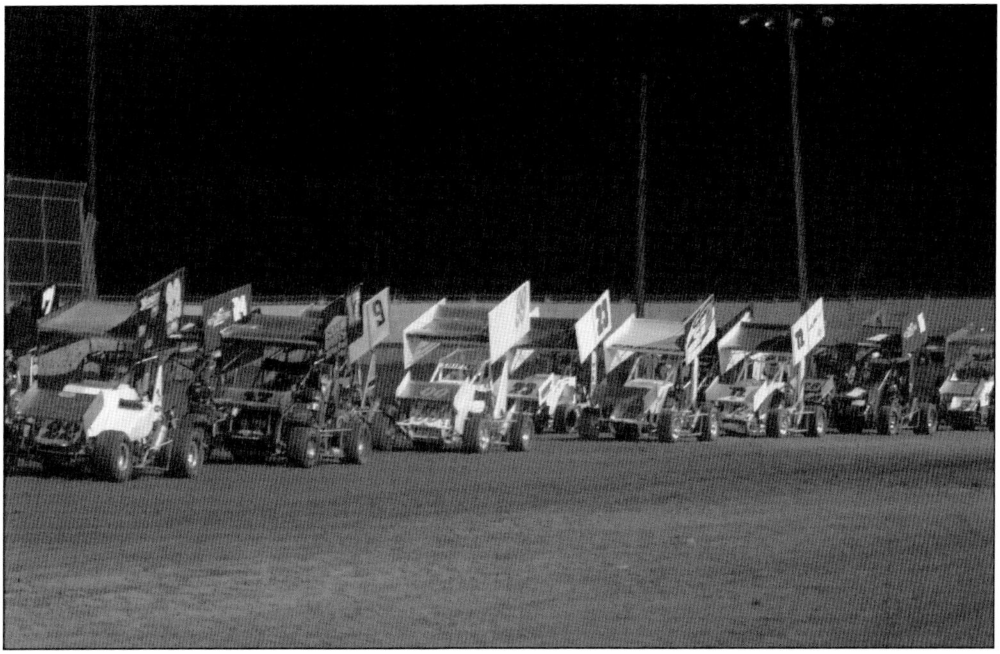

This lineup of winged mini sprints on parade has a fascinating symmetry to it. This will not be the case once the race begins and the cars spread out. Mini sprints are powered by motorcycle engines and are very lightweight, coming in at less than 1,000 pounds. With their high horsepower to weight ratio, these cars are very fast and compare to dwarf cars. (Courtesy of Don Iverson.)

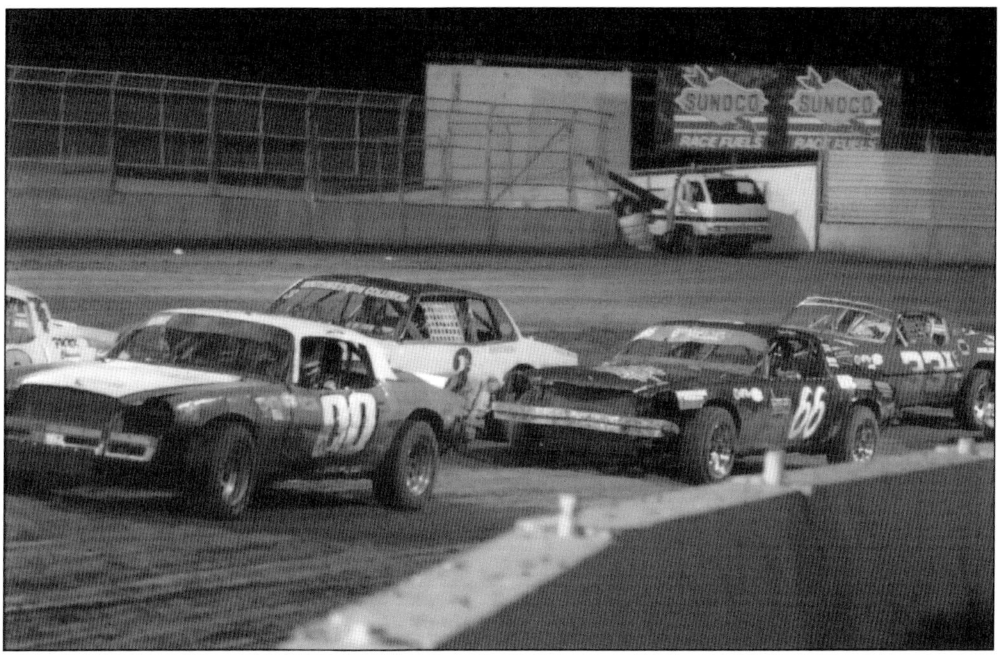

Factory stocks, led by Larry Price, an SCRA Hall of Famer, followed by Justin Upton in No. 66, Danny Pearson in No. 3, and Bobby Taylor in No. 33, roll into turn four at Manzy. When the green flag flies, every driver will punch the accelerator to the floor and charge down the front straight nose to tail before they slide into turn one. (Courtesy of Don Iverson.)

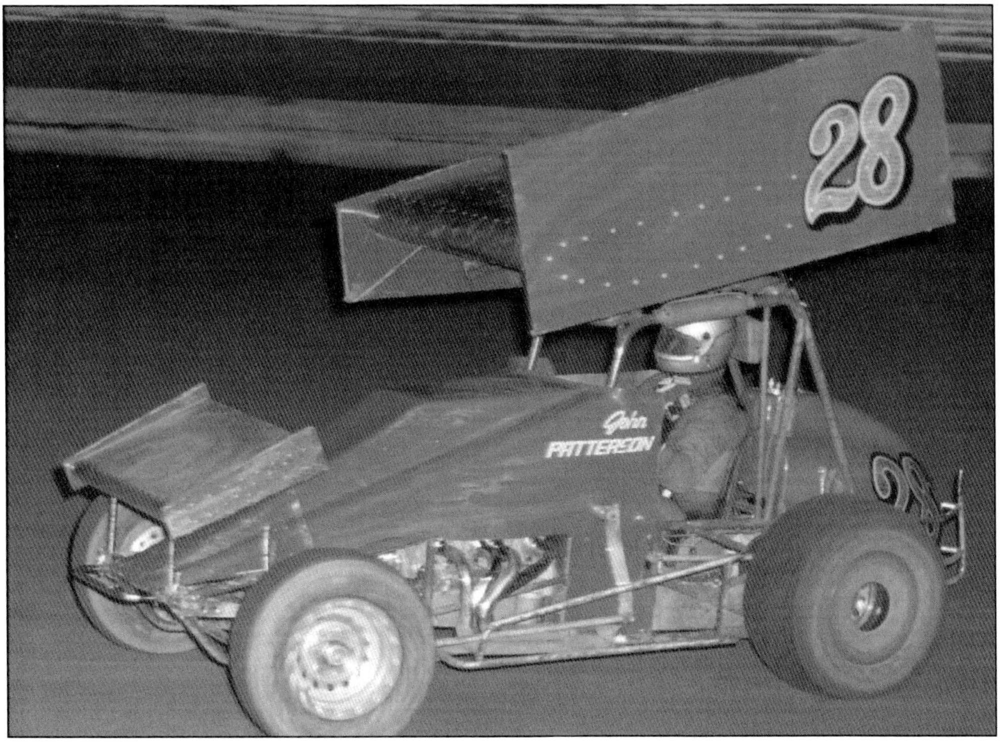

John Patterson purchased Manzy's house car in 1984, which had been raced by Lealand McSpadden, and completely rebuilt it, as shown above. Patterson taught himself to drive by copying the best driver on the track, who, at that time, was McSpadden, known locally as the "Tempe Tornado." After a year, Patterson found that the key to success was to tamp down the adrenalin and relax. After four years of speed and becoming one with his car, Patterson was driven from the sport for lack of funds. He said selling his car was like "losing a child." (Both, courtesy of John Patterson.)

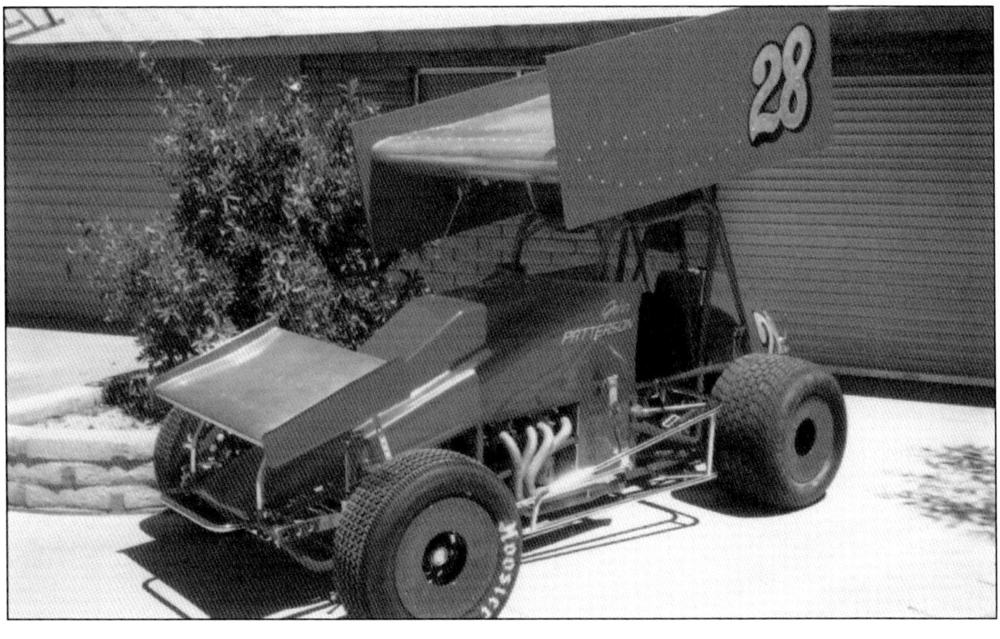

Manzy was always a draw for local celebrities, like Bruce St. James of radio station KTAR FM 92.3 in Phoenix. St. James, however, was one of the few who actually strapped himself into a sprint car and competed on a regular basis. Pictured here is St. James in No. 7k. (Courtesy of Don Appley.)

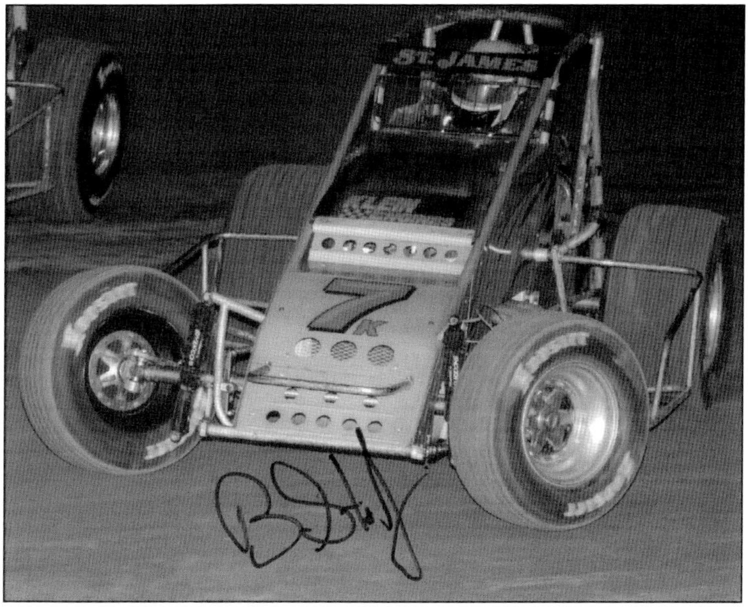

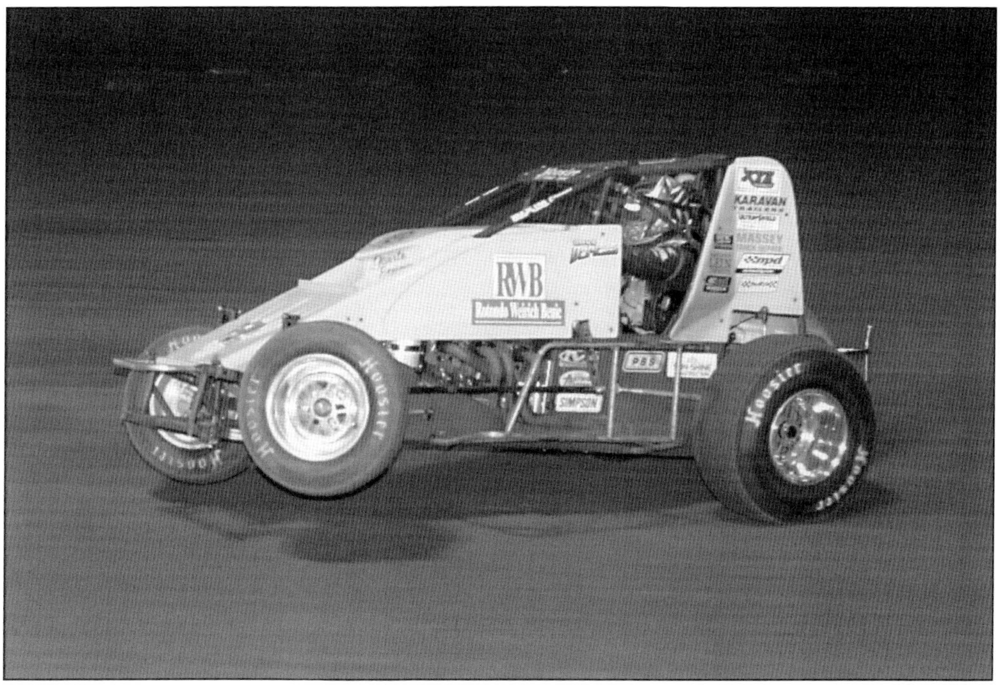

Dave Darland of Kokomo, Indiana, is wheeled up at the 2008 Western World Championships. Darland, one of only five sprint-car drivers to win the USAC's Silver Crown, National Sprint Car, and National Midget Championships, is the type of competitor that was drawn to the Western World Championships every November. (Courtesy of Don Iverson.)

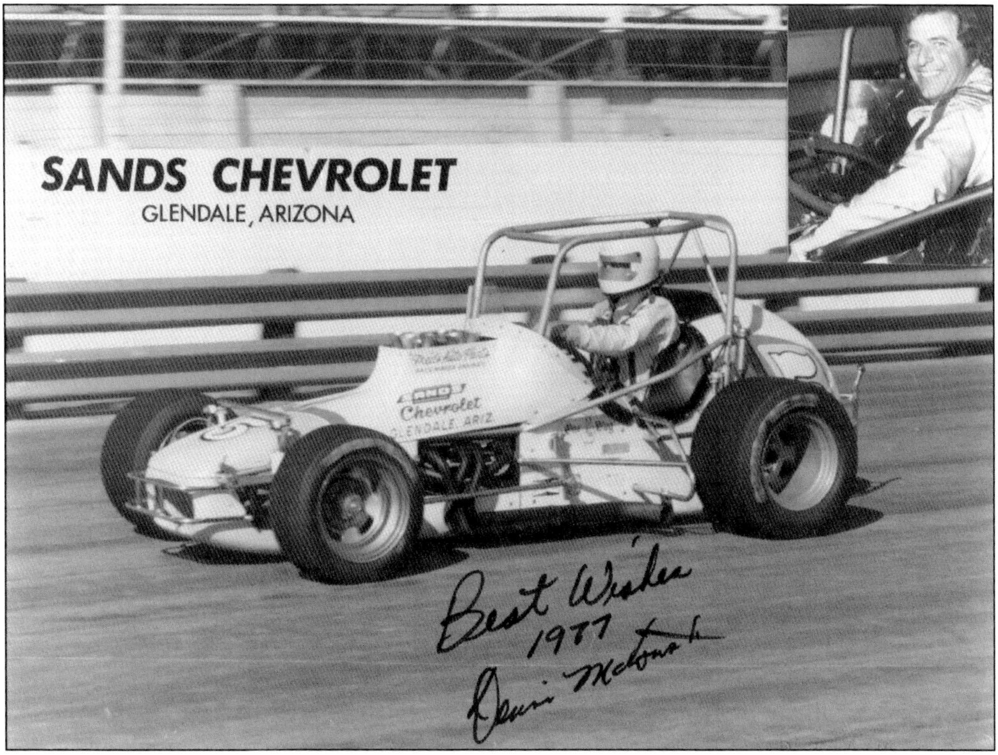

Dennis Matousek, a Manzy star in the 1970s and 1980s, is shown driving the Sands Chevrolet sprint car. One of his nicknames was "Dennis the Menace." Matousek and Sands Chevrolet in Glendale were loyal contributors to Manzy up to the end. (Courtesy of Don Appley.)

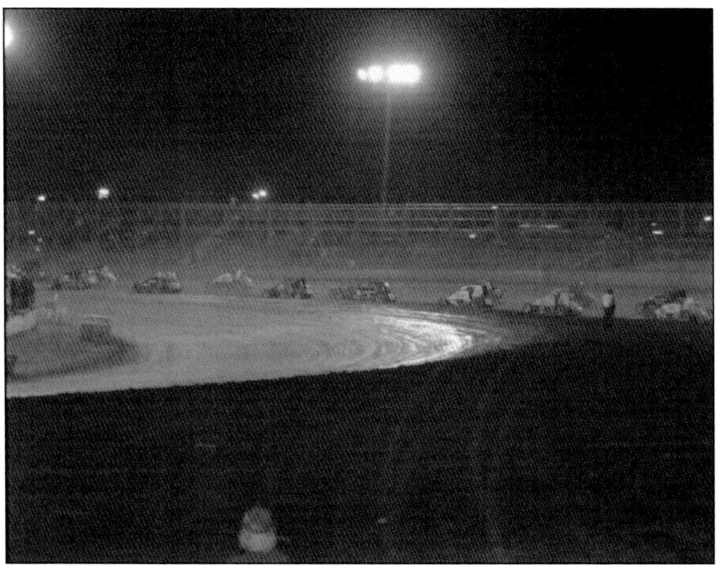

This image shows sprint cars rumbling out of turn four of the half-mile track on the parade lap at the Western World Championships on November 7, 2008. The track lights are reflecting off the wet clay of the third-mile track, which reveals the degree of banking in turn four, one of the reasons that the Manzy track is an exciting and fast surface on which to race. (Courtesy of Don Iverson.)

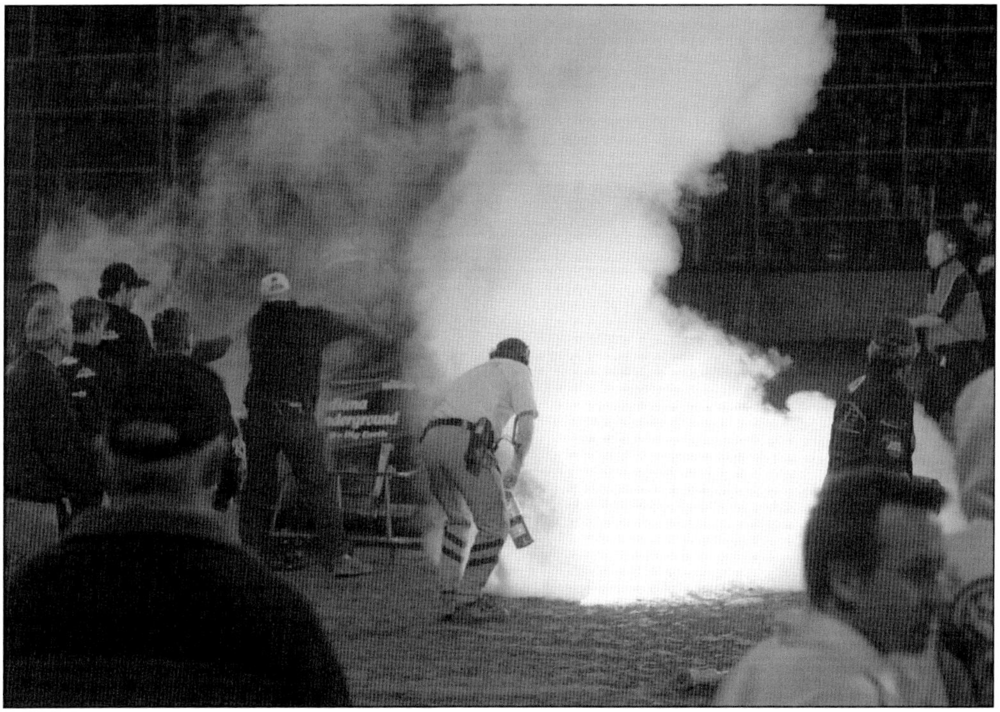

Above, the driver bolts out of the cockpit as the fire safety crew works fast and feverishly to extinguish the flare-up. Below, on the front straight, the driver is already coming out the top of the car as the flames leap up the back. The fire safety crew is already hosing the fire. Fire is the great fear of all race-car drivers; their fireproof gear adds only seconds to the margin of safety. (Both, courtesy of Don Iverson.)

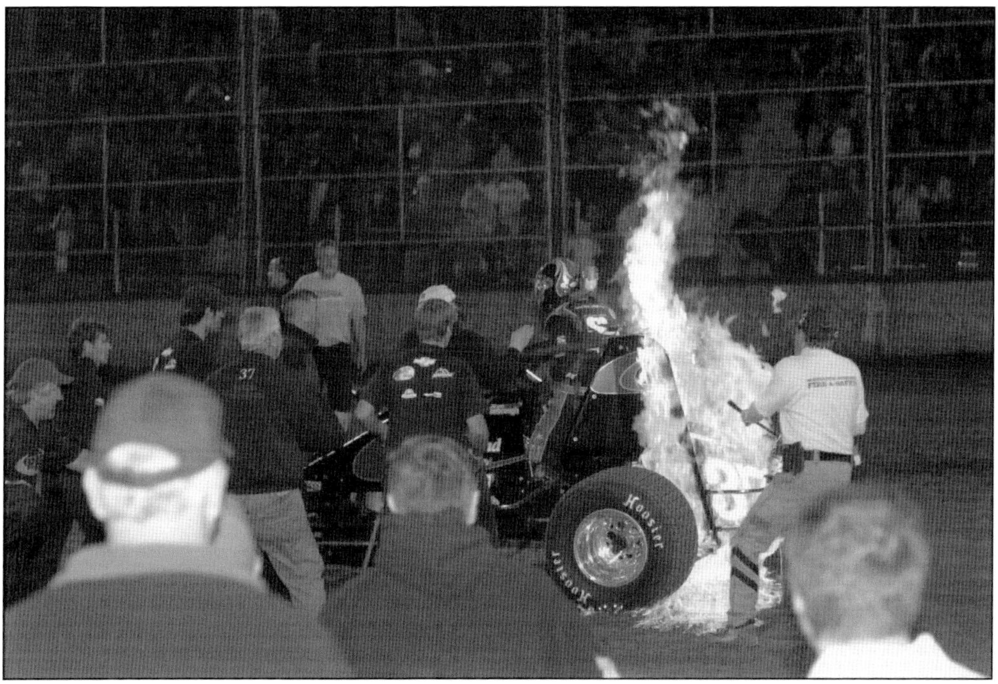

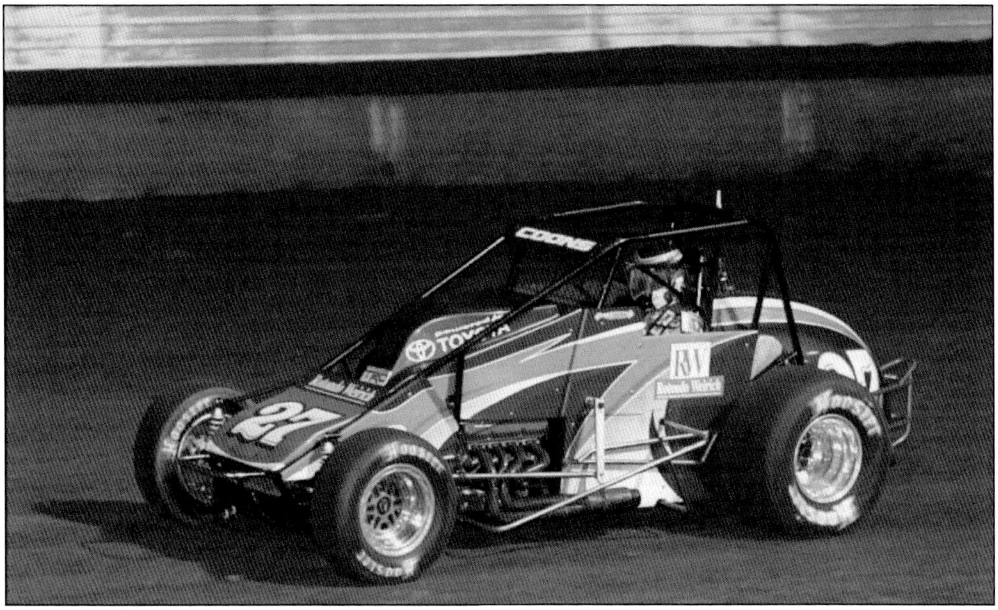

Jerry Coons Jr., originally from Tucson, is seen racing the No. 27 Rotondo-Weirich Silver Crown car. Coons Jr. was only the fifth driver to win the USAC Triple Crown, which consists of winning all three USAC national championships: Silver Crown, National Sprint Car, and National Midget. (Courtesy of Don Iverson.)

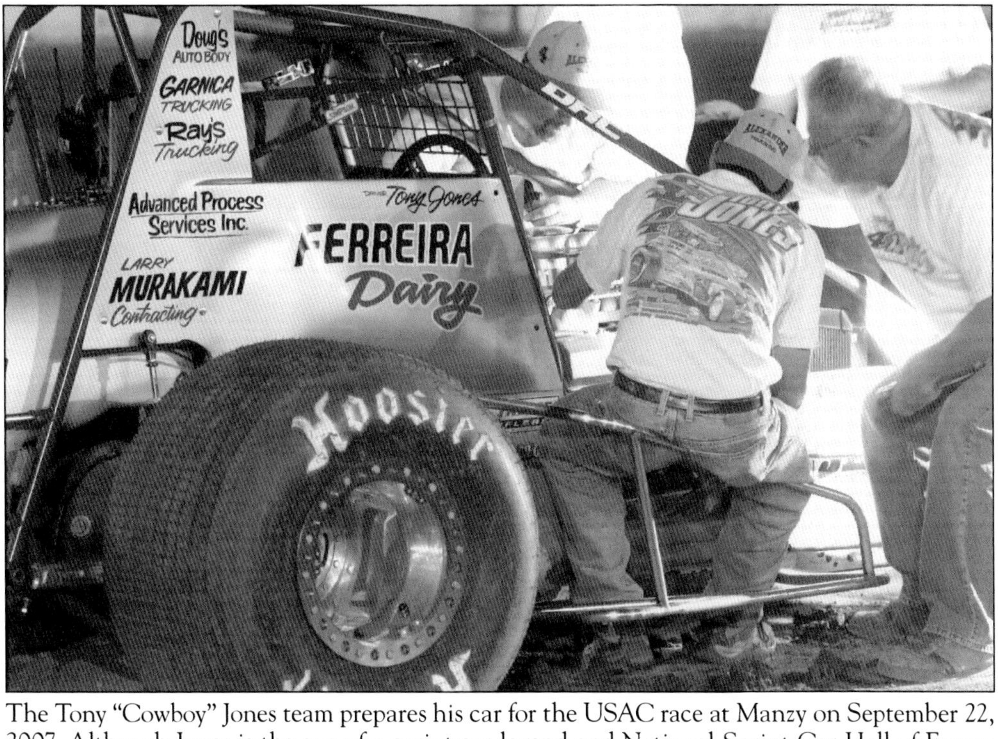

The Tony "Cowboy" Jones team prepares his car for the USAC race at Manzy on September 22, 2007. Although Jones is the son of a sprint-car legend and National Sprint Car Hall of Famer, Bubby Jones, Cowboy is so good that he has developed his own reputation as a top sprint-car racer in the country. (Courtesy of Don Iverson.)

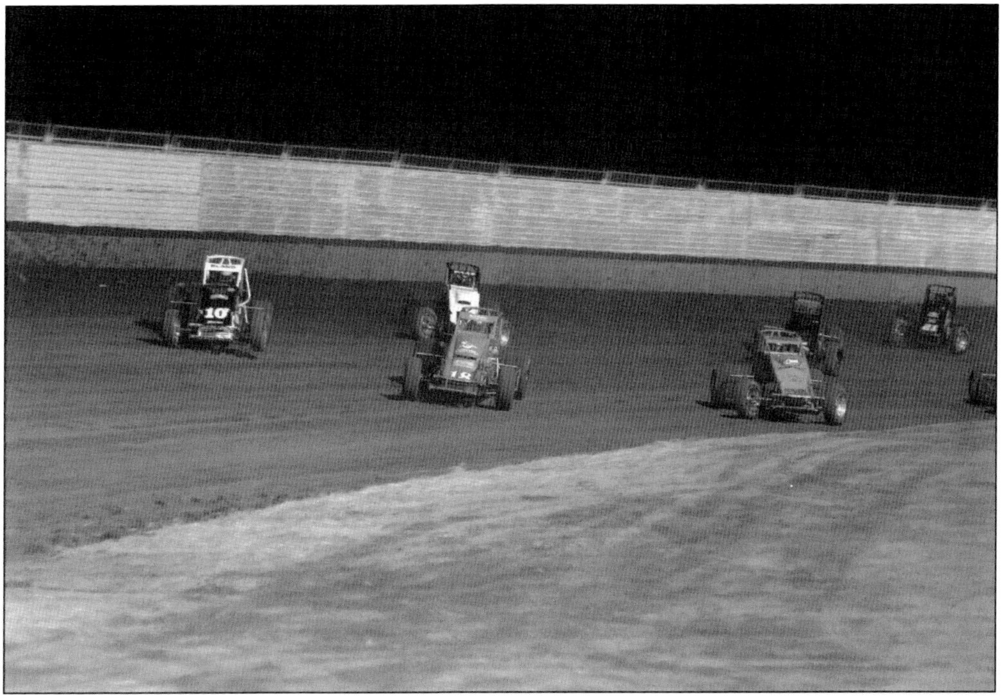

Shown above is the kind of action that keeps fans on the edge of their seats at the Western World Championships. The adrenaline hooks the fans as much as it does the drivers. Racing on the short tracks is where the action is pure and simple. The pace is so fast, the track so slippery, and the competition runs so tightly together that the slightest error by a driver results in the type of crash seen below in the same Western World Championship race. Sprint cars are so lightweight and powerful that sky-high rides and barrel-rolls are common. (Both, courtesy of Don Iverson.)

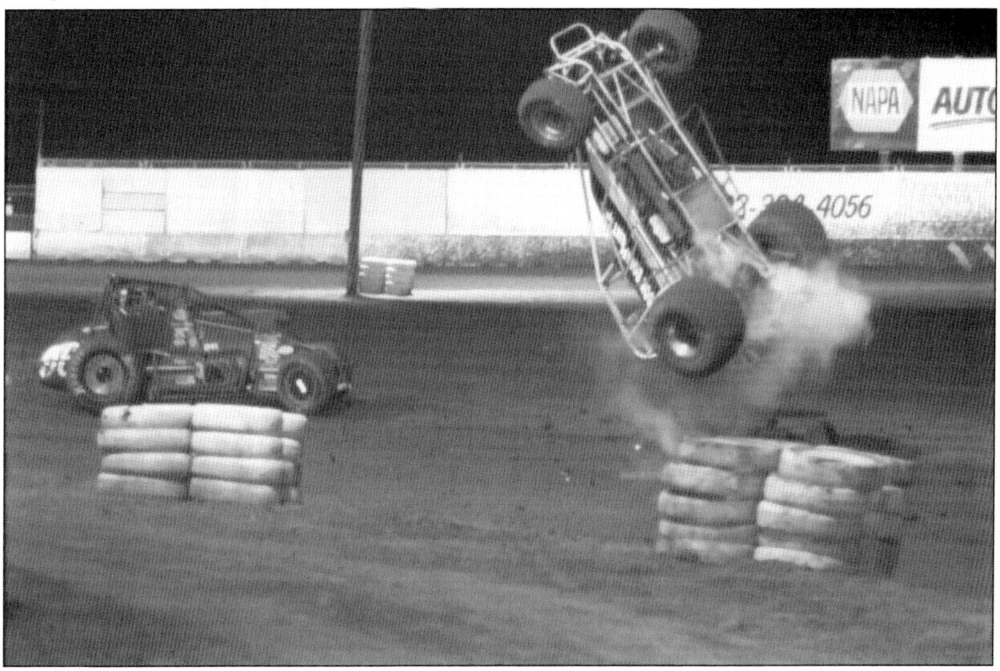

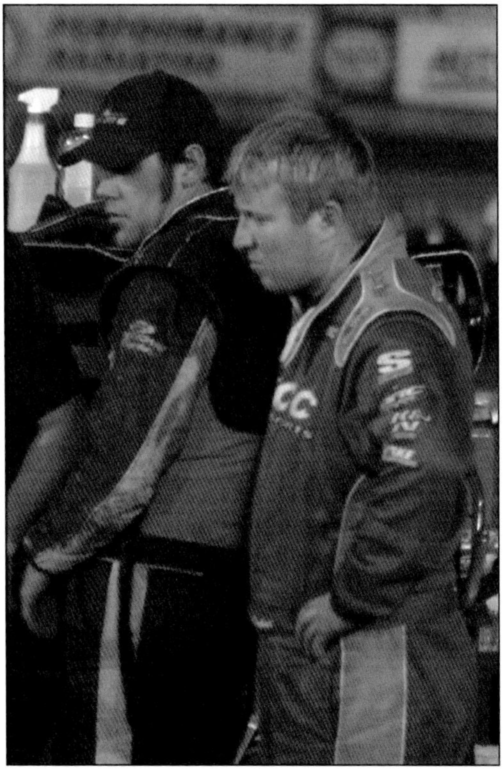

Pictured here are Mike Martin (left), a sprint-car owner and driver from Yuma, and Jesse "The Rocket" Hockett of Warsaw, Missouri. Both Martin and Hockett made regular appearances at Manzy's sprint-car events. Hockett was killed on May 26, 2010, in an accident at his garage while working on an electrical box. (Courtesy of Don Iverson.)

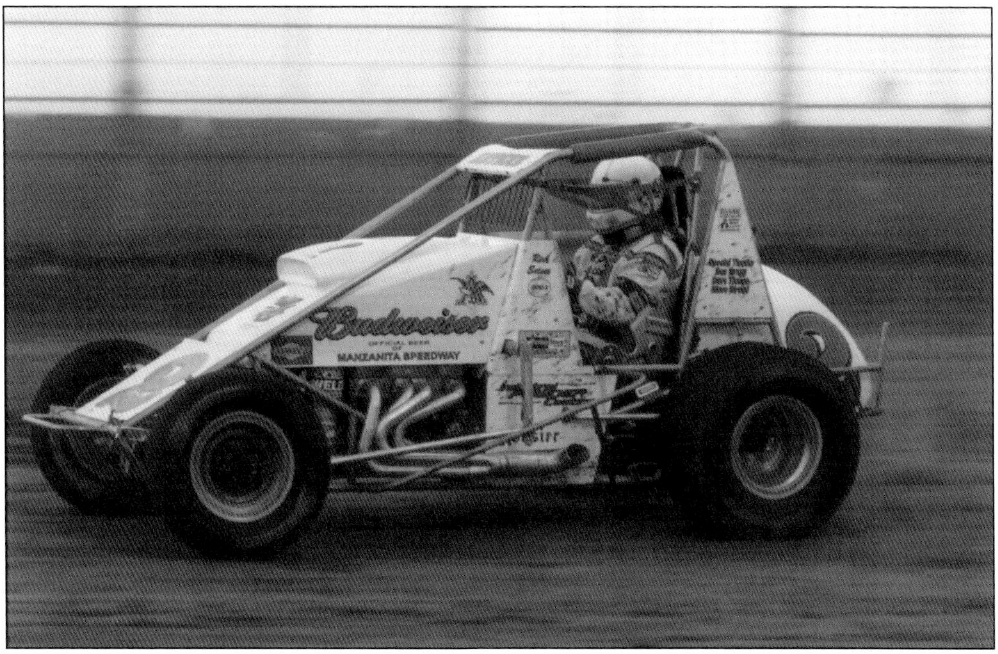

Driving the No. 2 Budweiser sprint car is Rick Setser, a longtime Manzy competitor in several divisions. After a serious accident racing a dwarf car, Setser moved to the sidelines, serving as pit steward and part-time announcer. Setser was fearless on the track and always maintained total control of events in the pits. He was a racer's racer. (Courtesy of Rick Setser.)

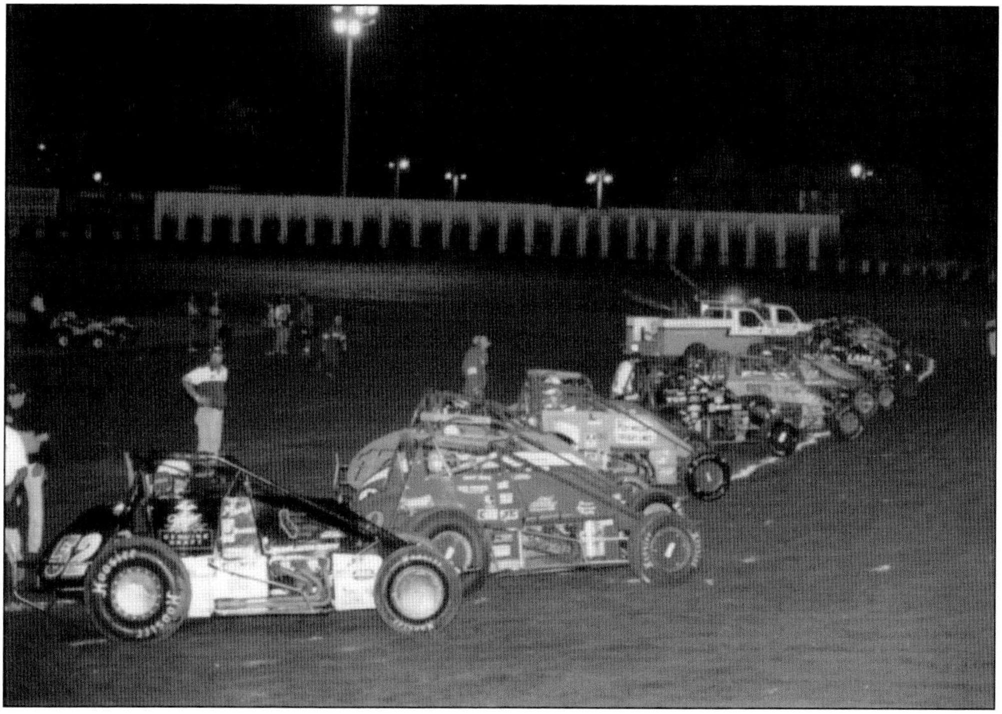

Above, non-winged sprint cars are lined up to do battle on September 2, 2000. As powerful as these cars are, they cannot move until a push vehicle lines up behind each car and pushes it until the engine starts. Sprint cars have no transmission; they are direct drive from engine to rear wheels. Below is a close-up of a sprint car, somewhat diminutive in appearance but with a monster motor beneath the tiny hood. (Both, courtesy of James A. Fargo.)

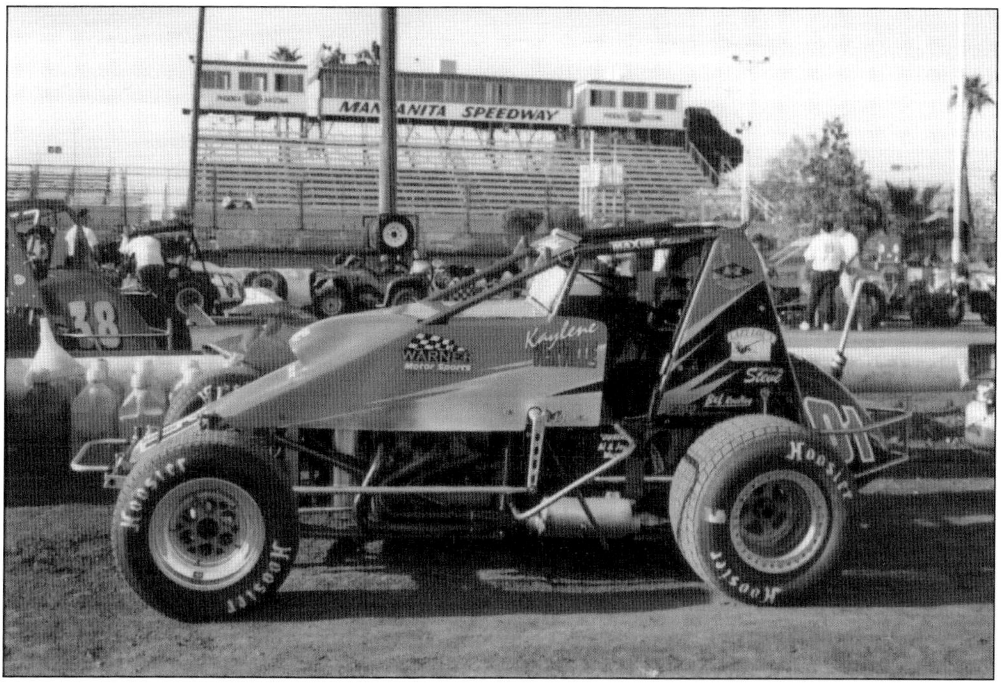

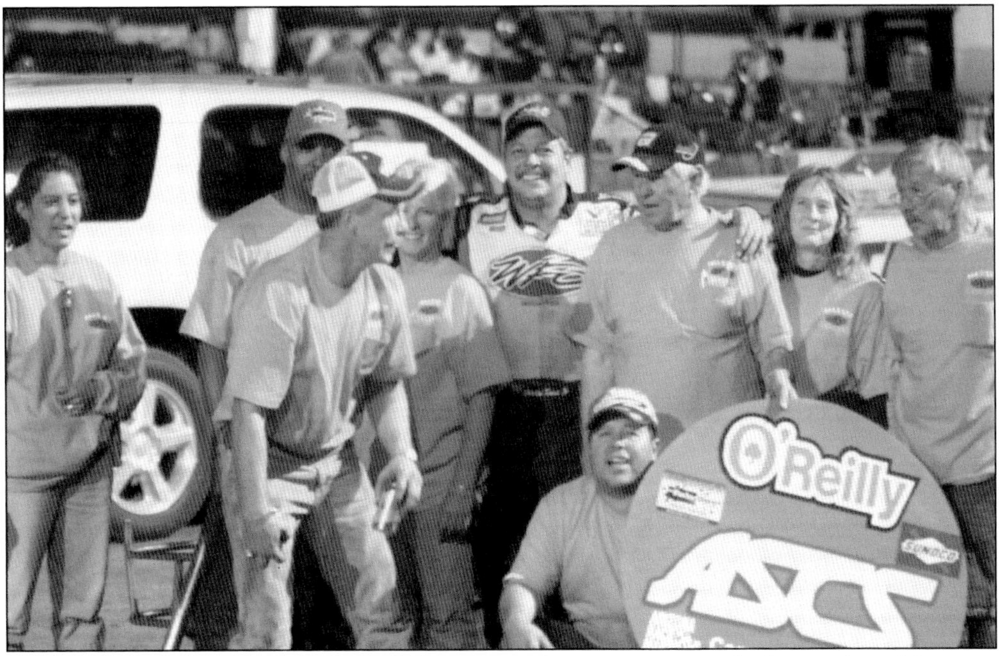

Charles Davis Jr., standing in the middle wearing the racing gear and a big smile, celebrates a victory at Manzy with family and members of the Massey Race Team in 2008. Davis Jr. has been racing since 1991 and is considered one of the best drivers in Arizona and in the West. His hero is Lealand McSpadden. (Courtesy of Don Iverson.)

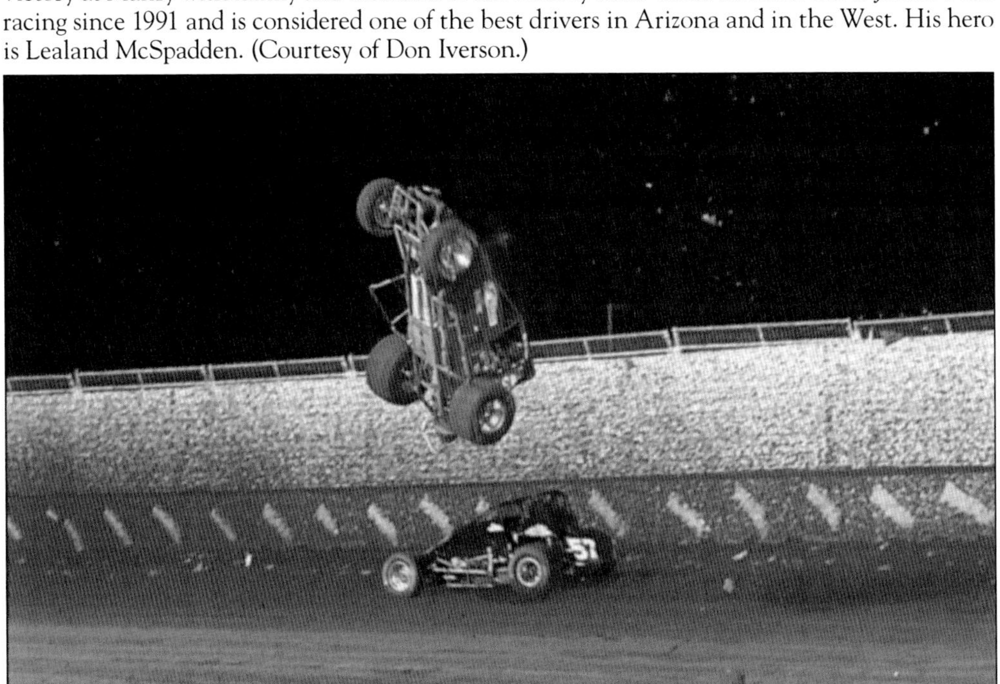

This sprint car goes airborne while No. 57 races underneath on Manzy's half-mile track at the Western World Championships in November 2008. Sprint cars by definition are rockets on wheels. They weigh about 1,200 pounds while sporting 600-plus horsepower. This kind of power on a lightweight chassis is a recipe for spectacular action on the track. (Courtesy of Don Iverson.)

Three

The Top Guns

Everyone knows racing is dangerous, which is the major reason why most people do not do it. So what motivates a person, protected only by a roll cage, a fire suit, gloves, shoes, and crash helmet, to strap himself or herself into a stripped down car of some type, powered by a high-performance engine, and then race pedal to the metal with 20 or more like-minded daredevils around an oval dirt track?

It is a given that racing and an adrenaline rush go hand in hand. Just the anticipation of the race sends the heart racing; it is absolutely nerve-wracking to sit side by side in line with the other cars in the race-staging area with the engines rumbling, awaiting one's turn to charge onto the track. The reality is that the driver feels better after the race begins.

The adrenaline rush is probably one reason why people engage in this sport; however, it makes one jumpy and prone to errors. The drivers who can conquer this nervous energy, converting it into a calm control, appear to be the most successful. The true professionals become one with the car, racing like they are out for a Sunday afternoon drive in the park. Those less fortunate individuals, the majority of racers, fight the wheel as they maneuver around the track, almost looking for a wreck in which they can participate.

Mistakes are part of racing, particularly dirt-track racing, because it is somewhat like driving on ice. The winners make the fewest mistakes. Many NASCAR drivers will admit that dirt racing requires the greater skill. A few years ago, a television camera caught Tony Stewart steering his car with his knees while he took a drink of water going almost 200 miles per hour at the Brickyard 400 in Indianapolis. One cannot do that on a dirt track. The speed is too great, and the tracks are too short. Well, maybe Tony Stewart could do it; after all, he came out of the dirt-track sprint-car ranks.

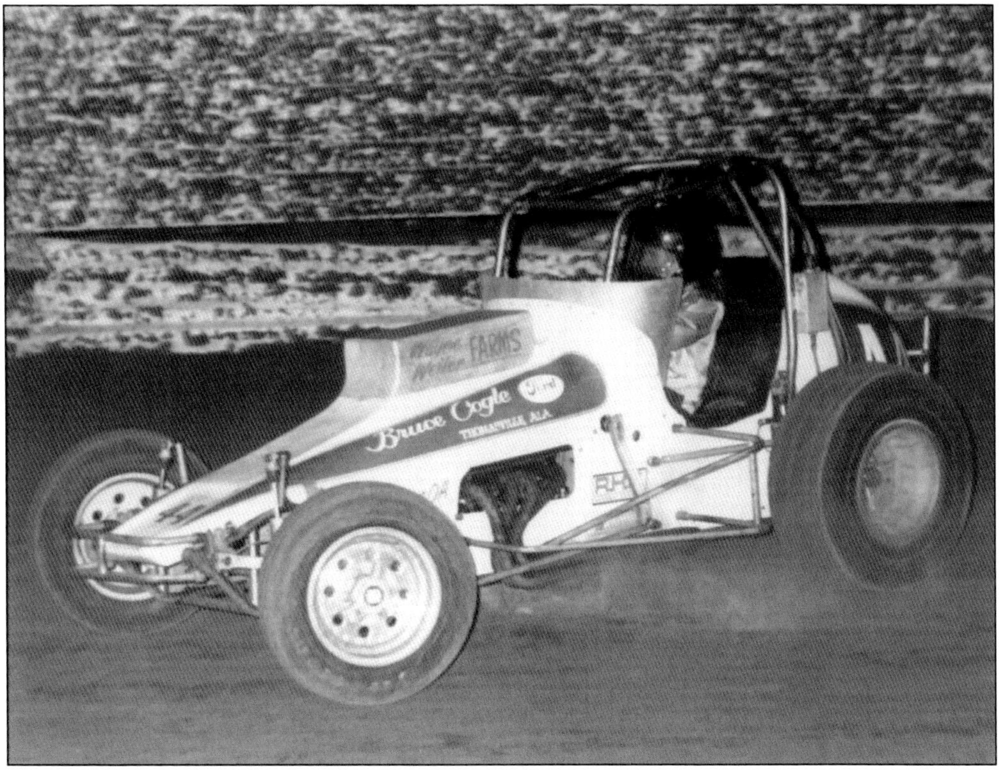

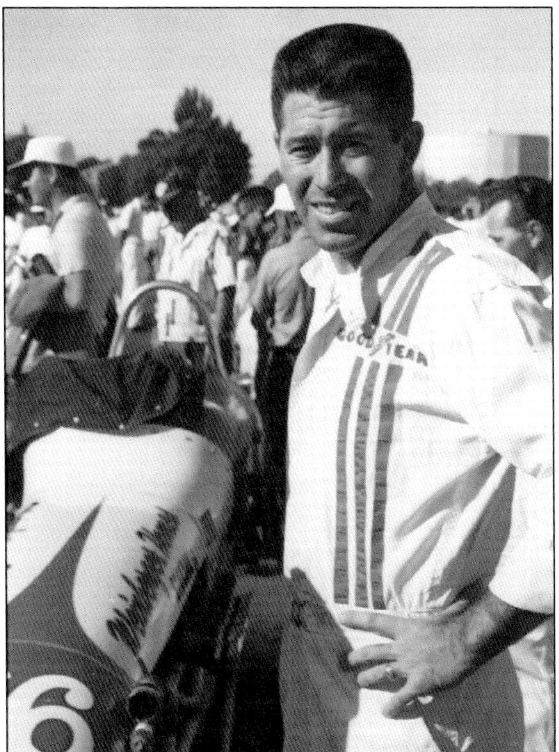

Pictured above is Wayne Weiler in the Weiler Farms' modified stock. Weiler continued moving up the ranks until he made his first appearance in the Indianapolis 500 in 1960. He raced in the Indy 500 again in 1961 but ended his USAC career the next month after a sprint-car crash in Terre Haute, Indiana. Weiler was one of the top drivers to come out of Arizona. (Courtesy of Don Appley.)

Roger McCluskey had racing talent that took him from jalopies to sprint cars and, ultimately, to the Indianapolis 500, in which he raced 18 times beginning in 1961. He also raced several times in the NASCAR Grand National Series. McCluskey and his good friend Hank Arnold were charter inductees to the Arizona Motorsports Hall of Fame. (Courtesy of Don Appley.)

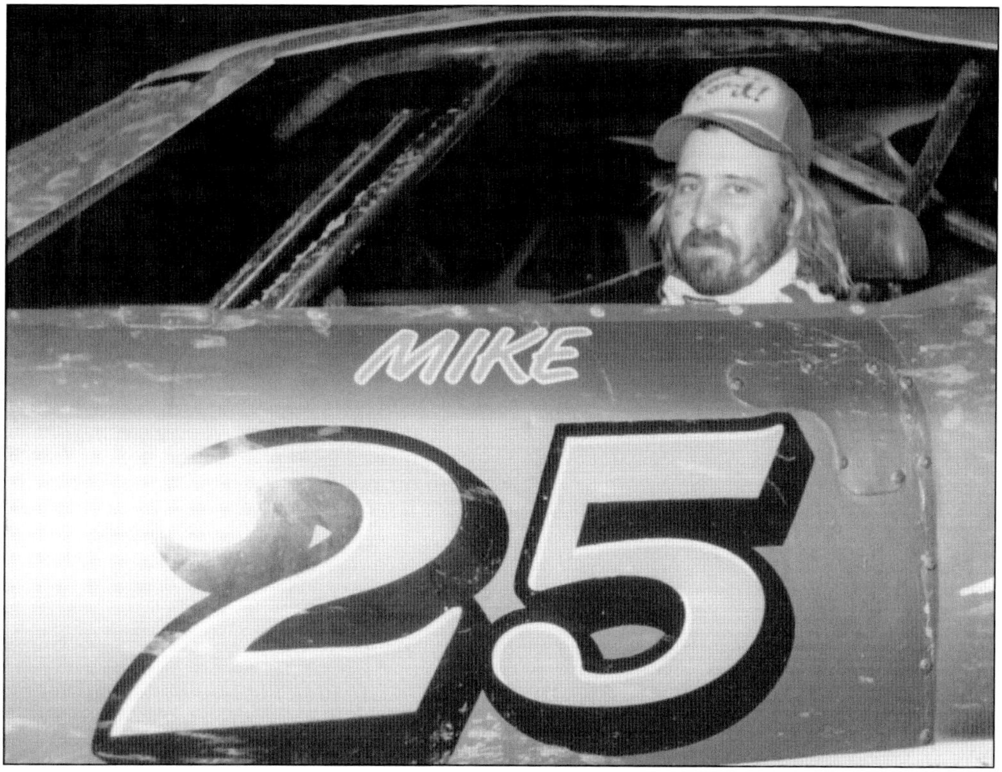

After several years of racing, Mike Lubanovich won the 1993 SCRA Street Stock Division Championship and then retired from racing. He said, "I wanted to be the champ, but after that I wanted to own a house and car. I realized I couldn't do that and continue racing." (Courtesy of Mike Lubanovich.)

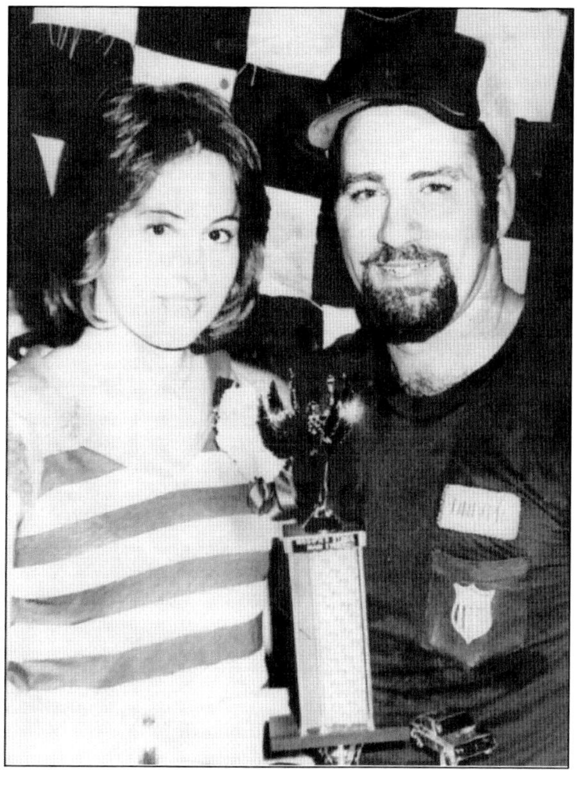

John Craig, on the right, receives a trophy from an unidentified trophy girl in 1973. Craig, a 1961 graduate of Camelback High School in Phoenix, began racing at Manzy in 1969 and was elected to the inaugural board of directors of the SCRA. In 1971, Craig, along with Ralph Hertel and Gary Belcher, was instrumental in founding the Modified Stock Division of the SCRA. Craig was inducted into the SCRA Hall of Fame in 2007. (Courtesy of Winston Brown Jr.)

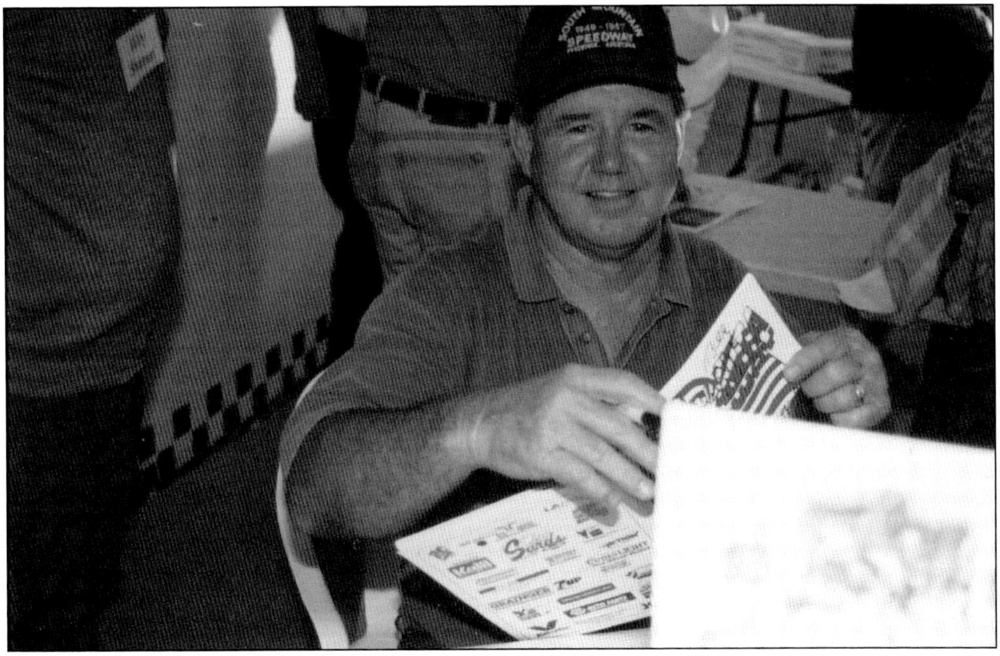

Above, Lealand McSpadden signs autographs at a celebrity event at Manzy on September 1, 2000. McSpadden was the leading Manzy lead-foot for three decades, from 1972 through 1996. He is a member of both the Arizona Motorsports Hall of Fame and the National Sprint Car Hall of Fame. In 2000, the *Arizona Republic* ranked McSpadden as the fifth top driver in Arizona over the past 100 years. Below, at a later autograph session on September 16, 2000, are two other racing greats, Gary Bettenhausen on the left and Billy Vukovich on the right. (Both, courtesy of James A. Fargo.)

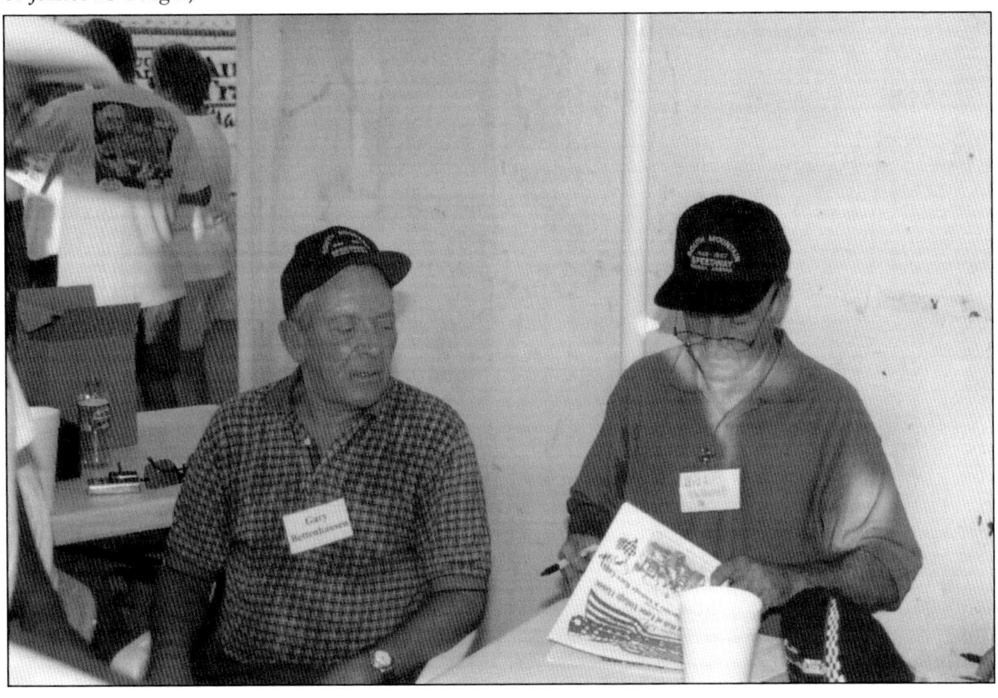

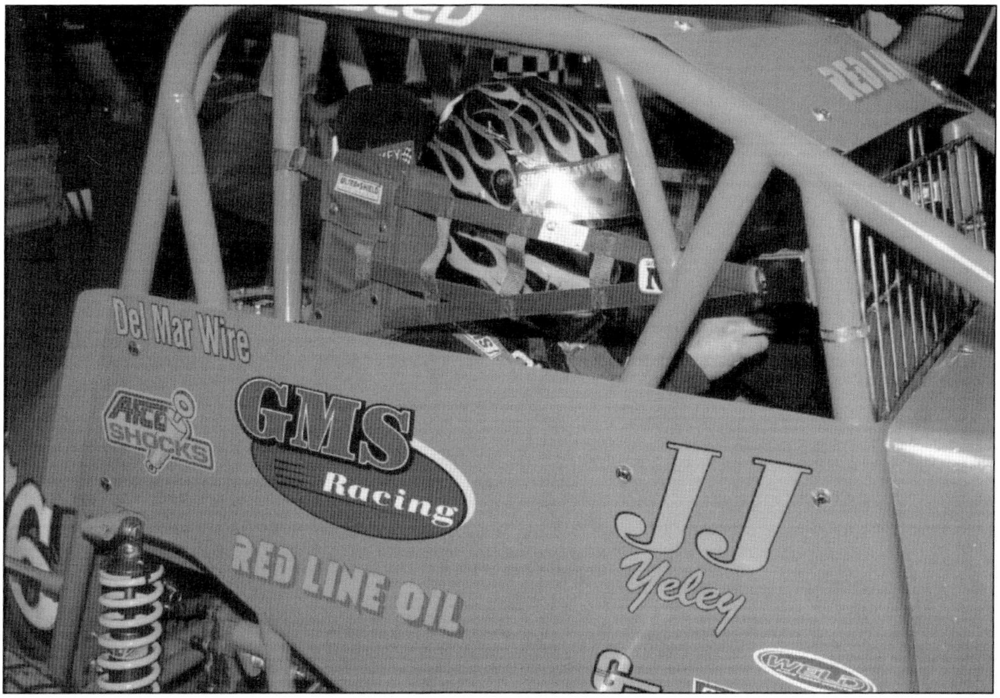

J.J. Yeley is one of the young guns from Phoenix who blew through Manzy on his way to the top of stock-car racing. By 2003, Yeley had already accomplished all there was to achieve in sprint cars and moved to NASCAR in 2004. Above, Yeley prepares for a sprint-car race at Manzy on February 4, 2000. Below, Yeley powers through turn four at Manzy in the 2007 Winter Super Late Model Championships. (Above, courtesy of James A. Fargo; below, courtesy of Don Iverson.)

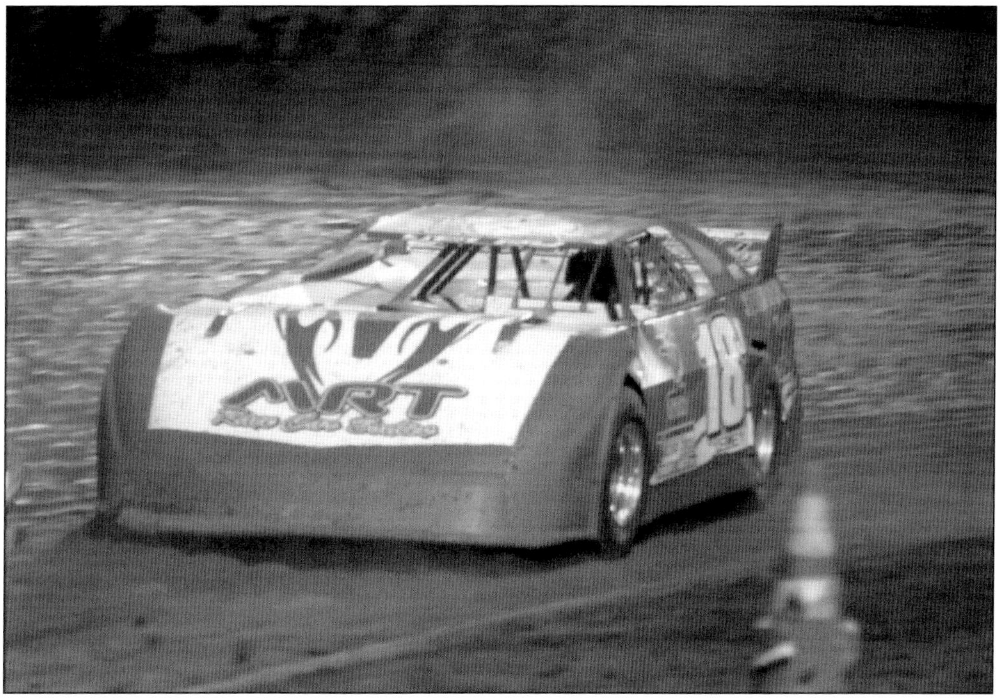

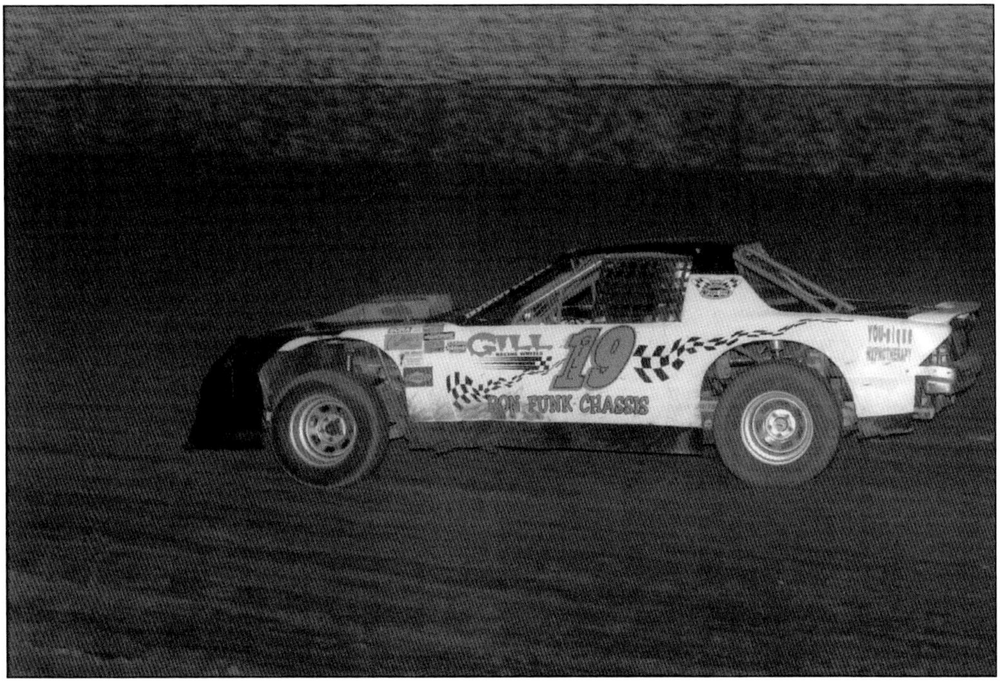

Kenny Gill, shown here in No. 19, is a frequent winner in the SCRA Super Stock Division. Gill has been racing since 1992 and won the last short-track super stock race before Manzy's closing in 2009. Gill won the SCRA Super Stock Division Championship in 2005 and 2006. In addition, he also won the SCRA Half-Mile Series in both those years. Gill is now preparing to enter the Southwest Late Model Series in 2012. (Courtesy of James A. Fargo.)

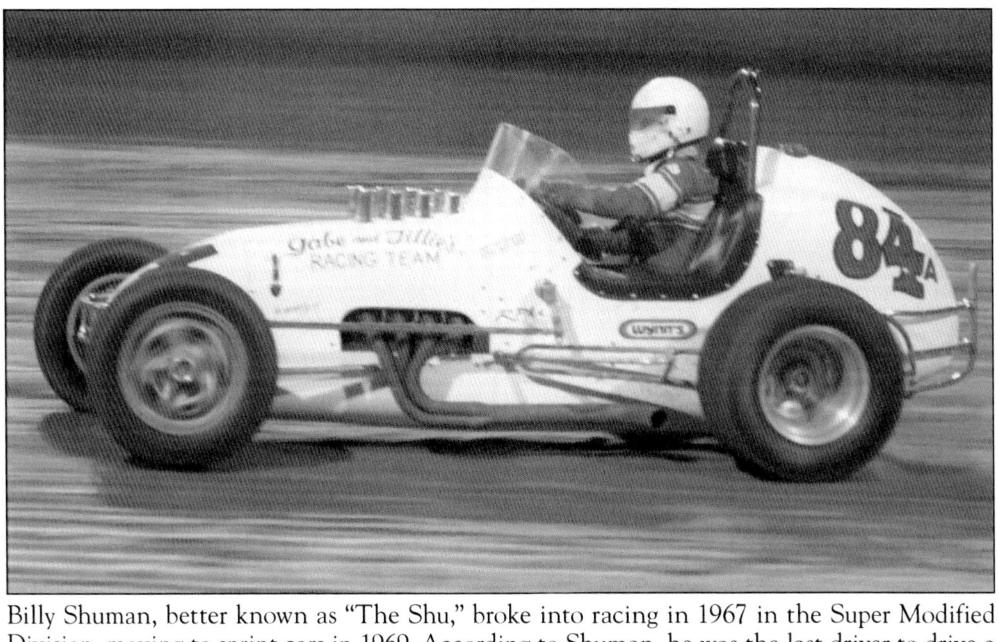

Billy Shuman, better known as "The Shu," broke into racing in 1967 in the Super Modified Division, moving to sprint cars in 1969. According to Shuman, he was the last driver to drive a sprint car at Manzy, doing so on February 10, 2010. This was by special permission after the track had been closed. (Courtesy of Don Iverson.)

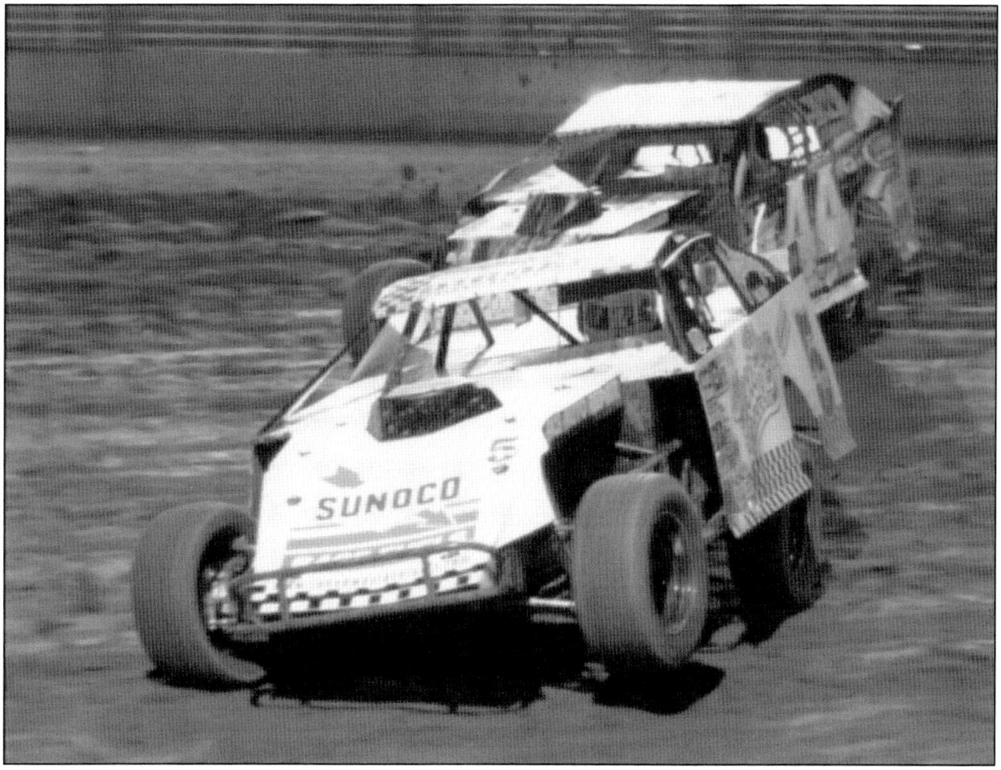

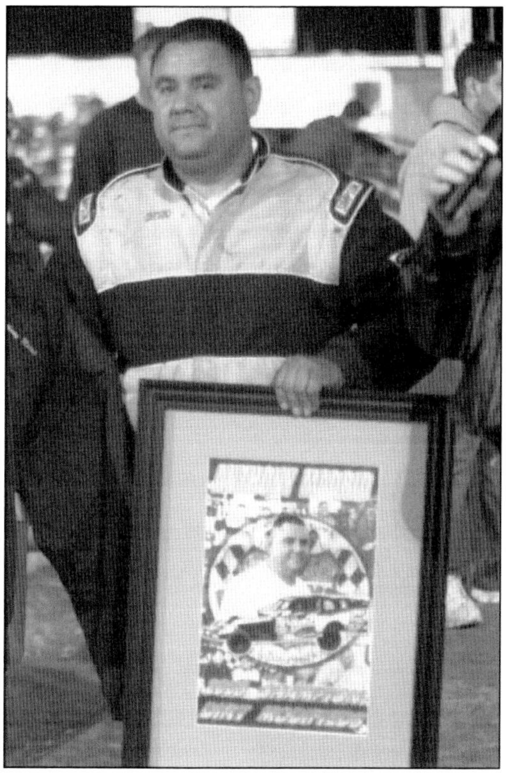

Above, Anthony Madrid, racing in the Flexi Flyer No. 5 dirt-modified car, was always a favorite to win regardless of the division in which he raced. In this photograph, Madrid is trying to hold off another top driver, Jason Knoll. Below, Madrid has been presented with a plaque celebrating his 2008 dirt modified championship. By the time Manzy closed in 2009, Madrid had won championships in bombers, factory stocks, super stocks, dirt modifieds, sport mods, and trucks. He is the only driver in Manzy history to win championships in two divisions in the same season in consecutive years, 2004 and 2005. (Both, courtesy of Don Iverson.)

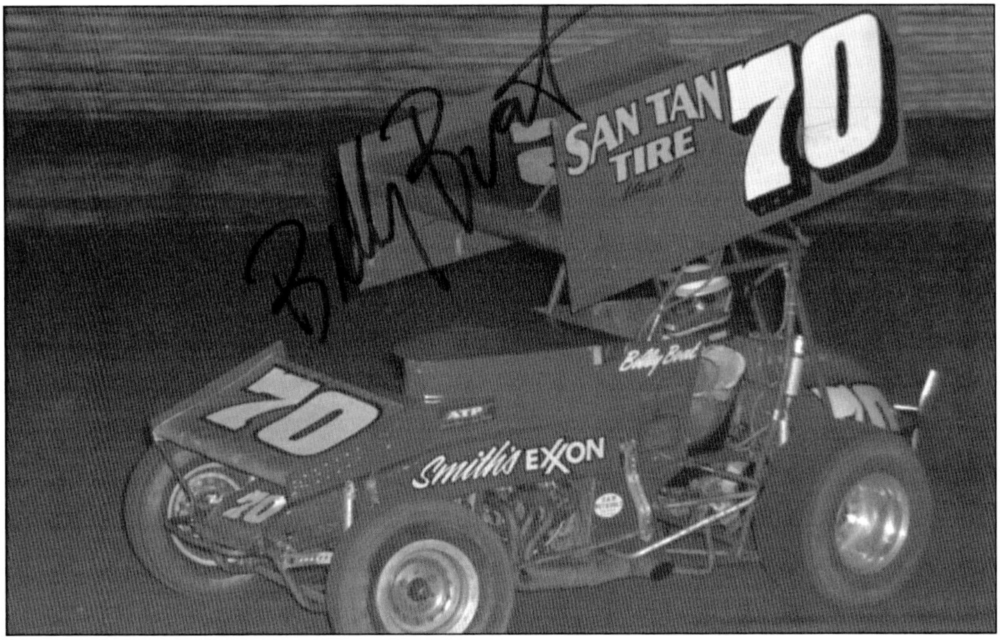

Above, Billy Boat is shown racing the No. 70 winged sprint car in May 1988 prior to his emergence on the national stage of automobile racing. Boat moved from the USAC to the Indy Racing League in 1997 and made his first start in the Indianapolis 500. He started on the pole in the 1998 race. Today, Boat owns and operates Billy Boat Performance Exhaust in Phoenix. Below, Boat's son Chad holds the winner's trophy for a winged mini sprint race. Under the tutelage of his father, Chad Boat is currently climbing the ladder of major-league racing. (Both, courtesy of Don Appley.)

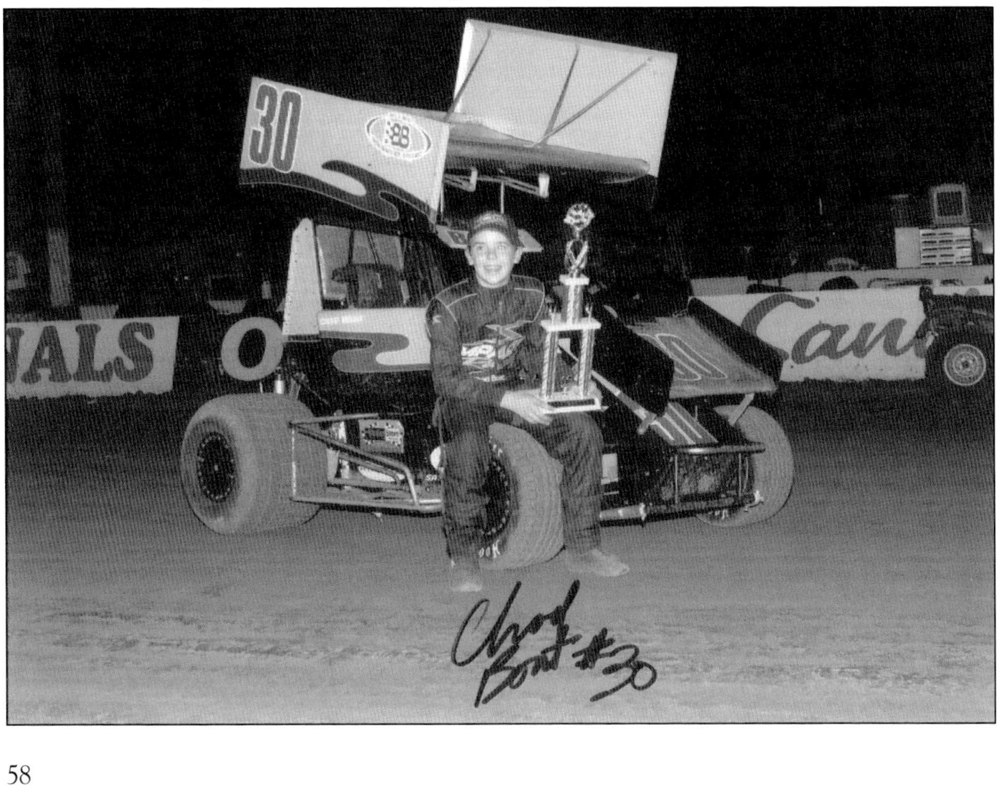

At right is Kevin Cain, arguably the best dwarf-car driver in Arizona with six championships. Kevin, his brother Casey, and their parents, John and Joan, manufacture more dwarf cars than anyone in the United States at the Dwarf Car Company Inc. in Phoenix. Below is a group of dwarf-car champions at Manzy, including No. 12, Pat Henesey; No. 11, Heather Henesey; No. 35, Jeff Hock; and No. 10, Helen Henesey. (Both, courtesy of Don Iverson.)

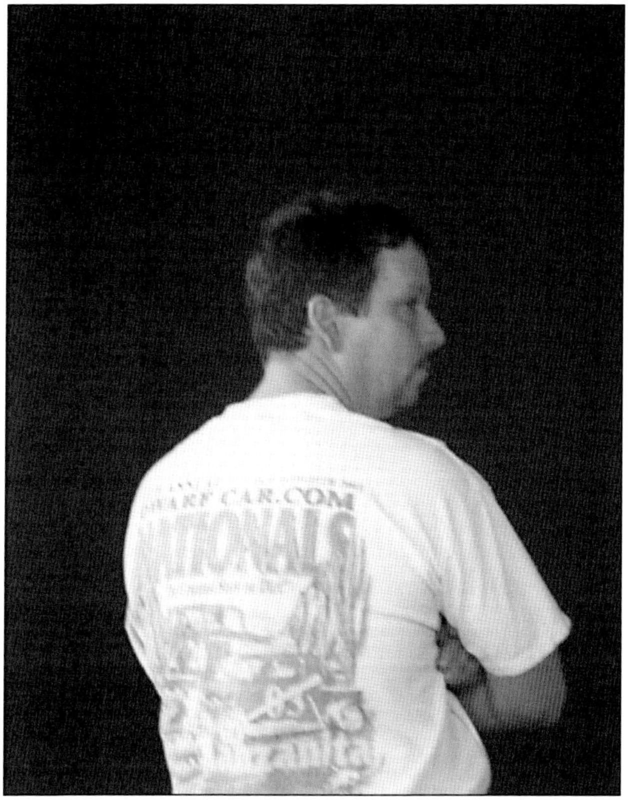

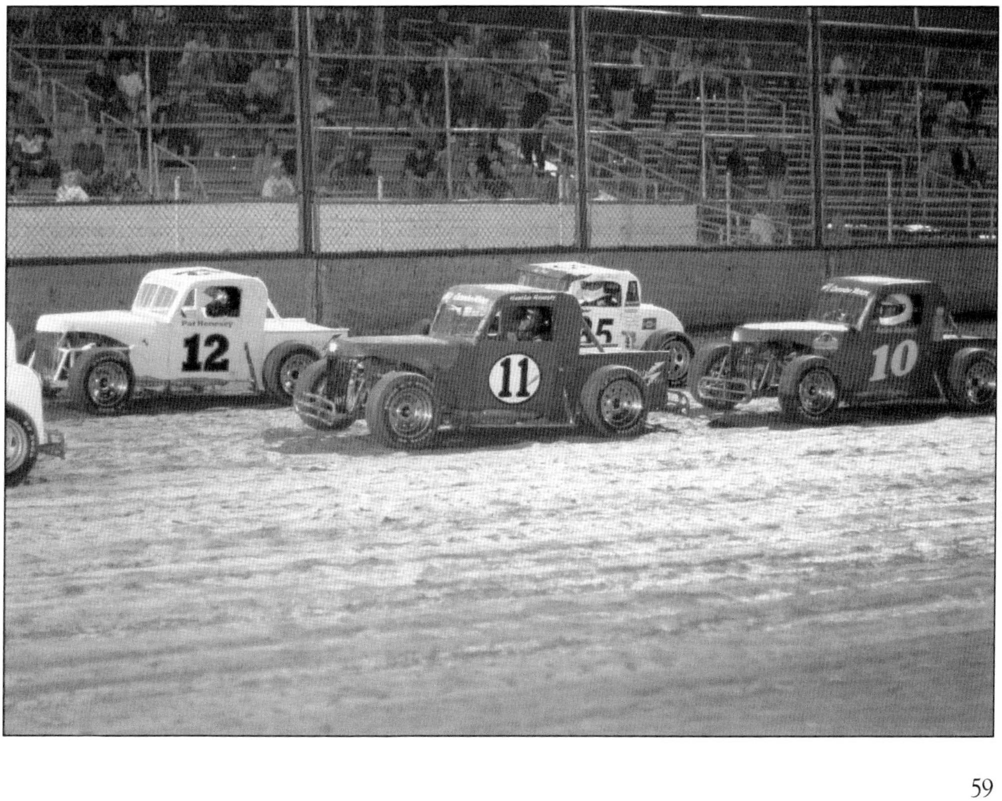

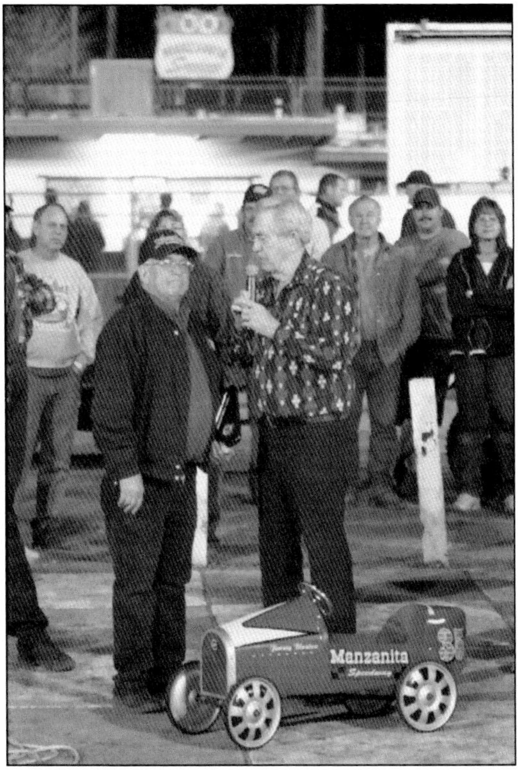

Announcer Windy McDonald, a Hall of Famer, has a little fun with another member of the Arizona Motorsports Hall of Fame, Jimmy Blanton, with the presentation of a toy race car. Blanton, the good sport that he is, took it all in stride. In addition to being a top sprint-car driver, Blanton for many years owned Arizona Race Mart, which was a key supplier to Phoenix racers. (Courtesy of Don Iverson.)

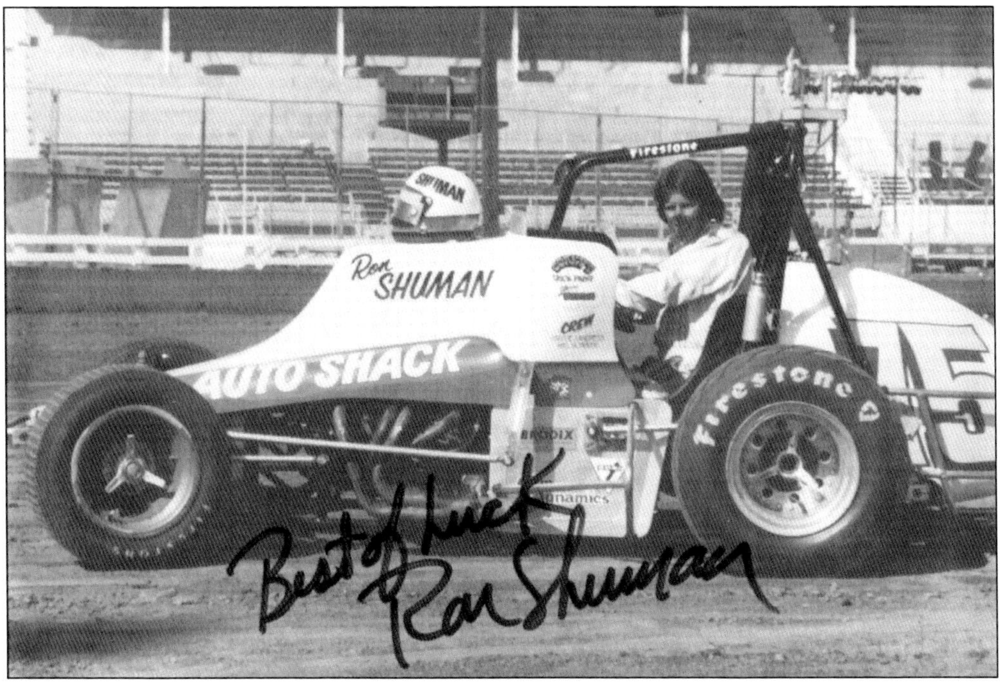

Ron Shuman sits in his No. 75 sprint car. Both Shuman and his older brother Billy have been inducted into the Arizona Motorsports Hall of Fame, Billy in 1994 and Ron in 2001. Ron was also inducted into the National Sprint Car Hall of Fame in 2003. (Courtesy of Don Appley.)

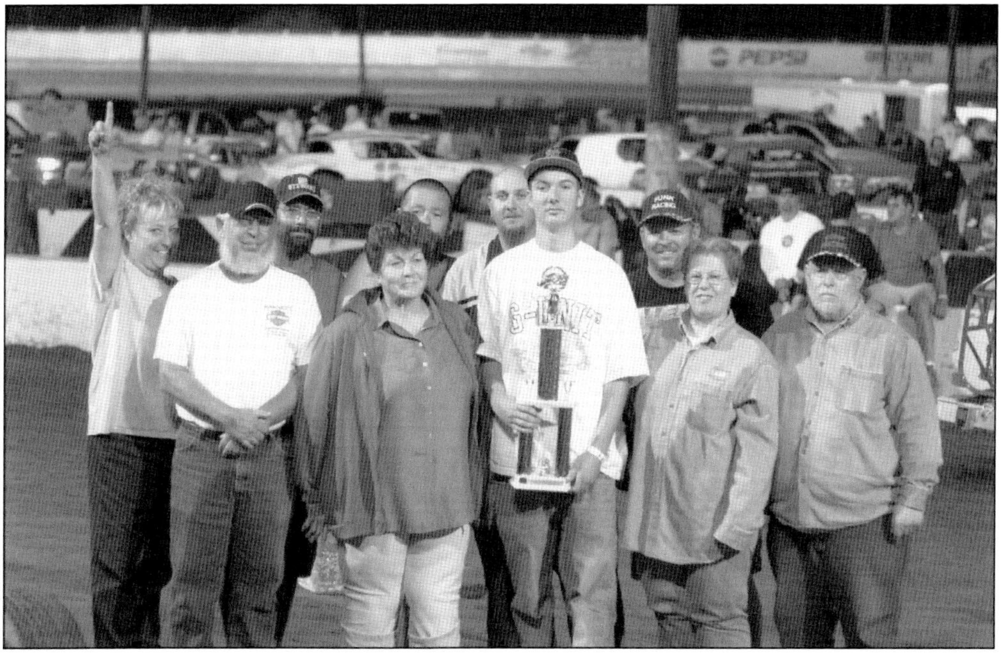

Pictured are, from left to right, (first row) Shawna Funk, her parents Leo and Ann Berard, Garrett Funk (2009 SCRA Sport Mod Division champion), and Garrett's grandparents, Pat and Dan Funk; (second row) Billy Dodd, Mike Spilgenbauer, Joe Nesbitt, and Ron Funk. Shawna and Ron Funk are the proud parents of Garrett Funk. (Courtesy of Don Iverson.)

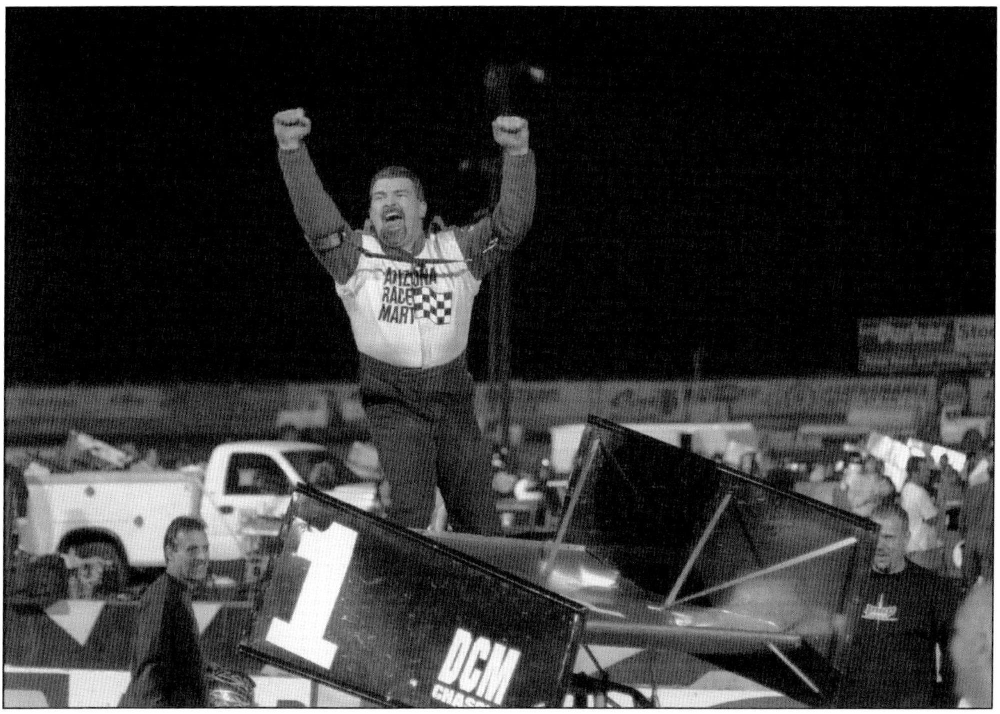

Kiley Fellers celebrates a mini sprint win at the Kaiser in 2008. Fellers went on to win the 2008 mini sprint division championship. (Courtesy of Don Iverson.)

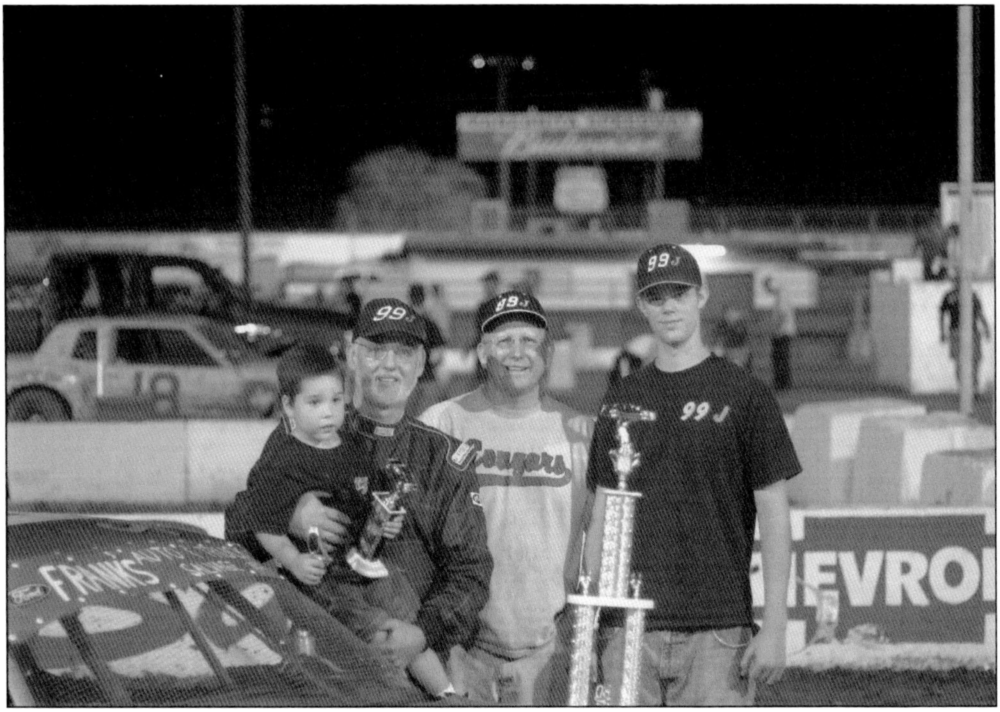

Pictured after a race on May 25, 2008, are, from left to right, an unidentified young boy, winning driver Bobby Erdman, Rich Clucas, and Jamie Woody. Erdman, a mechanical engineer, is a three-time SCRA champion, winning the factory stock title in 1991 and 1992 and the super stock crown in 1998, after which he retired from racing. Erdman came back in 2007 and continues to race with the SCRA. He is a member of the SCRA Hall of Fame. (Courtesy of Don Iverson.)

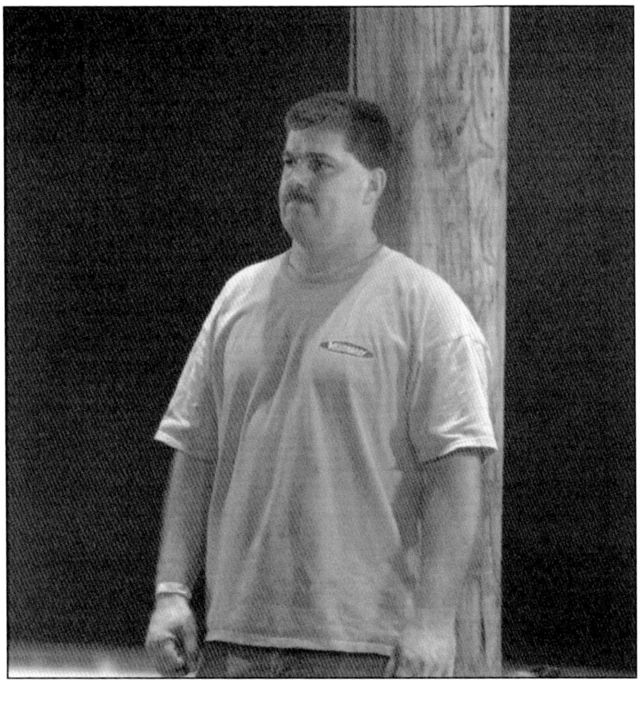

Father of a racing family, Ricky Thornton Sr., himself a three-time dirt-modified champion, seems preoccupied as he watches his son Ricky Jr. race at Manzy on September 14, 2007. Ricky Jr. has already won a dirt modified championship, and his younger brother Justin is on the way up. (Courtesy of Don Iverson.)

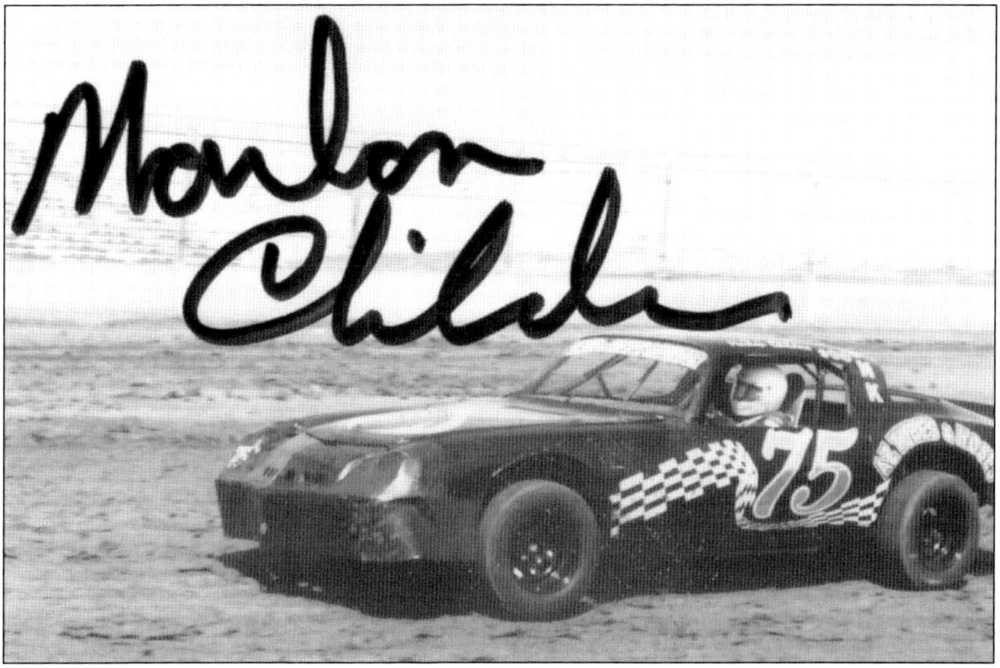

Marlon Childers, a 2005 inductee into the SCRA Hall of Fame, had won four championships by the time he retired from racing in 2007. Childers played baseball, basketball, and football at South Mountain High School in Phoenix. After high school, he played third base on a Phoenix semiprofessional baseball team that lost only one game over three years. His most enduring memory and greatest loss was when Melvin, his older brother, was killed on his 21st birthday in combat in the Vietnam War. (Courtesy of Don Appley.)

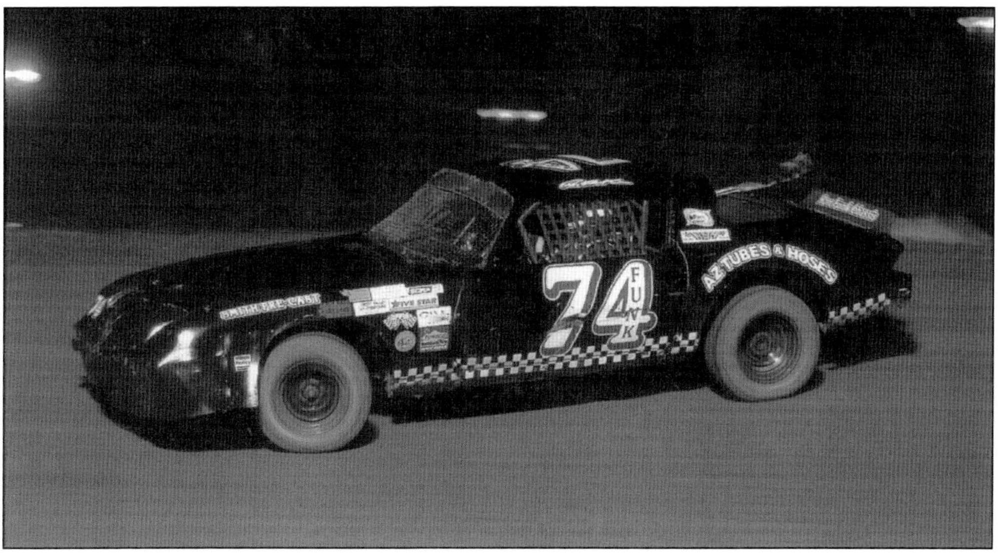

In the words of SCRA Hall-of-Famer Ron Funk, driver of No. 74, "I have been fascinated with race cars from my earliest memory." His parents, Danny and Pat Funk, had occupied the same seats at Manzanita Speedway for 38 consecutive years when it closed in 2009. The winner of numerous racing awards, Funk is also a premier race-car builder in Phoenix. His wife, Shawna, is his most passionate fan. (Courtesy of Shawna Funk.)

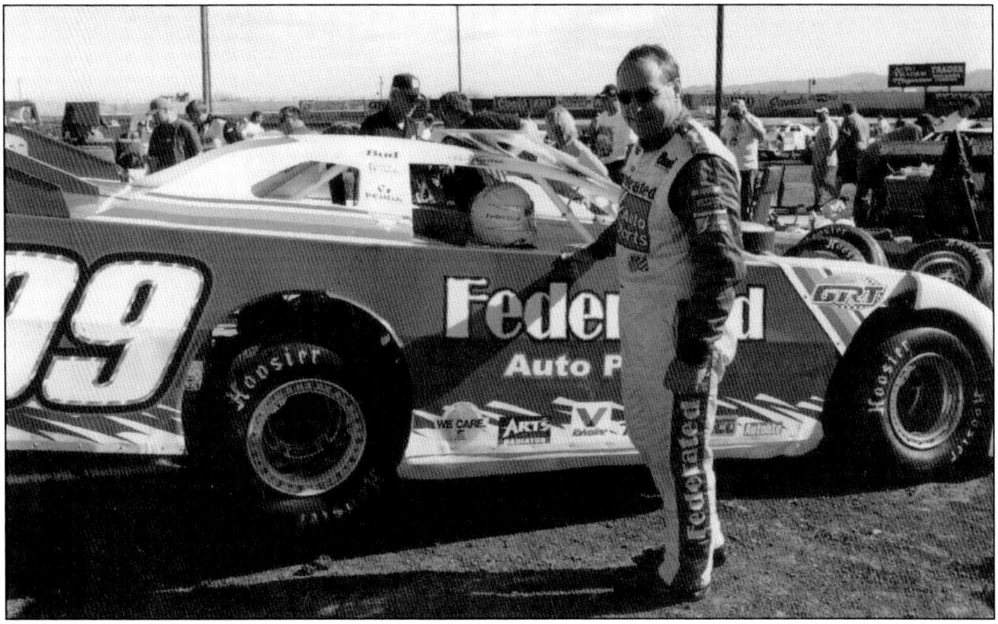

Ken Schrader is a former NASCAR star who now races part-time with the NASCAR Camping World Truck Series but finds time to race on dirt tracks in Super Late Model races all over the country. Schrader will drive any type of race car. He even participated in a celebrity Bomber Division race at Manzy several years ago. He spun out, finishing out of the money. (Courtesy of James A. Fargo.)

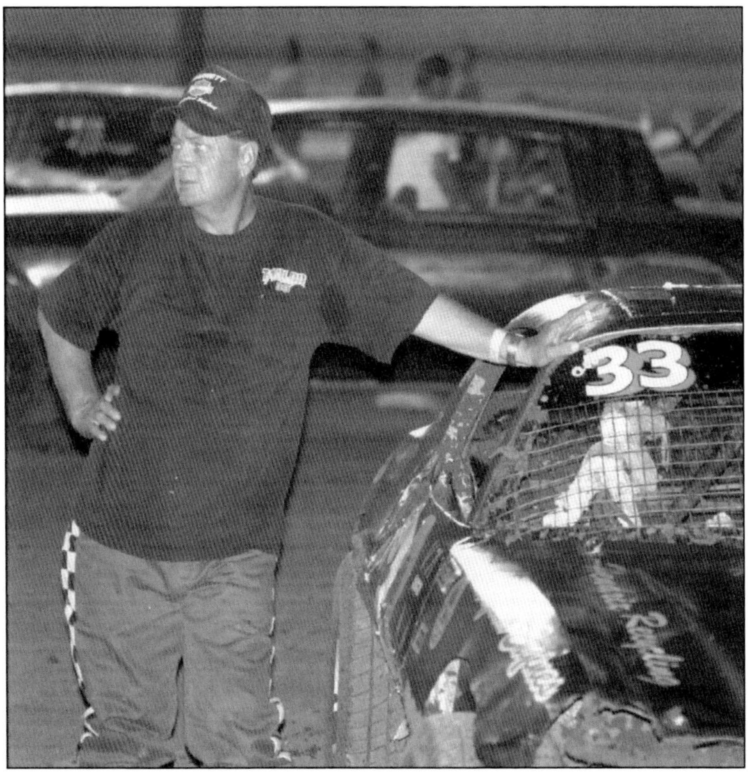

Three-time SCRA champion and Hall-of-Famer Bobby Taylor relaxes next to his No. 33 between races. Taylor is one of the most popular drivers in the SCRA Factory Stock Division, and his driving performance belies the old adage that "nice guys finish last." Taylor sees racing as entertainment and says, "I like being part of the show." (Courtesy of Don Iverson.)

Larry Price said that he bought his first car, a 1951 Chrysler, for $5 at age 12, "so I would have something to work on . . . I have always been attracted to cars." He began racing at Manzy in 1970, buying a 1958 DeSoto for $50, which he named the "Silver Bird." Price won the 2000 SCRA Factory Stock Division Championship and was inducted into the SCRA Hall of Fame in 2006. Price has mentored untold dozens of racers in the sport. (Courtesy of Don Iverson.)

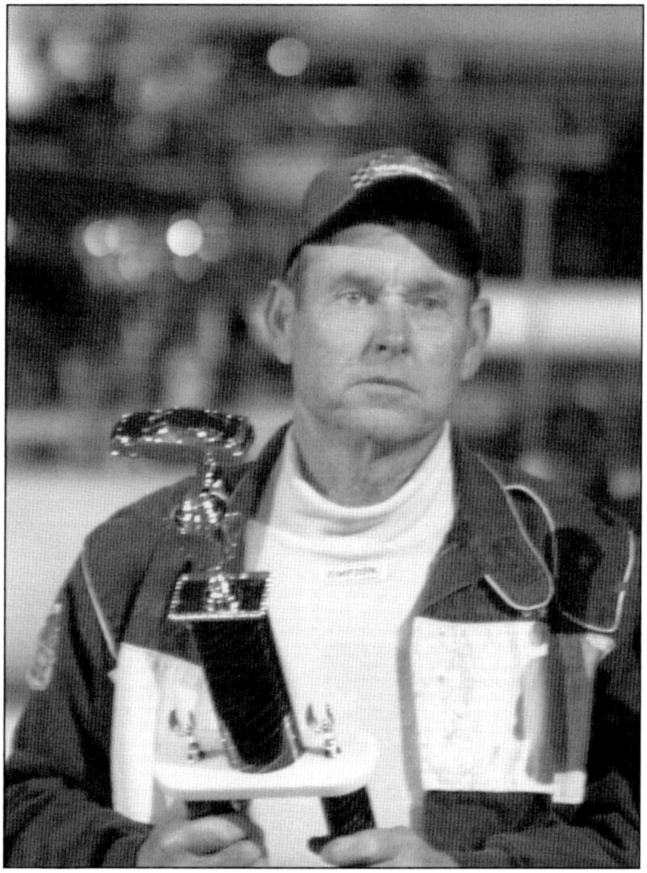

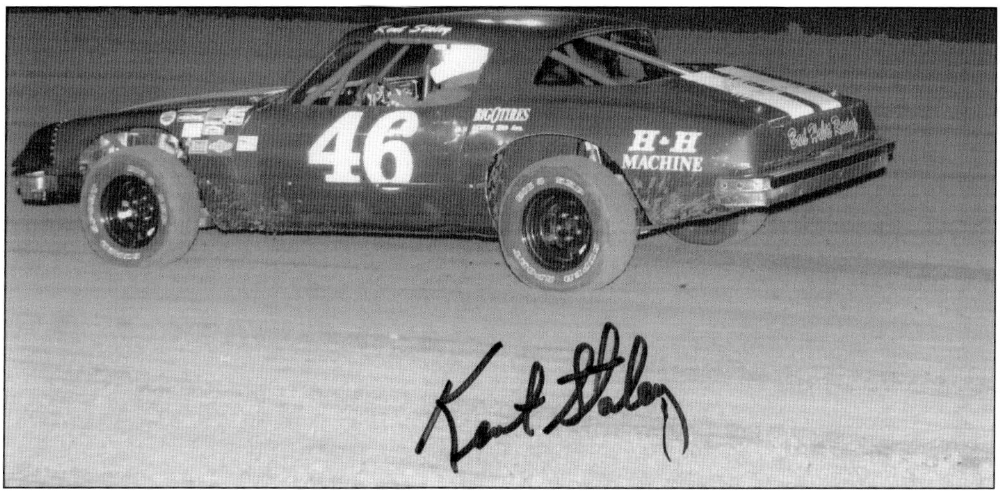

Kent Staley won three stock-car championships in Albuquerque, New Mexico, before moving to Phoenix in 1983. He won the 1990 SCRA Super Stock Division Championship at Manzy and was inducted into the SCRA Hall of Fame in 2007. Staley's wife, Beverly, was the official scorekeeper at Manzy for 25 years. At the end of the Manzy run, Staley was the unofficial captain of the Bad Habit Racing Team, comprised of his son Reeve, James Pautot, and Clint Fouts. (Courtesy of Don Appley.)

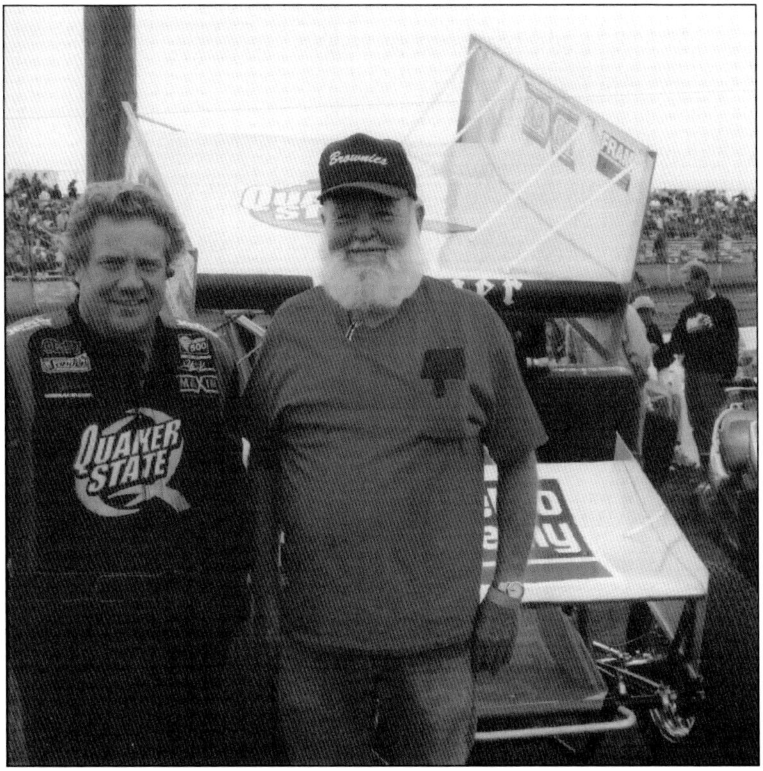

Steve Kinser, on the left, is a legend in World of Outlaws sprint-car racing. Currently, he has 20 World of Outlaws Championships, 12 wins of the Knoxville Nationals, and was inducted into the National Sprint Car Hall of Fame in 2005. Winston Brown Jr. (right) caught up with Kinser at Manzy in February 2004 and traded a cap for Kinser's shirt. (Courtesy of Winston Brown Jr.)

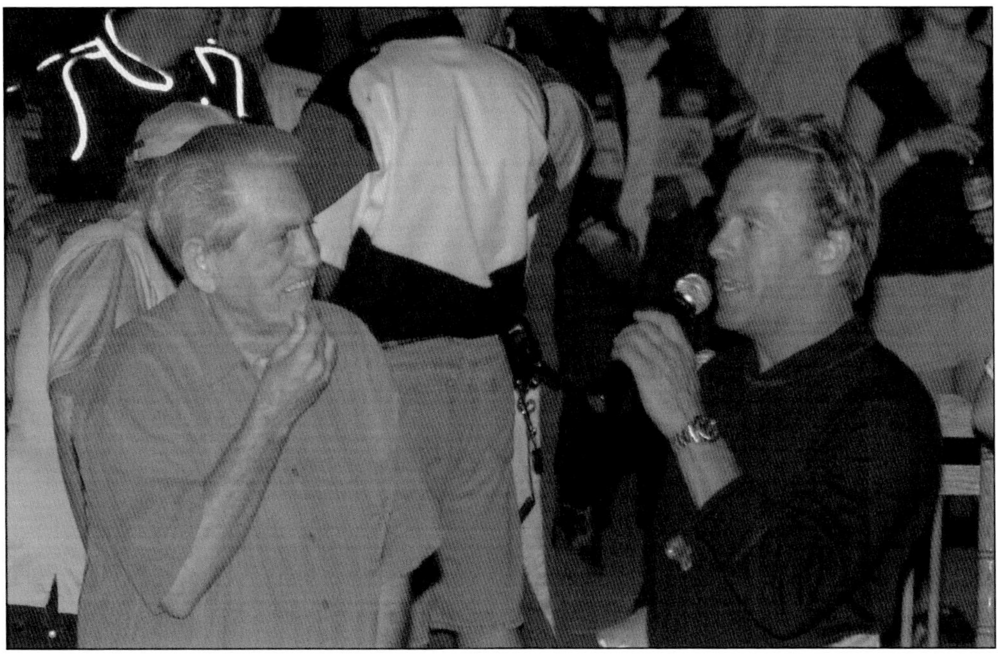

Announcer Windy McDonald, an Arizona Motorsports Hall of Famer (left), is interviewed by Scott Pasmore, the news anchor of the KTVK-TV show *Good Morning! Arizona*. McDonald became a full-time announcer at Manzy in 1957 and, with a little time off here and there, stayed until the end. (Courtesy of Don Iverson.)

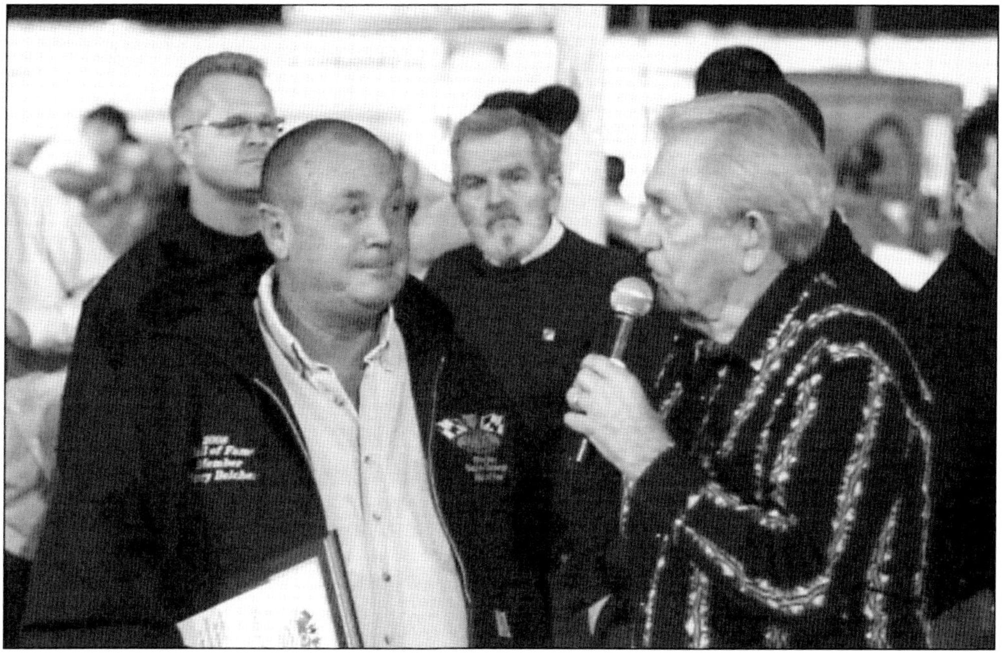

Pictured on the left, Terry Belcher Sr., the most prolific winner in Manzy history with over 200 wins and a 2007 inductee into the SCRA Hall of Fame, is being interviewed by announcer Windy McDonald. Notice that Belcher is wearing the SCRA Hall-of-Fame jacket. (Courtesy of Don Iverson.)

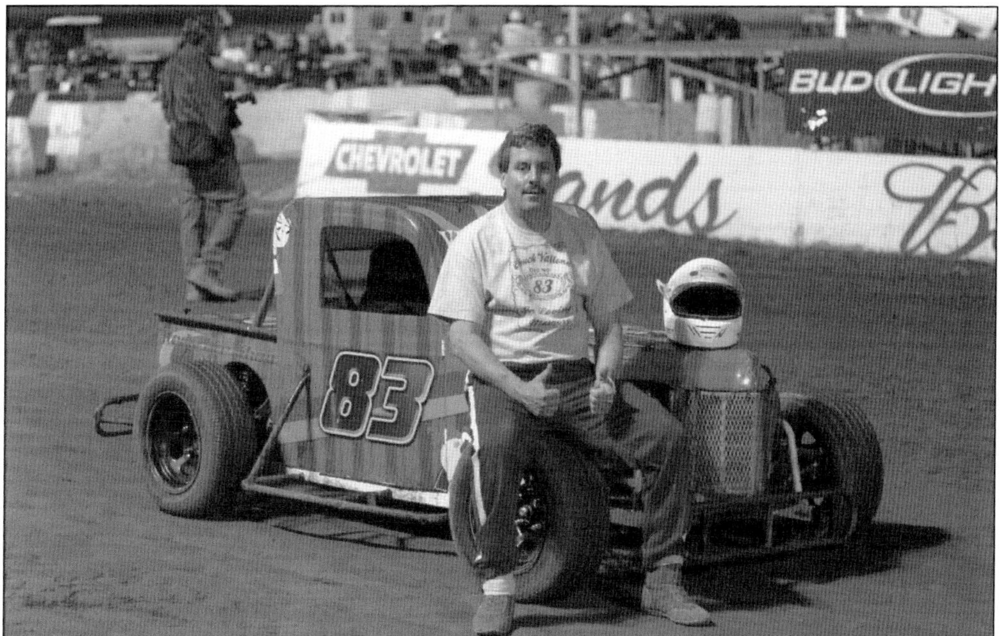

Dwarf Car Series champion Casey Cain drives the Chuck Vallone truck in honor of Vallone at the 2008 Dwarf Car Nationals. Chuck Vallone died of a heart attack in the pits after his heat race just a month earlier. Cain is a member of the dwarf-car manufacturing family in Phoenix. (Courtesy of Don Iverson.)

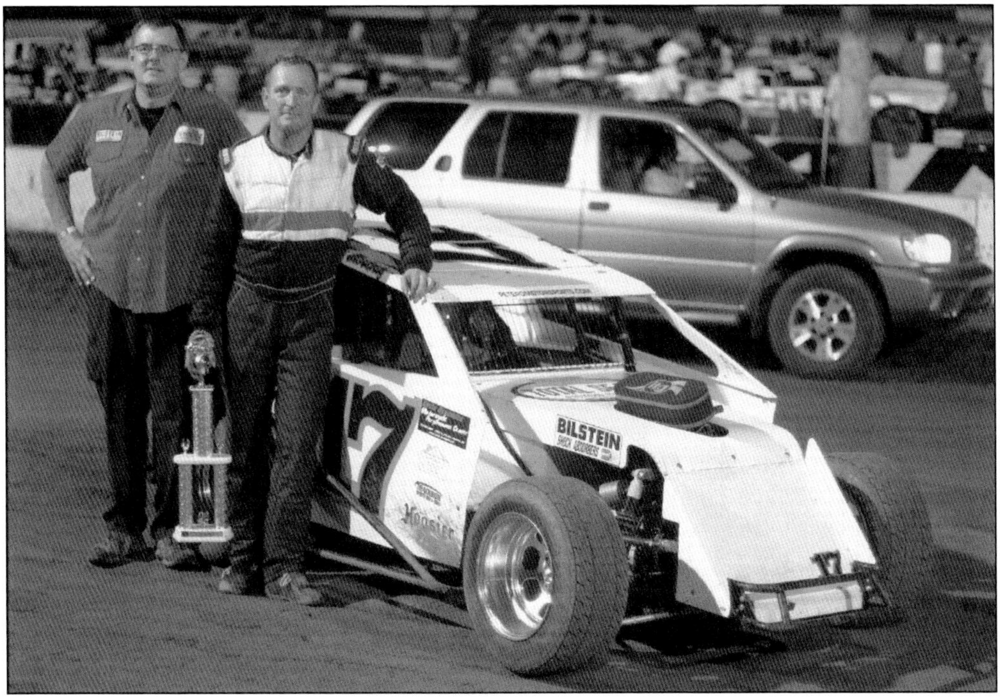

Steve Moriarty was the winning driver in this mod lite race in 2008. Moriarty is no rookie. He raced motorcycles for 13 years, owning several New England championships with 60 wins. Steve raced in the American Motorcyclist Association Pro Superbike series and also drove shifter karts. He won the over age 35 championship in Englishtown, New Jersey, in 2005. After moving to Arizona, Moriarty switched to dwarf cars and mod lites. (Courtesy of Don Iverson.)

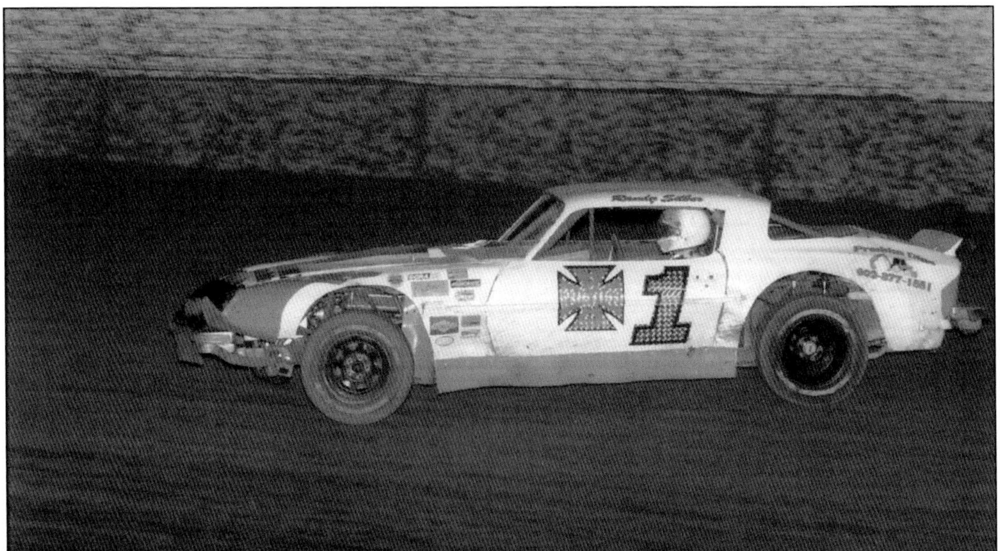

The tradition at Manzy is for the most-recent champion driver to display No. 1 on his race car the season following the championship run. Shown here is Randy Silber's 2005 super stock car displaying the No. 1, which he earned by winning the 2004 SCRA Super Stock Division Championship. (Courtesy of James A. Fargo.)

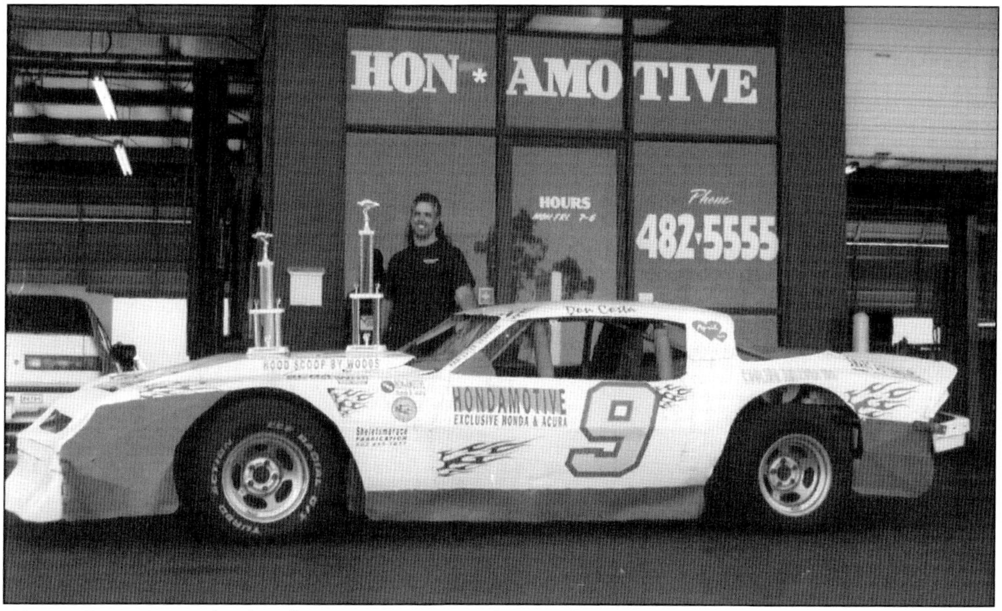

Above, Don Costa displays his No. 9 super stock, which always shows pride of ownership. Costa began racing in 1995 and has over 50 wins, including the 2007 SCRA Super Stock Division Championship as well as the 2008 SCRA Half-Mile Challenge Championship. Costa's entry into racing led to his exit as a drummer from Phoenix rock bands The Visitors and Evergrey. Shown below, standing in front of No. 9, are Kenny Gill; Drew Costa, son of Don; Don Costa; and Stacey Thares after a good night of racing. (Both, courtesy of James A. Fargo.)

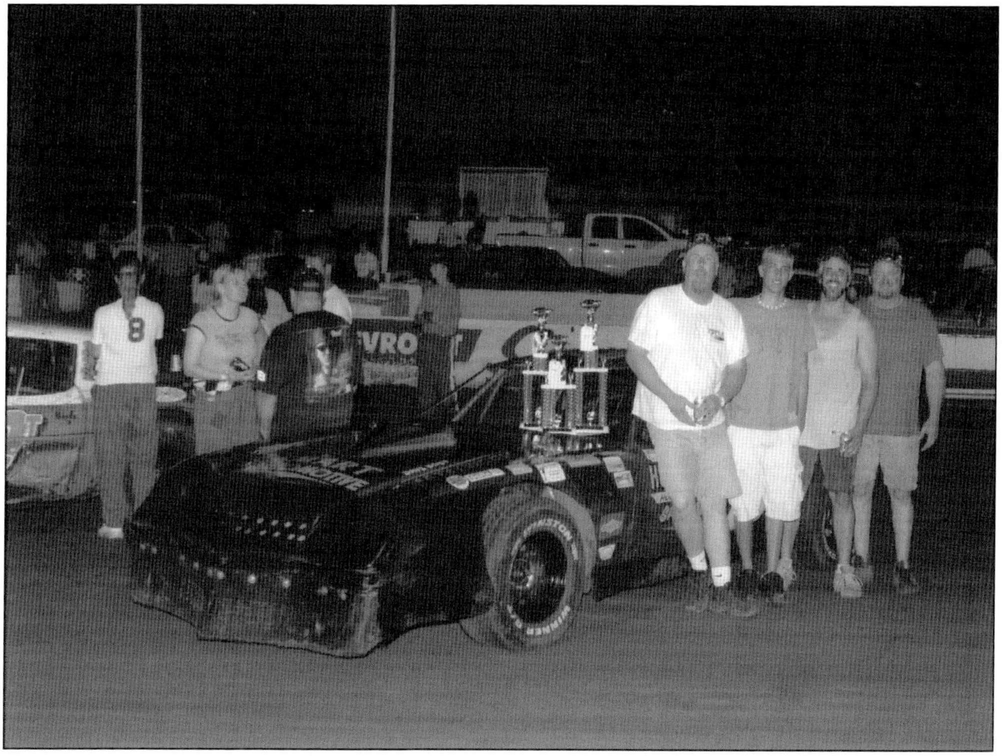

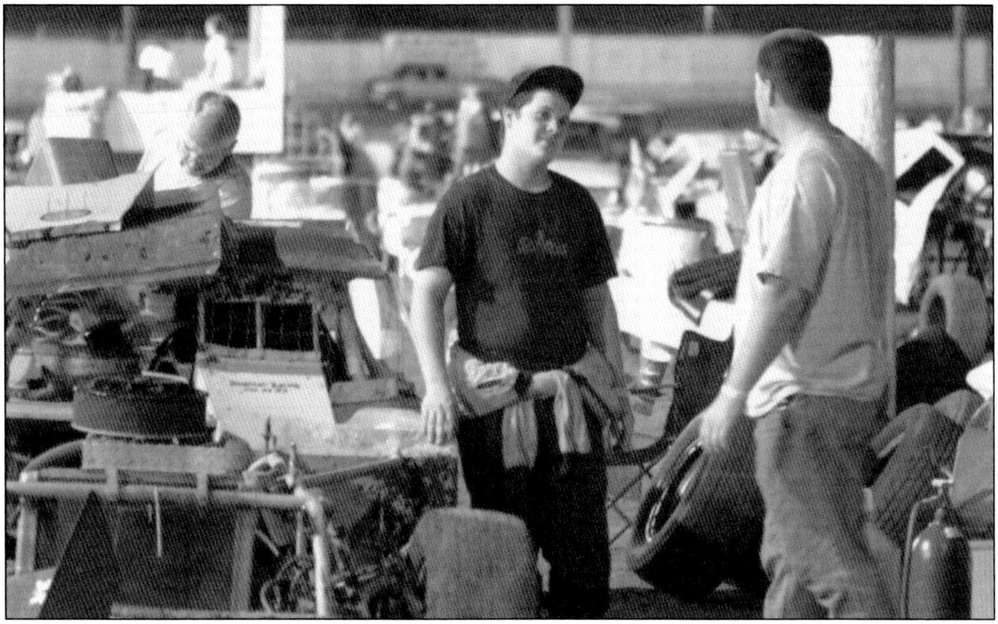

Ricky Thornton Jr., wearing the cap, receives advice from his father, Ricky Thornton Sr., before a dirt-modified race. Thornton Jr. earned Rookie of the Year honors in the SCRA Factory Stock Division in 2005 as a 14-year-old, moved to the dirt modifieds at age 15, and won the championship at age 16. Ricky Thornton Sr. was a three-time dirt-modified champion. He continues to race, but is devoted to assisting his sons, Ricky Jr. and Justin, in their racing careers. (Courtesy of Don Iverson.)

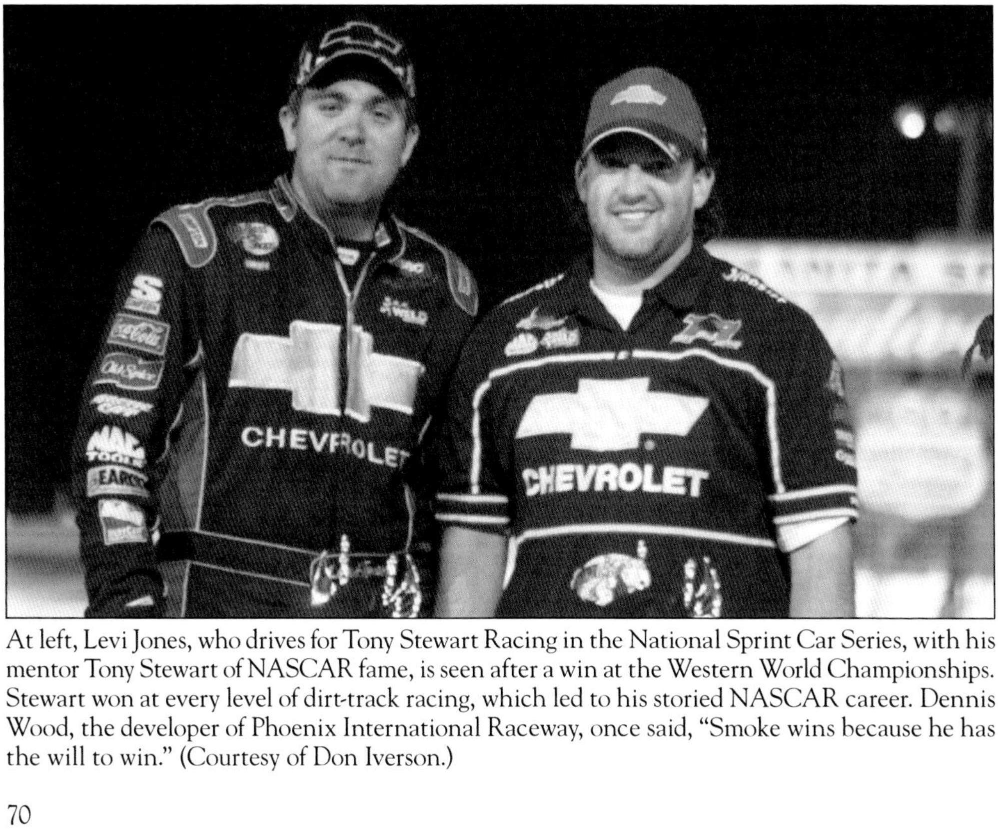

At left, Levi Jones, who drives for Tony Stewart Racing in the National Sprint Car Series, with his mentor Tony Stewart of NASCAR fame, is seen after a win at the Western World Championships. Stewart won at every level of dirt-track racing, which led to his storied NASCAR career. Dennis Wood, the developer of Phoenix International Raceway, once said, "Smoke wins because he has the will to win." (Courtesy of Don Iverson.)

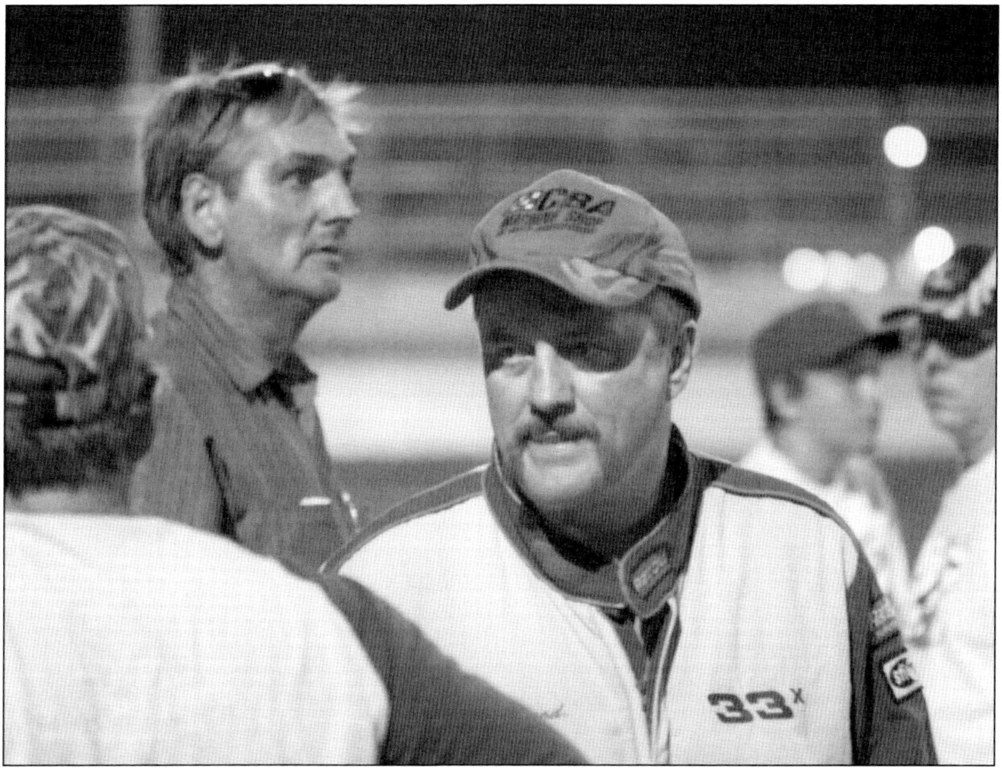

Pictured in the center foreground is factory stock driver Jody Henderson on September 7, 2007, at Manzanita Speedway. Henderson holds five championships from the now defunct Central Arizona Raceway in Casa Grande, Arizona, and is the defending 2010 SCRA champion. Henderson was the president of the SCRA in 2010. (Courtesy of Don Iverson.)

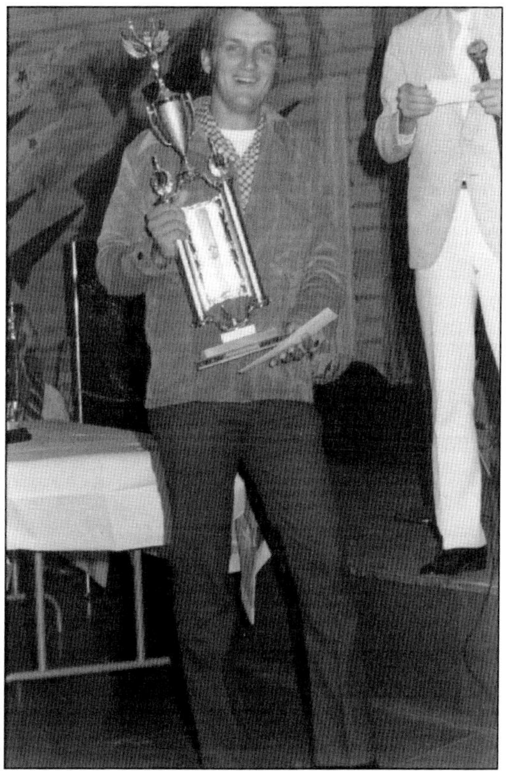

Pictured here is 16-year-old Phil Hertel with his first championship trophy in 1969. Hertel was a tag-a-long with his father, Ralph, and several other drivers who met in a bar on Broadway Road in Phoenix to organize the Stock Car Racing Association. Phil Hertel has performed in almost every capacity at Manzy, from racing to maintenance, concessions to announcer, pit steward to fuel vendor, and more. (Courtesy of Phil Hertel.)

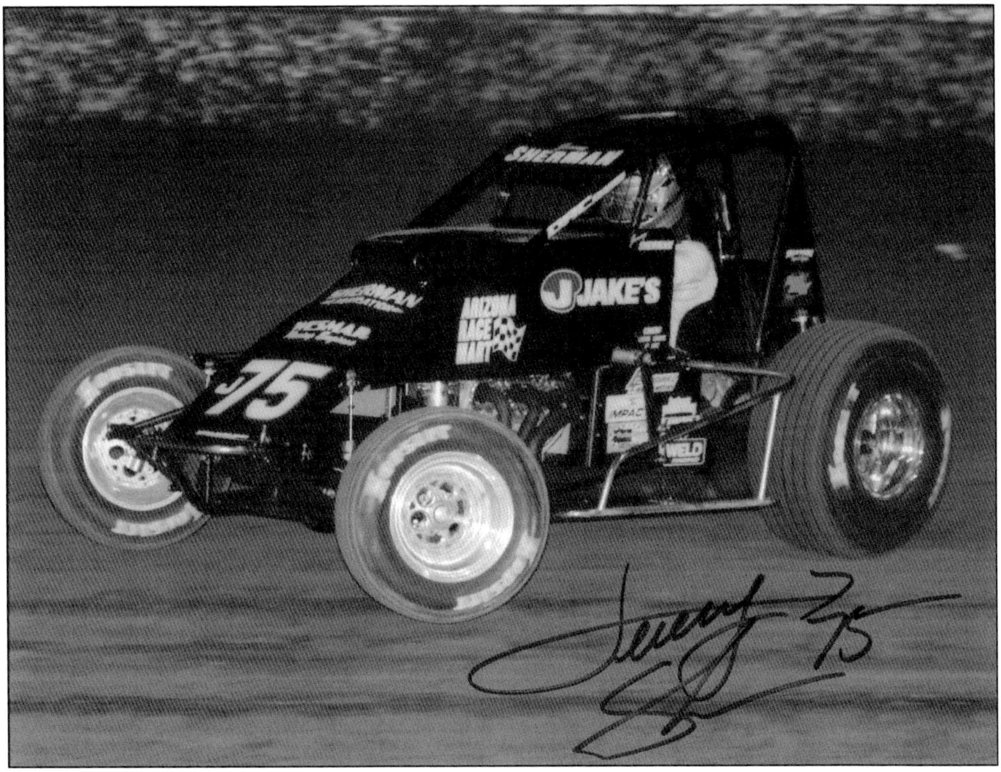

Jeremy Sherman, also known as the "Shermanator," is one of the top sprint-car drivers in Arizona. Sherman has over 100 career wins, including Western World Championships in 2001, 2002, and 2003. (Courtesy of James A. Fargo.)

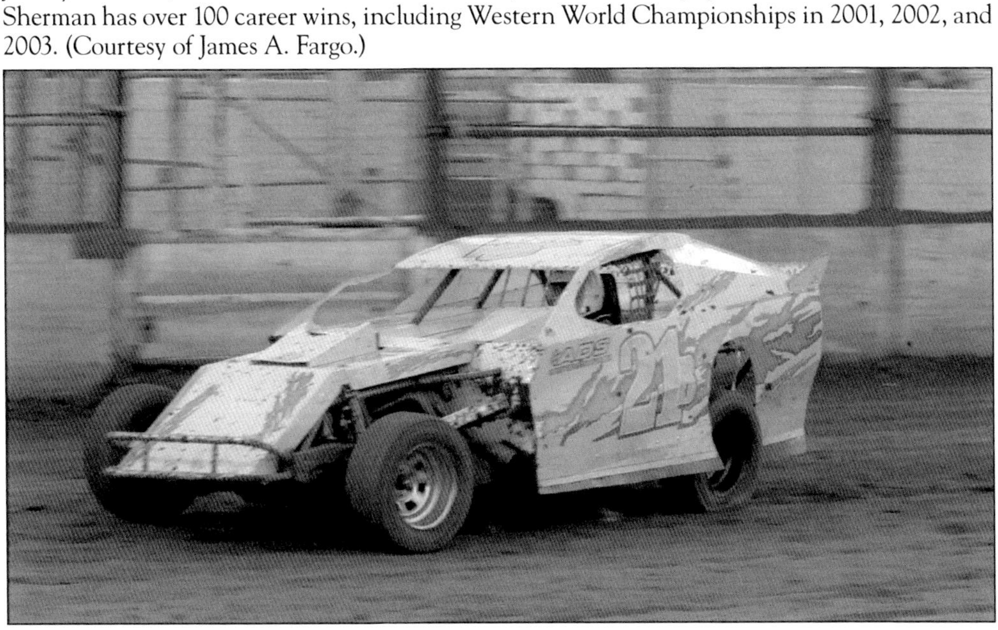

Charging down the front straight into turn one in dirt modified No. 21B is Terry Belcher Sr. Notice the downward force on the outside rear tire, which indicates that Belcher is in the gas. There is no one more competitive than Belcher; however, he has said that he is so comfortable in a race car that "he could almost go to sleep." (Courtesy of Don Iverson.)

Four

The Stock Car Racing Association

In 1968, the Phoenix Racing Association began trying to start a claimer stock-car division. Finally, in 1969, a small group of race-car advocates, including Buck Crum, Dale Hershey, Jack Bushell, and Ralph Hertel and his 15-year-old son Phil, met at Bill's 86 Club at 1525 West Broadway Road in Phoenix. The group sat in a corner booth, eating peanuts and drinking beer (young Phil had a soda pop), ultimately concluding that they needed to split off from the Phoenix Racing Association and form their own organization. The guys pointed to Hertel and said, "Ralph, you're going to lead us." Ralph was older than the typical race-car driver, and his maturity and attitude had earned their respect. Better yet, Hertel had a way of getting things done.

With Hertel at the helm, the Phoenix Claimer Racing Association, officially organized on December 26, 1969, approached Manzanita Speedway to get on its schedule. Because the new group could not guarantee a significant number of race cars initially, it was permitted to run exhibition races with no purse. The first race consisted of a field of five cars, and to make it interesting, Hertel put up $25 out of his pocket. As the car count increased, Hertel negotiated a purse structure with the speedway. At the same time, Ralph's wife, Jean, formed a support group called the "Claimettes," which organized bake sales and raffles to raise money for the association's points fund. Ralph Hertel was elected posthumously to the SCRA Hall of Fame.

After Hertel got the group off the ground, the drivers elected John Bushell as president, Ralph Hertel as vice president, Bea Crum as secretary-treasurer, and Don Moore, John Craig, Len Ward, Larry Dagley, and George Posey as directors. Later, the group changed its name to the Stock Car Claimer Association, finally incorporating as the Stock Car Racing Association on September 12, 1972.

The Stock Car Racing Association, more commonly called the SCRA, is unique among racing organizations, at least in Arizona, because it still exists! Race-car drivers by nature are independent; nevertheless, they form associations, become dissatisfied, break apart, and form more associations. The SCRA is made up of the same type of drivers: aggressive, competitive, and somewhat cantankerous. Regardless, this association has survived every obstacle all these years. Manzy is gone forever, but the SCRA motors on as a stock-car touring series.

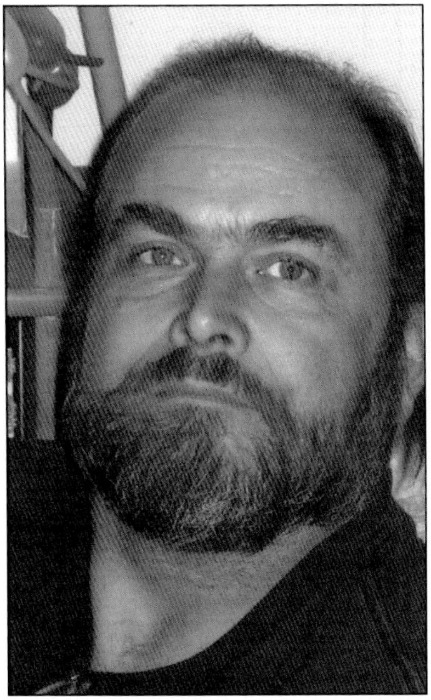

Joe Atkinson has been a race-car owner, crew chief, and crew member for race teams belonging to NASCAR West, USAC, and SCRA. In addition, he heads up the Atkinson Motorsports team, which includes his son Aaron, who holds a Masters of Automotive Engineering degree from the University of Michigan, and his daughter Sarah, a graduate of Arizona State University. Both Aaron and Sarah have spent time behind the wheel. Joe is the current president of the SCRA, a position he has held in three separate years. (Courtesy of Joe Atkinson.)

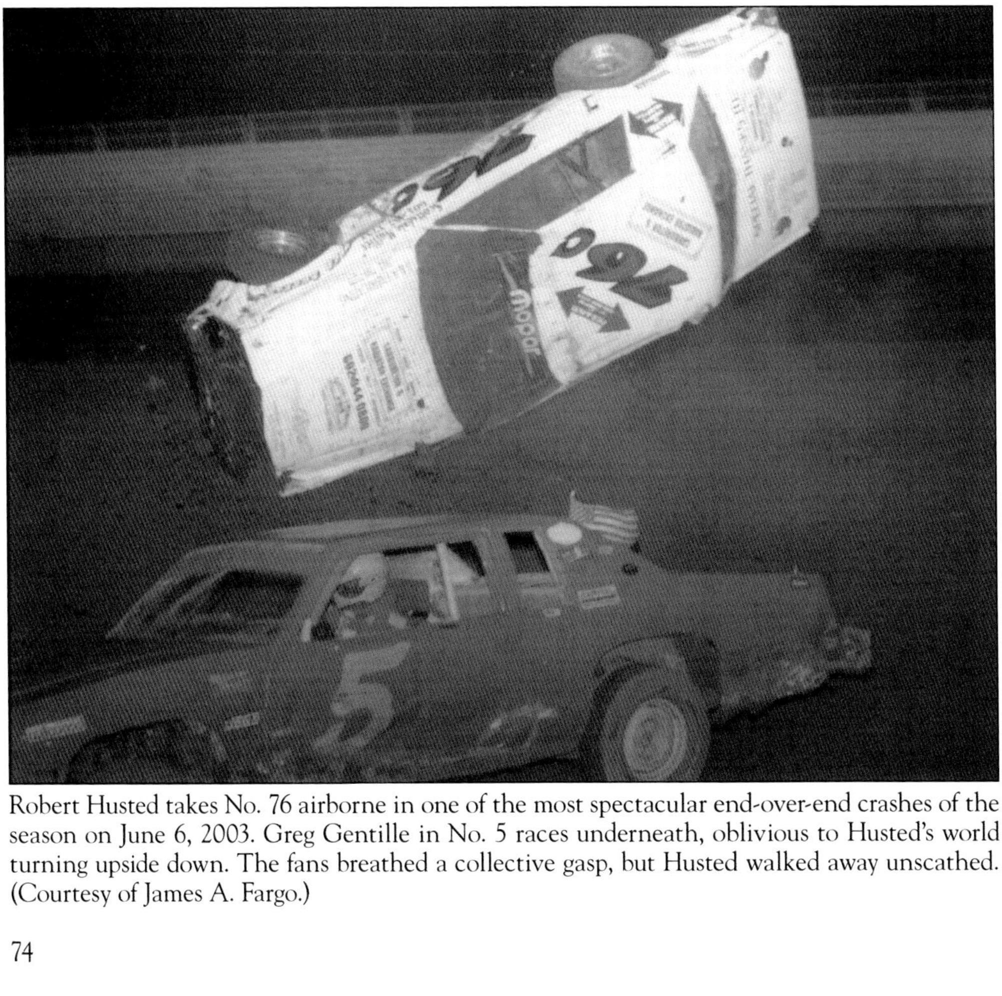

Robert Husted takes No. 76 airborne in one of the most spectacular end-over-end crashes of the season on June 6, 2003. Greg Gentille in No. 5 races underneath, oblivious to Husted's world turning upside down. The fans breathed a collective gasp, but Husted walked away unscathed. (Courtesy of James A. Fargo.)

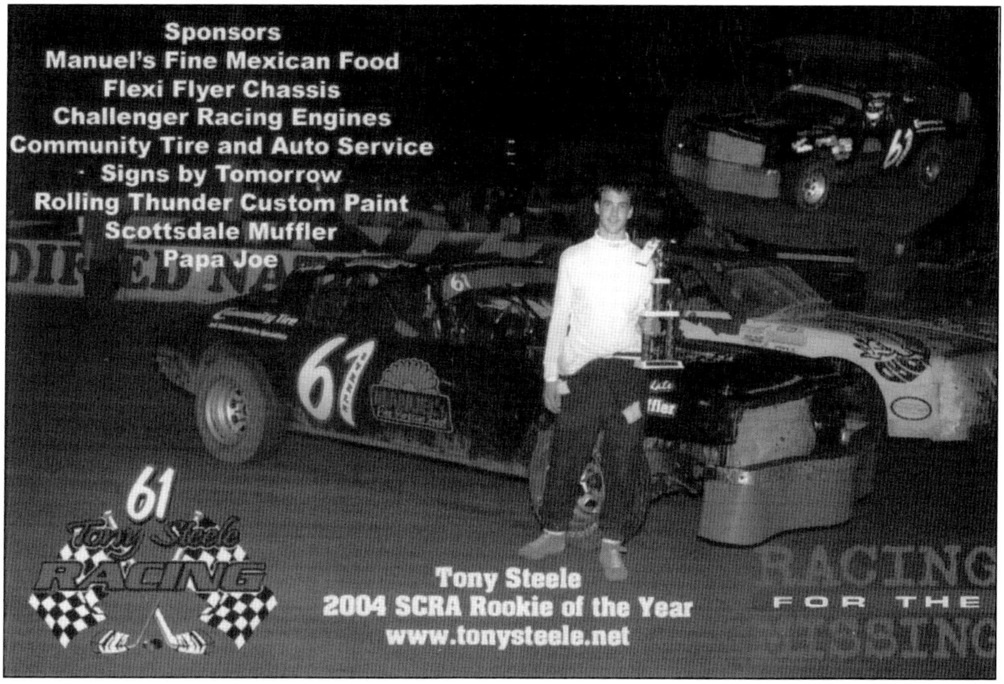

Tony Steele was a hockey player until he won an SCRA factory stock car in a raffle when he was 13 years old. Although he had to wait until age 14 to race at Manzy, Tony shocked his older competitors by finishing eighth in the SCRA standings and fifth at Canyon Speedway in the 2004 season. Tony is a tough competitor and currently races dirt-modified race cars. (Courtesy of Tony Steele.)

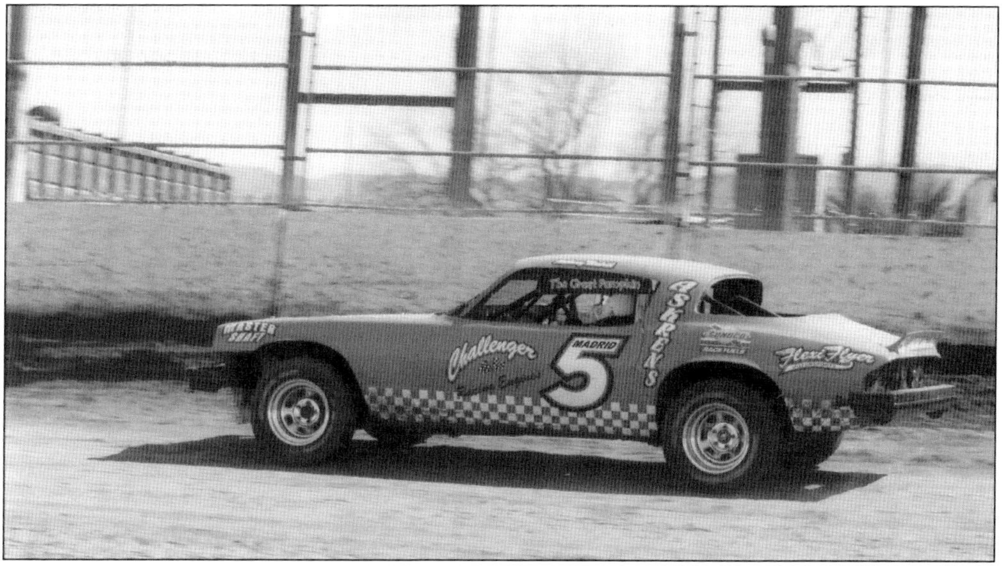

Anthony Madrid is shown here in the No. 5 factory stock in which he won the 2005 SCRA Championship. Madrid is one of Manzy's special stories, coming out of an early Manzy racing family. Mary and Benny Madrid, his grandparents, were around when Manzy was still a dog track. Since Madrid began his career at age 16 in 1992, he has won championships in numerous divisions. At the end, Anthony was the third winningest driver in Manzy history. (Courtesy of James A. Fargo.)

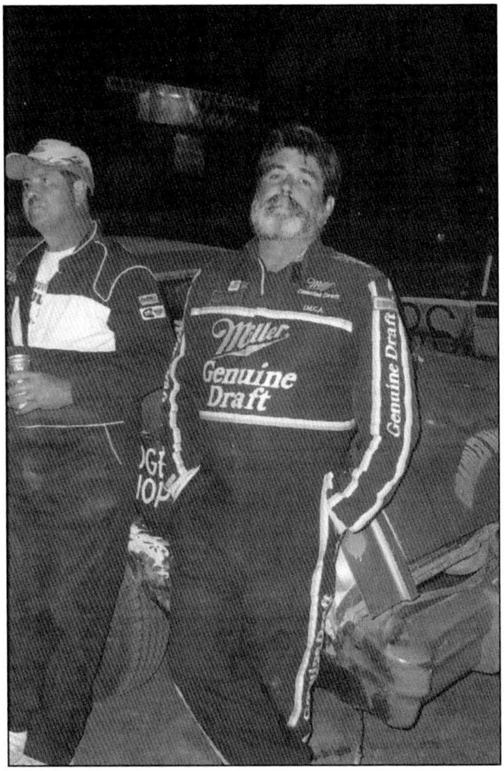

Looking relaxed after the races are Mark Millan (left) and his brother Bob Millan. Actually, the wind-down after an event is short-lived, as there is heavy work to be done in loading up the tools, supplies, and race cars before heading for home. (Courtesy of Don Iverson.)

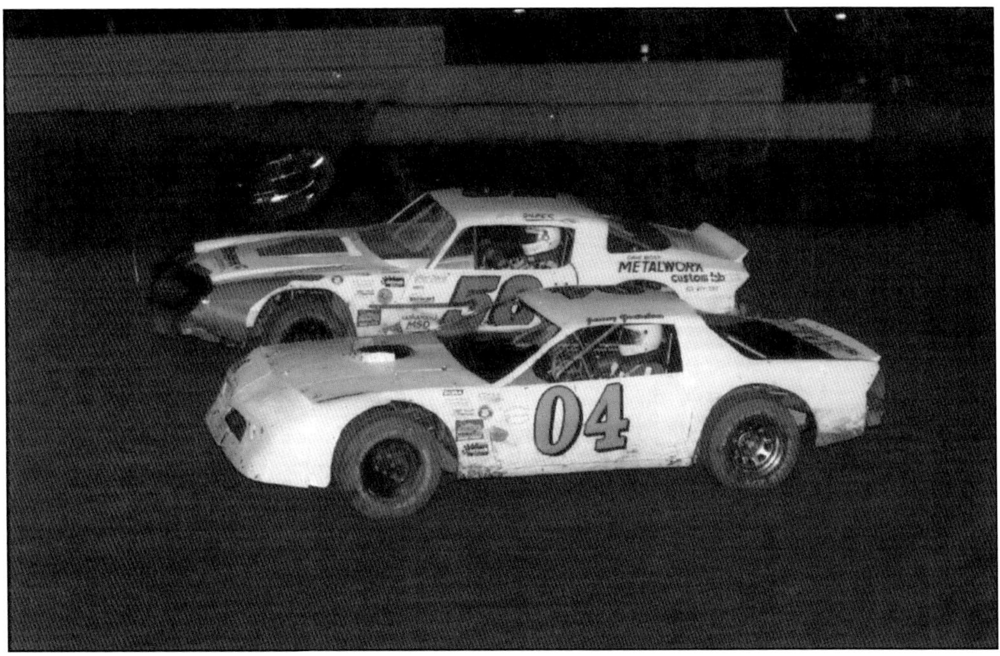

Hard charging 2004 SCRA Super Stock Division champion Randy Silber in No. 50 runs neck and neck with Jeremy Goetchius in No. 04 on the inside during a 2004 race. Goetchius lived to race and was always competitive in the super stock division. He was a mentor to Justin Upton during his run to the 2007 SCRA Factory Stock Division Championship. (Courtesy of James A. Fargo.)

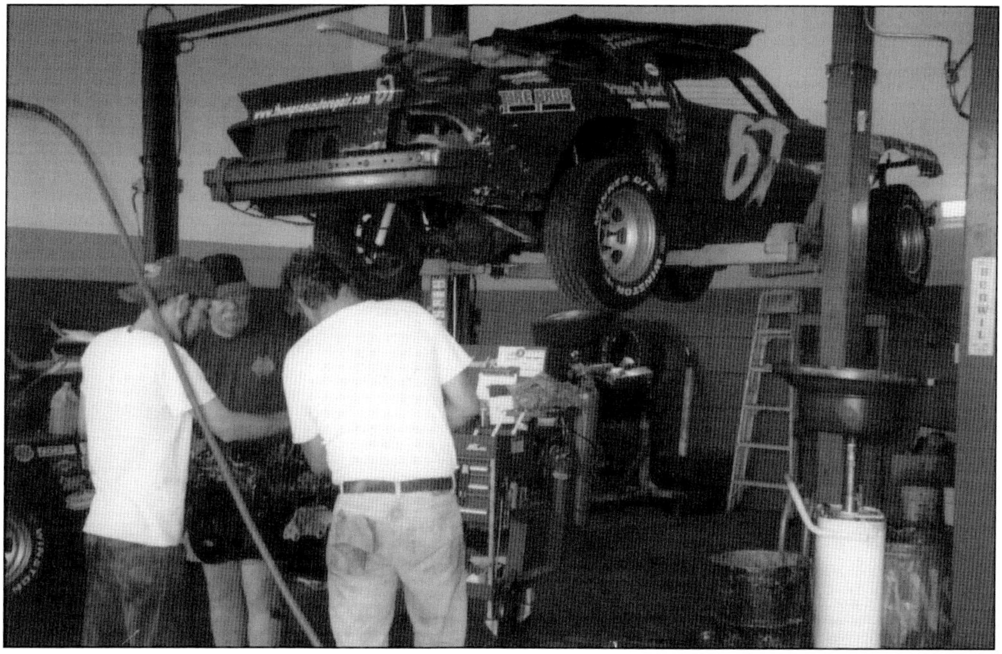

Jay Armstrong (left) and his father, Jim Armstrong (center), are helping Richard Kirn prepare No. 67 for the next factory stock race. Jay Armstrong was another outstanding driver in the factory stocks and dirt modifieds but did not race often enough to compete for a championship. (Courtesy of Jane Upton.)

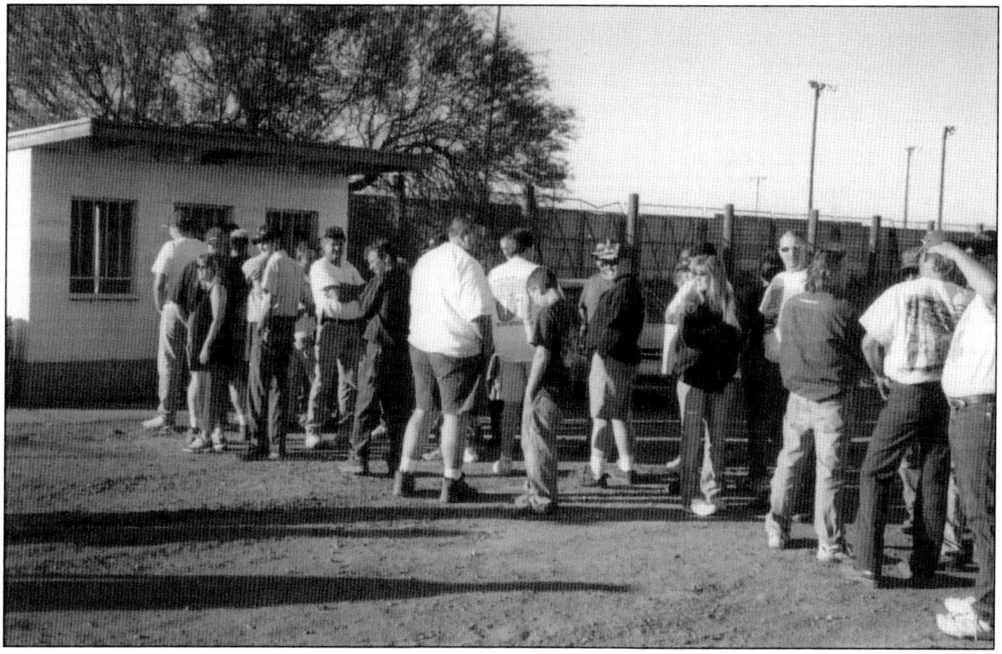

Drivers and pit crews are lined up at the pit booth to buy pit passes, which are more than double the price of general admission. Manzy's purses were always published to the drivers, and the promoter priced pit passes accordingly in an attempt to cover the costs of the race through the back gate. Profit comes from the fans coming through the front gate. (Courtesy of Jane Upton.)

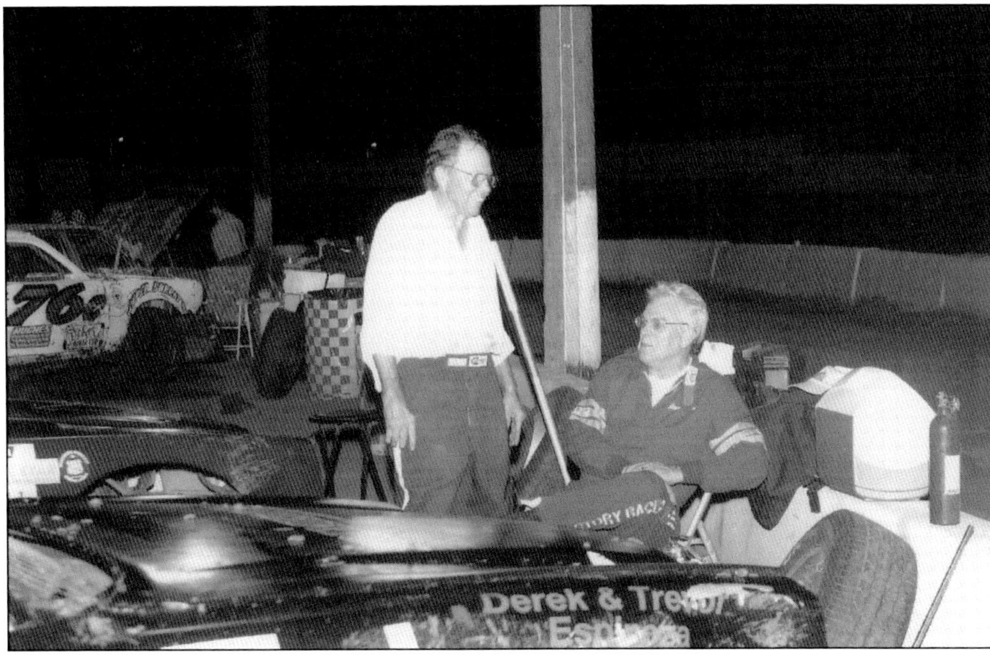

Tom Kozack (standing) visits in the pits with Larry Upton before the race. The pits are a place of friendly camaraderie until the green flag flies. Green flag racing is pure aggression, no holds barred, and with no mercy for the slowpokes. The attitude on the track is "get out of my way; I'm going to the front!" (Courtesy of Don Iverson.)

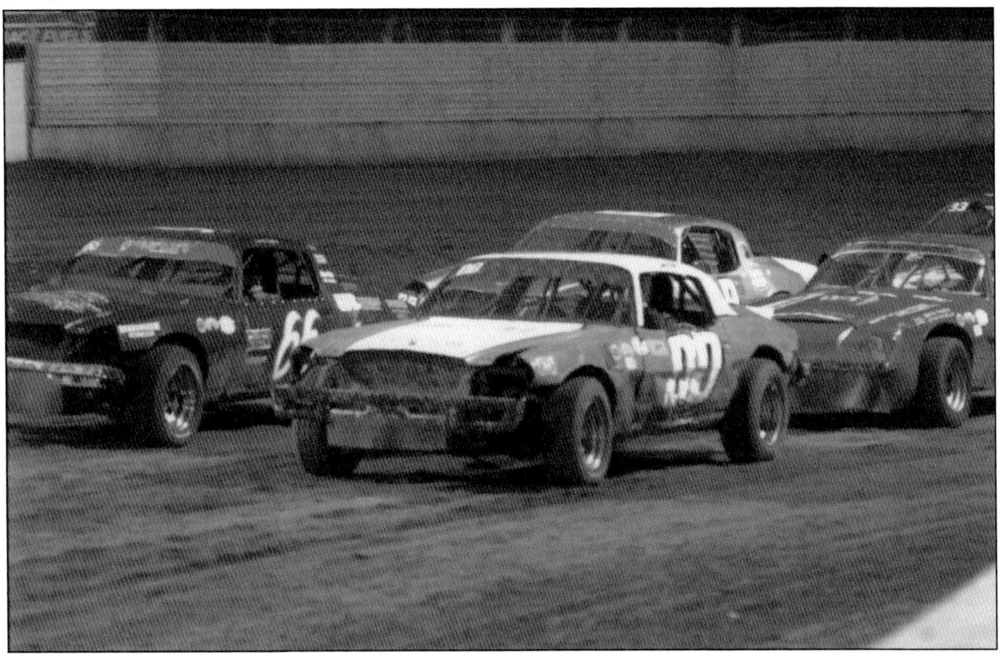

Factory stocks, led by Larry Price in No. 00, a 30-year racing veteran and SCRA Hall of Famer, roll into turn four at Manzy. When the green flag waves, every driver will punch the accelerator to the floor and charge down the front straight nose to tail before sliding into turn one, creating the illusion of a moving wall of metal. (Courtesy of Don Iverson.)

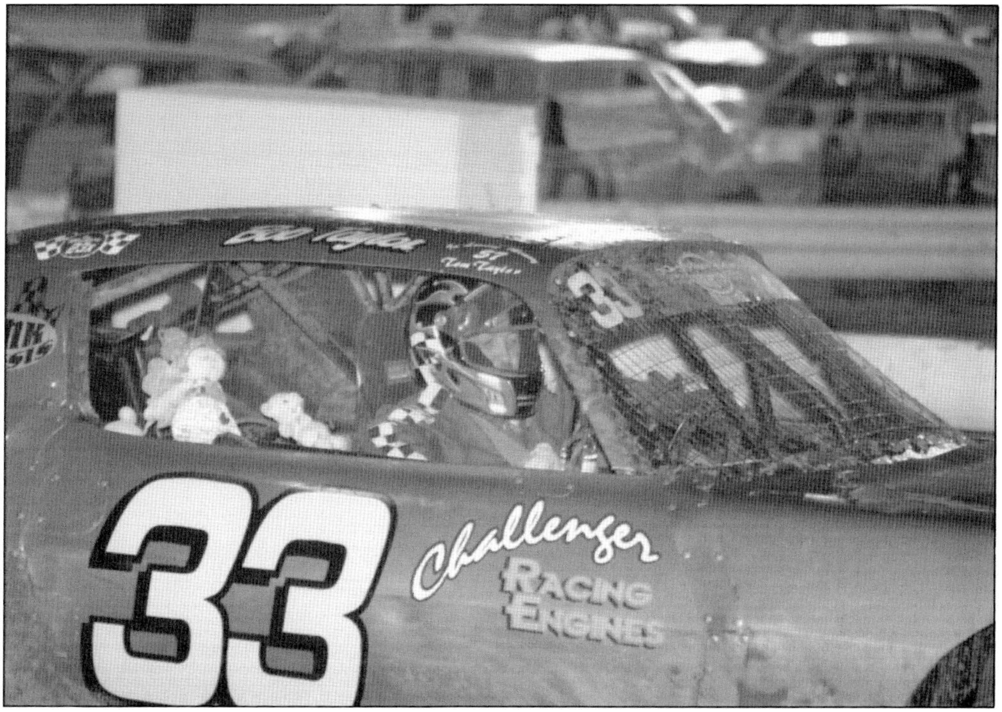

Bob Taylor, a three-time SCRA Factory Stock Division champion and Hall of Famer, is shown here in No. 33. Taylor faced the reality of racing in a 1991 crash in which his car hit an exploding fuel tank from another car. Taylor was engulfed in flames and spent three months recovering from his injuries. Nevertheless, Taylor states that during the off-season, his family sits around asking each other "What are we going to do tonight?" (Courtesy of Don Iverson.)

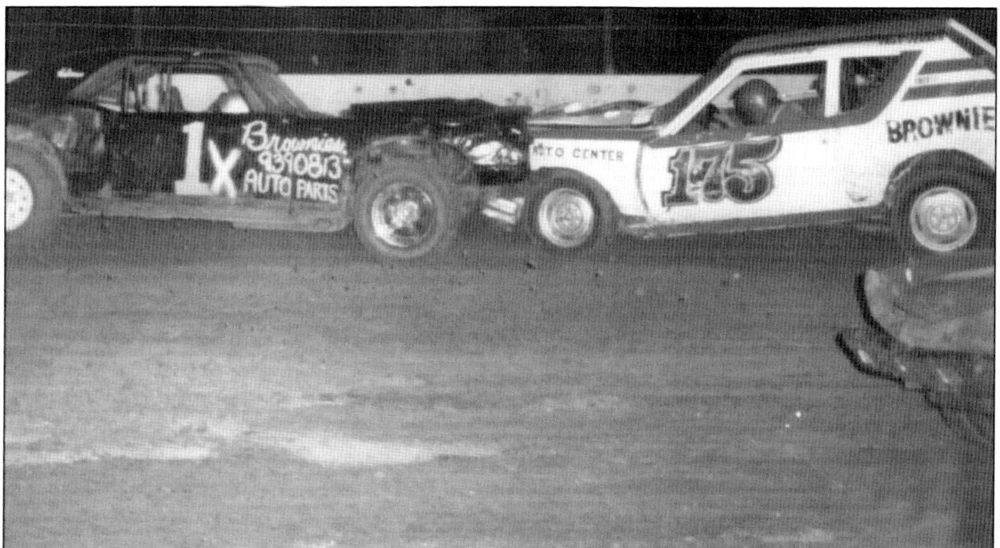

Mike Lubanovich in No. 175 plows head-on into No. 1x driven by Joanne Days in a 1988 race. This was in the days before the SCRA began requiring five-point shoulder harnesses; note that both drivers' helmets are down on the steering wheels. Brownie's Auto Parts was the sponsor of both cars. (Courtesy of Winston Brown Jr.)

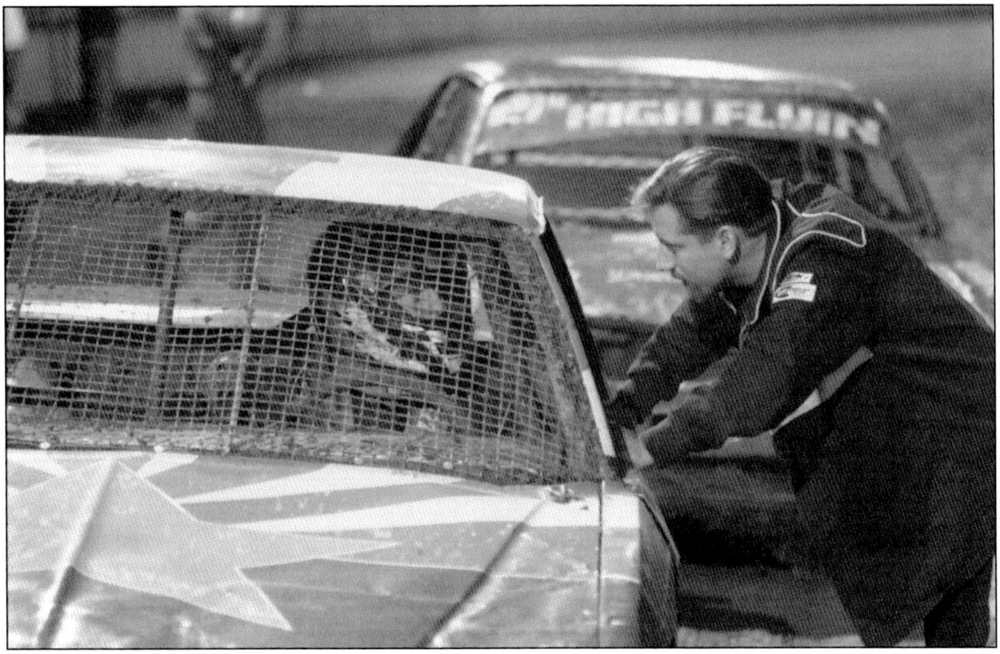

Above, Danny Pearson, leaning on the car, talks race strategy with Brent Radke prior to the trophy dash. Radke is driving factory stock No. 11, the 2008 SCRA raffle car, which he purchased from Larry Price. Below, celebrating after the race are, from left to right, Brent Radke, Jared Keener, Danny Pearson, and Pearson's pit crew members Shane Holcombe and Robert Lowrey. This was a special race for Pearson as it was the only time his father saw him race before he passed away. Pearson says, "A night of racing really takes the edge off of all the things that you can't control in your life." (Both, courtesy of Don Iverson.)

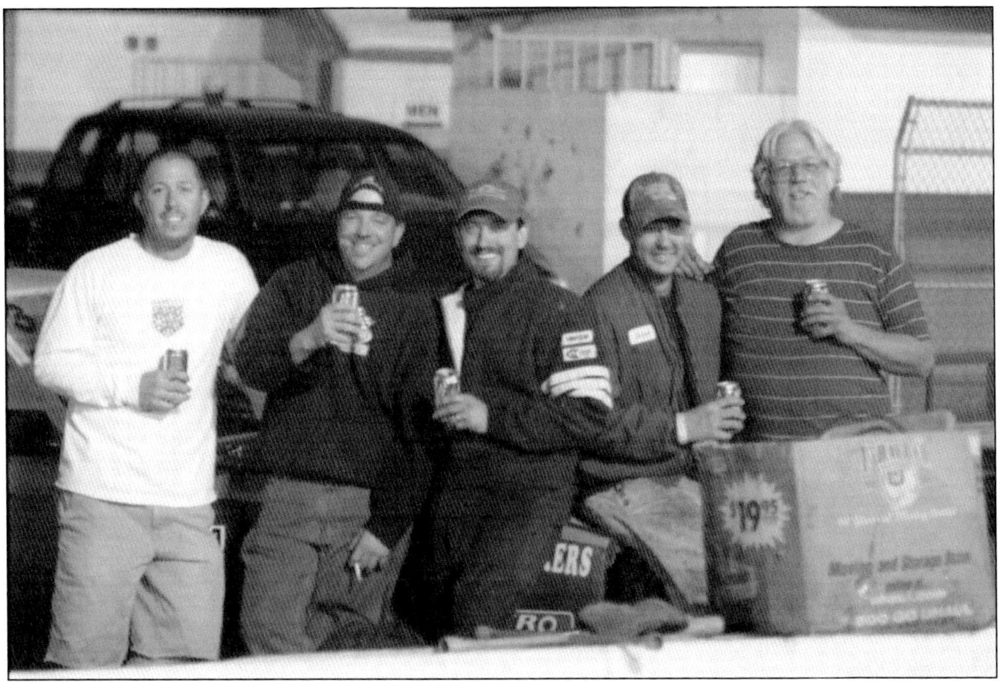

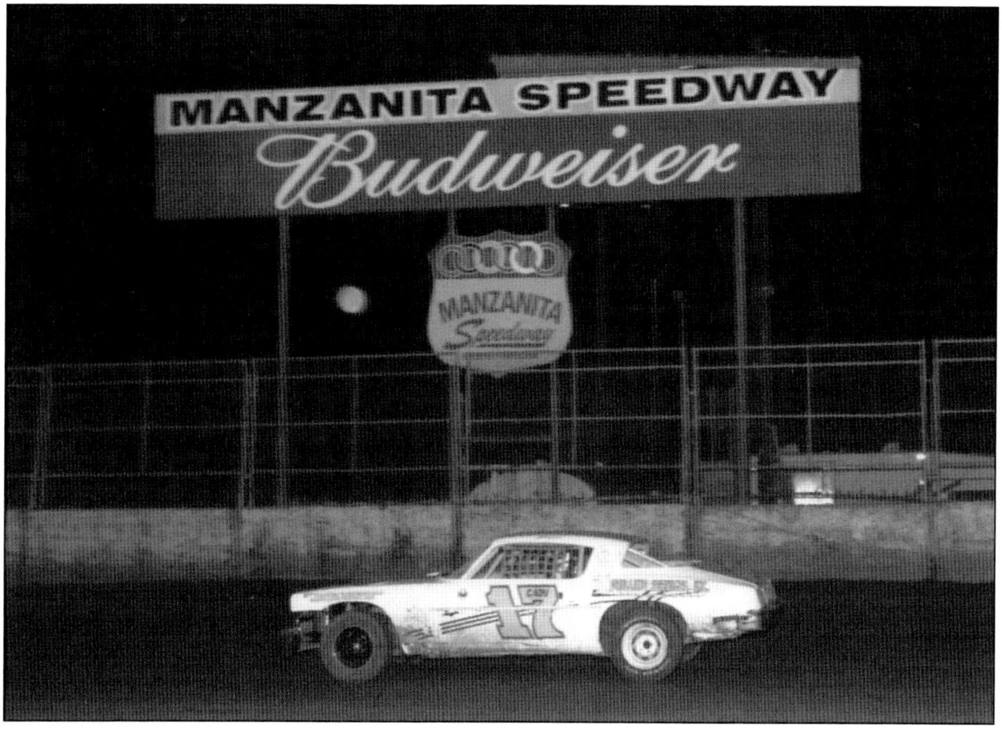

Brian Cady, a 17-year-old senior at Thunderbird High School in Phoenix, races beneath the Manzy sign during a stock-car race in 2009. Neither Brian nor his father, Clay, is a mechanic, but they wanted to be involved with something they could do together, and Brian chose racing. Brian is now a sophomore majoring in biology at the University of Arizona, but continues to race with the SCRA on weekends. (Courtesy of Clay Cady.)

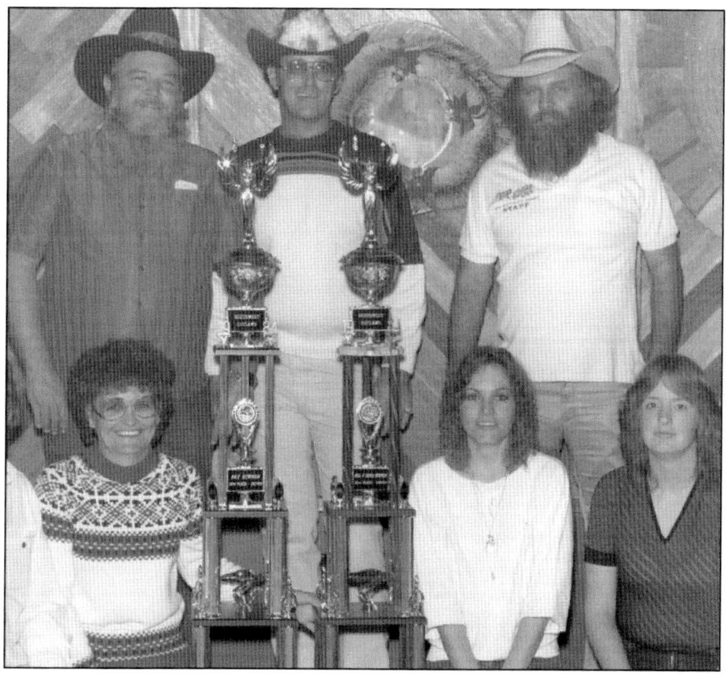

Pictured are, from left to right, (first row) Margaret Brown, Carla Bowman, and Carole Bowman; (second row) Winston Brown Jr., Doc Stevens, and Bill Bowman. The event was the SCRA banquet at the end of the 1984 season, which was when the SCRA raced with the Southwestern Outlaw Series. (Courtesy of Winston Brown Jr.)

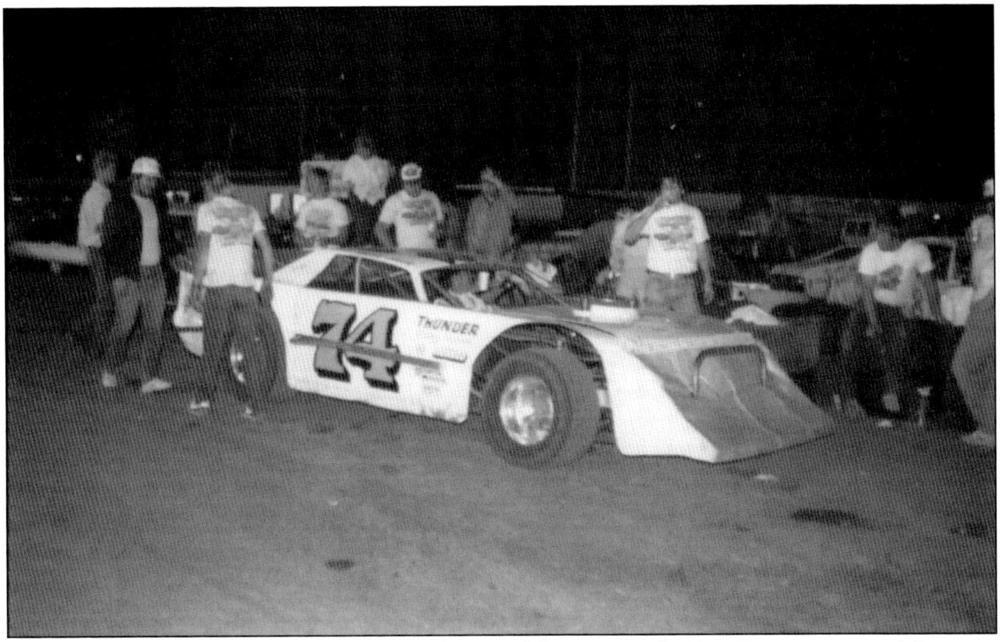

Carl Trimmer of Tucson sits in the No. 74 late model car around 1984. Trimmer, one of the most famous and prolific winners in Arizona, has raced for over 50 years with over 700 wins in main events and 34 championships in various types of cars. (Courtesy of Winston Brown Jr.)

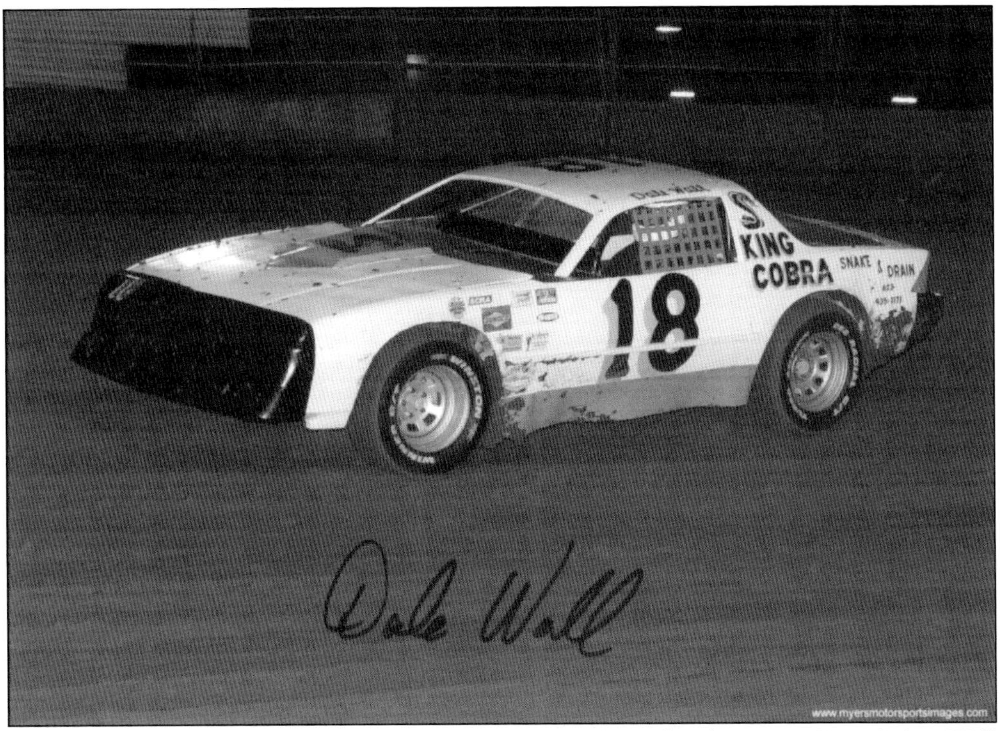

Shown in this photograph is longtime super stock racer Dale Wall in his No. 18 King Cobra. Wall was a member of the SCRA for many years and a consistent class act on and off the racetrack. Dale Wall loved being part of "the Show." (Courtesy of James A. Fargo.)

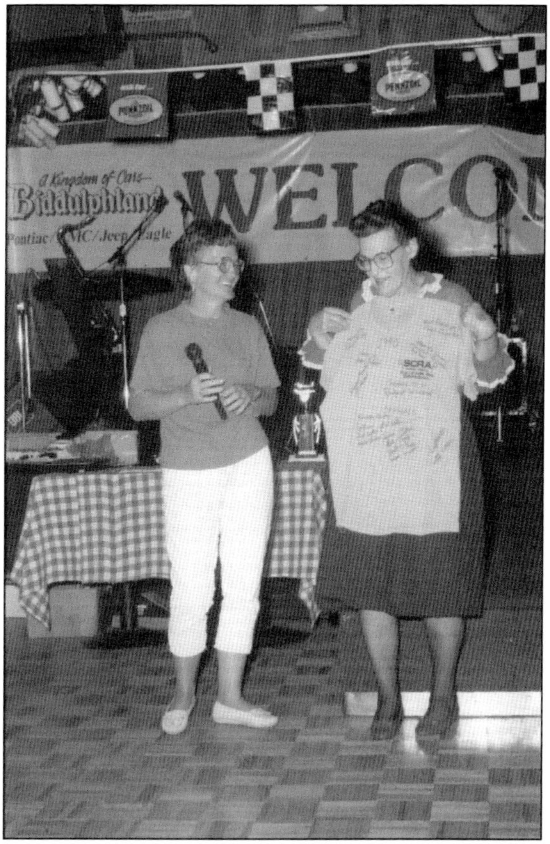

At right, Margaret Brown, a SCRA Hall of Famer, presents a t-shirt autographed by drivers of the SCRA to Marie Gray, wife of Ward Gray, one of the most honored of the SCRA's ranks. During Ward Gray's lifetime, he was a major contributor to the SCRA on many levels. Below, the trophies are lined up at the 1990 SCRA Championship banquet, which was held at Mr. Lucky's in Phoenix. (Both, courtesy of Winston Brown Jr.)

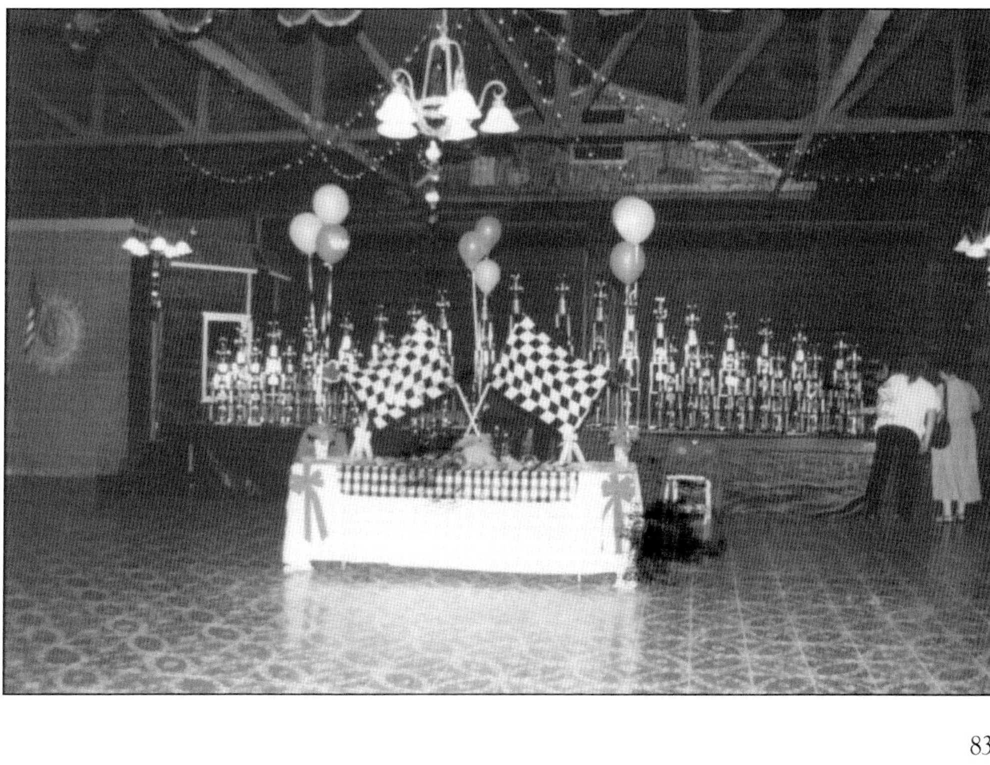

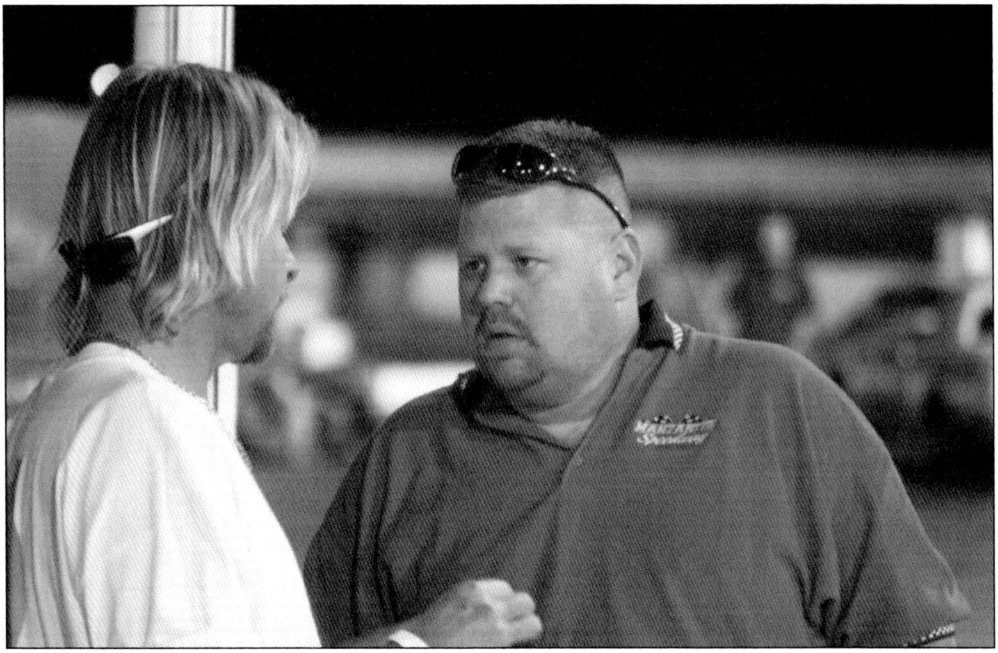

John Romero, on the right, talks to an unidentified man at Manzy. Romero raced in the Bomber Division and the Super Stock Division. Romero was one of the most popular drivers at the track, and fans loved his big bomber station wagon, with luggage strapped to the rack on top and cutouts of the kids in the back of the wagon. (Courtesy of Don Iverson.)

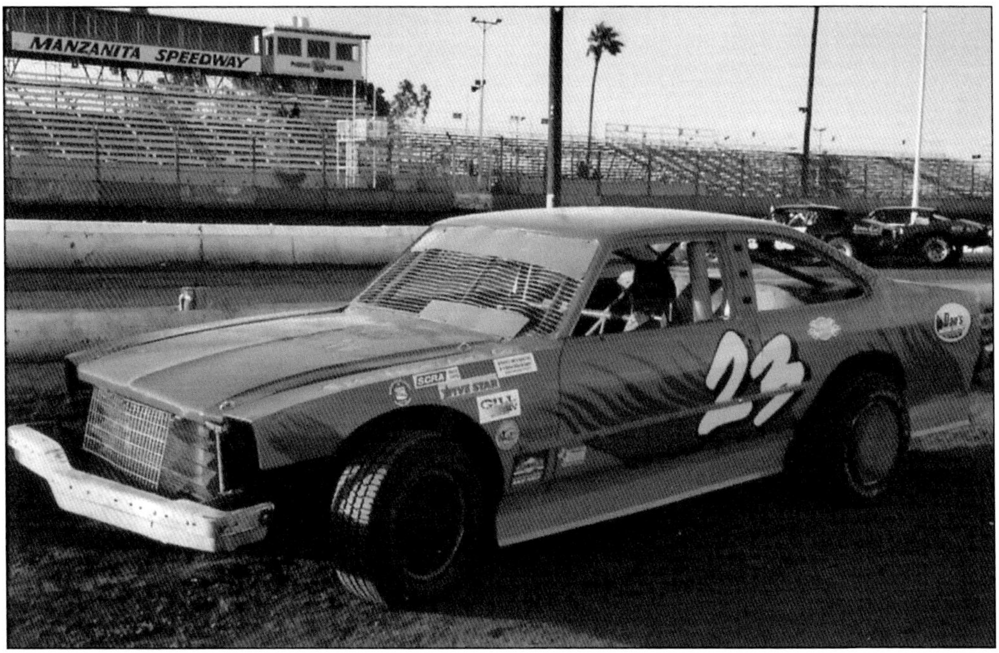

Chris McCurdy, No. 23, was known for his hard-nosed, intense, competitive driving style. Chris once said, "Part of my reputation comes from my desire to win; to do that you have to be aggressive . . . and patient. Sometimes aggressive wins out!" Today, McCurdy is supporting his son Chris Jr., who is making his own mark in racing. (Courtesy of James A. Fargo.)

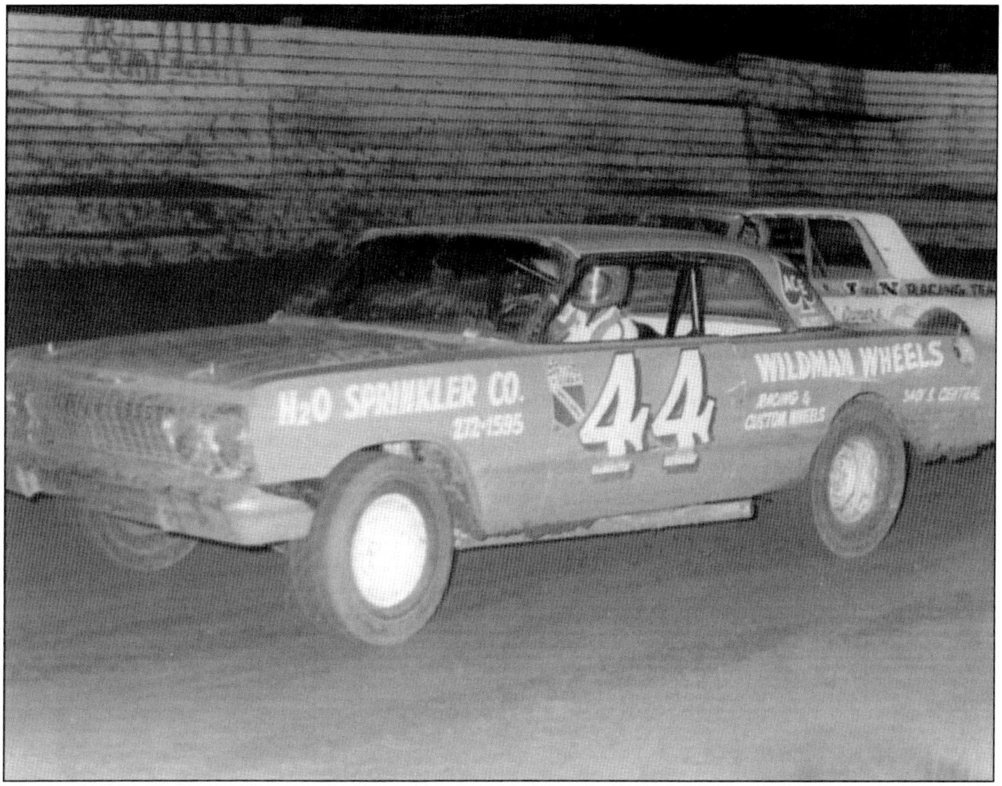

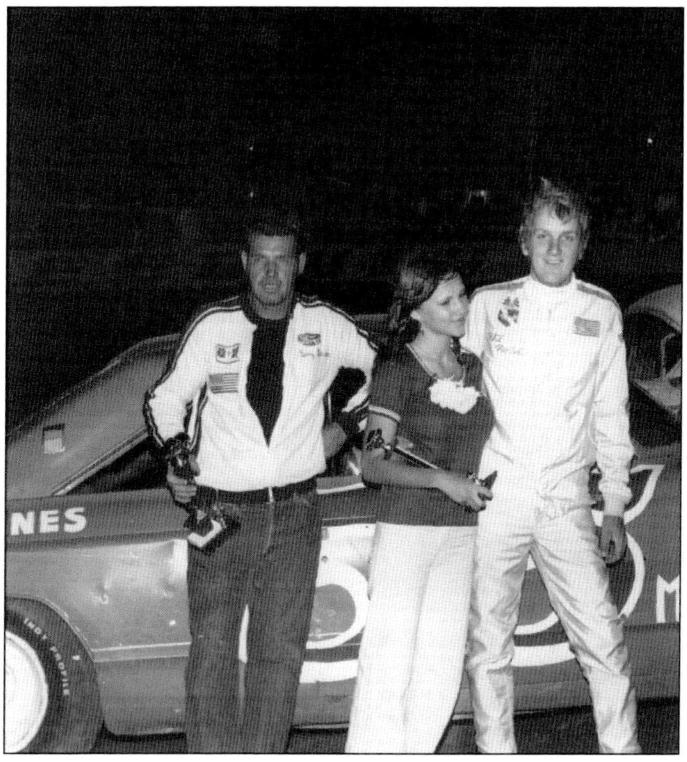

Above, Phil Hertel races No. 44, a 1963 Chevrolet. Hertel was 15 years old when he, along with his father, Ralph Hertel, and a group of men met to organize the SCRA. At right are Gary Belcher (left), a longtime Manzy driver and former SCRA champion and Phil Hertel, winners of the night's events, with an unidentified trophy girl. Belcher is the older brother and mentor to Terry Belcher Sr., the top racer in Manzy history. (Both, courtesy of Phil Hertel.)

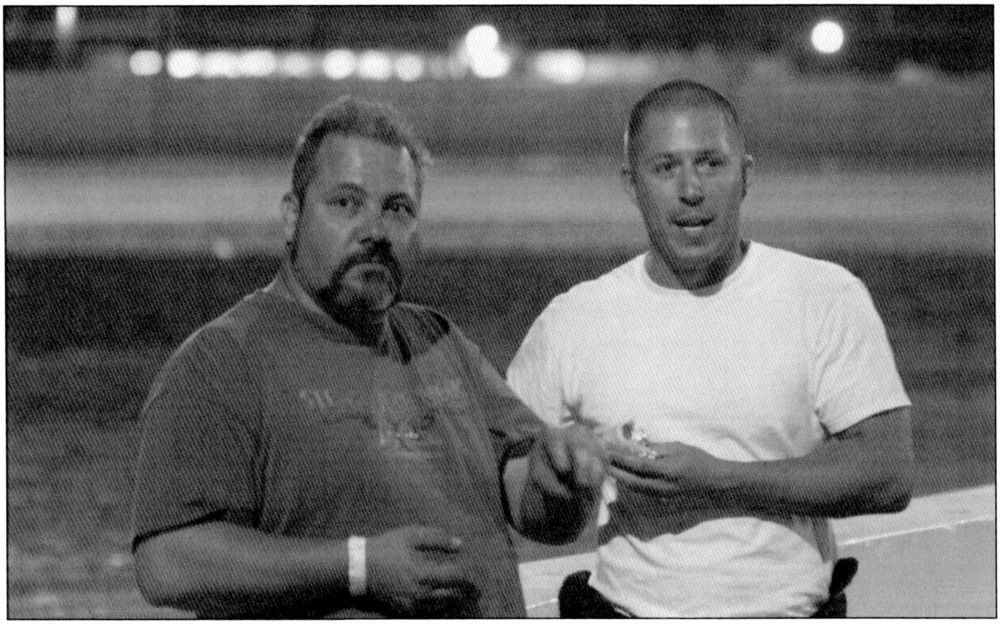

Rod Martinez, on the left, is the owner of Rod's Carbs in Phoenix and a longtime supporter of the SCRA and Manzy. Martinez is also the father of Matt Martinez, the young, up-and-coming driver of factory stock No. 23M, who holds several stock-car speed records at Manzy. Martinez became a dominating force in the SCRA in 2011. Brent Radke, on the right, was a driver in the SCRA's Factory Stock Division. (Courtesy of Don Iverson.)

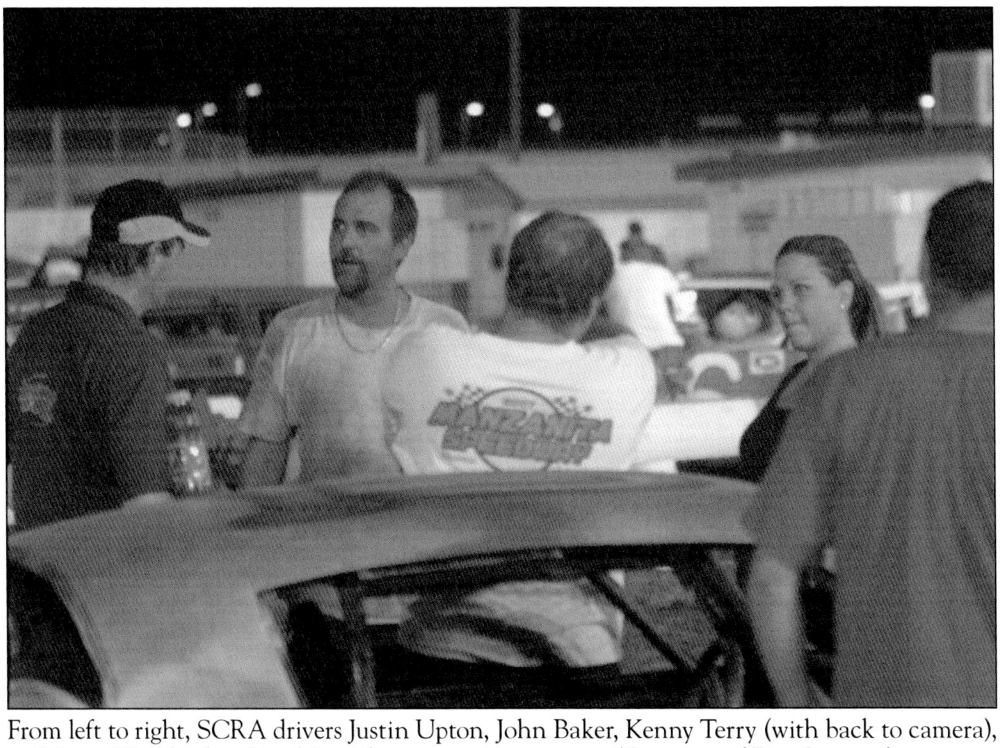

From left to right, SCRA drivers Justin Upton, John Baker, Kenny Terry (with back to camera), and Suzie Wood, a bomber driver, discuss prerace strategy. (Courtesy of Don Iverson.)

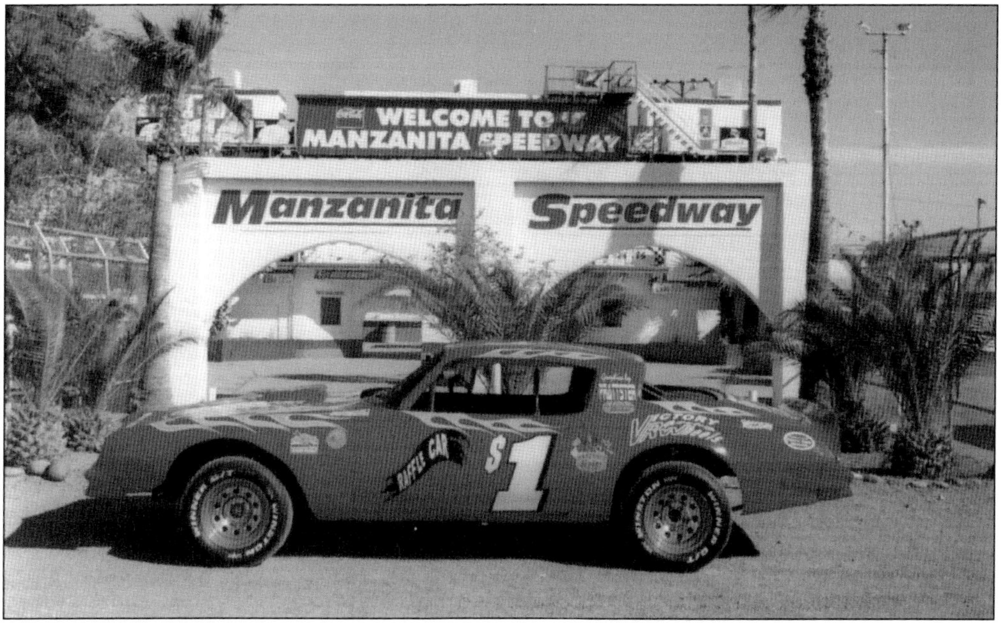

This is a 1978 Pontiac Trans Am built by Mary and Mike McCullough and Ray and John Reynolds. The car builders sold raffle tickets at $1, raising $9,406 for the SCRA points fund for the 2003 season. In addition, the McCulloughs and Reynolds raffled a motor and season tickets that raised another $5,000 for the fund. This is the car that 13-year-old Tony Steele won in which he earned Rookie of the Year honors in 2004. (Courtesy of James A. Fargo.)

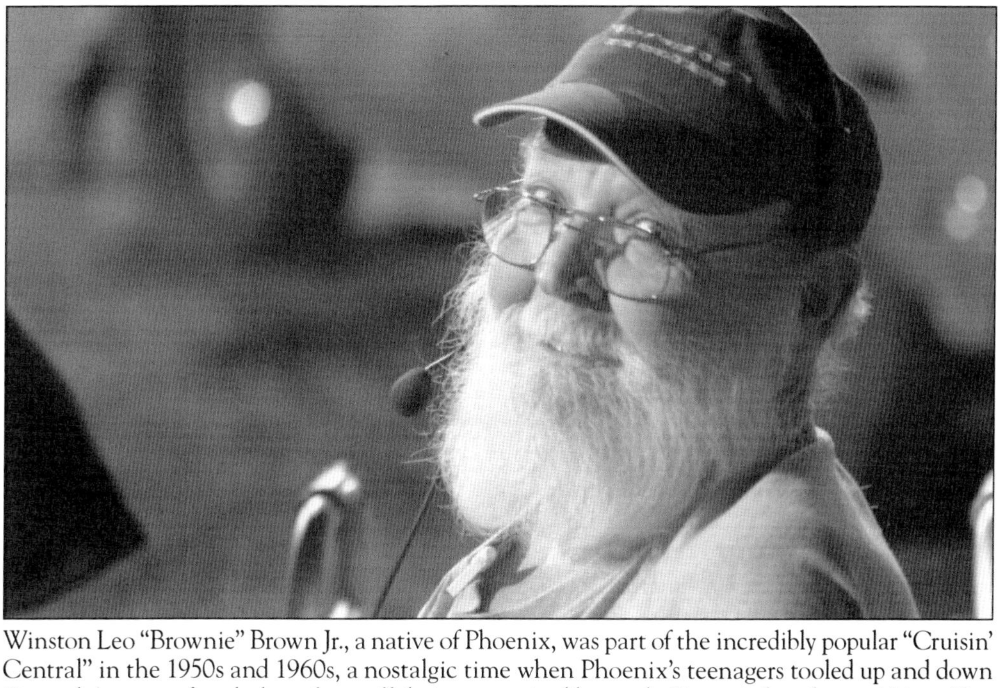

Winston Leo "Brownie" Brown Jr., a native of Phoenix, was part of the incredibly popular "Cruisin' Central" in the 1950s and 1960s, a nostalgic time when Phoenix's teenagers tooled up and down Central Avenue after dark to show off their customized hot rods. Brownie has devoted himself to the SCRA for over 30 years, earning induction into the SCRA Hall of Fame in 2005. (Courtesy of Don Iverson.)

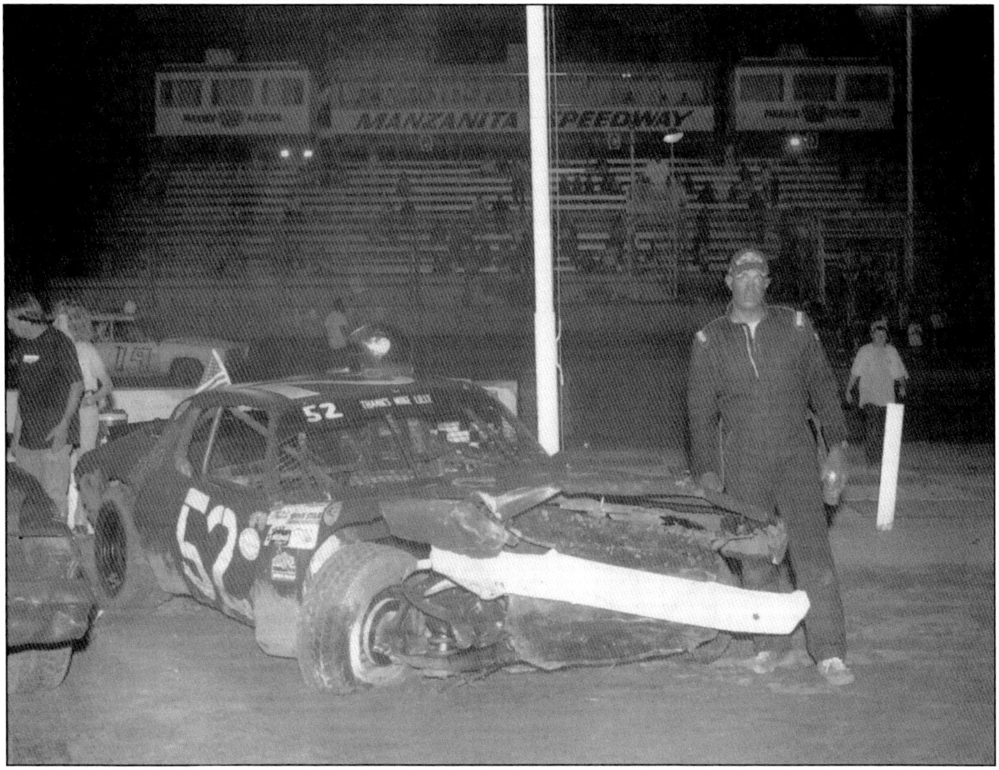

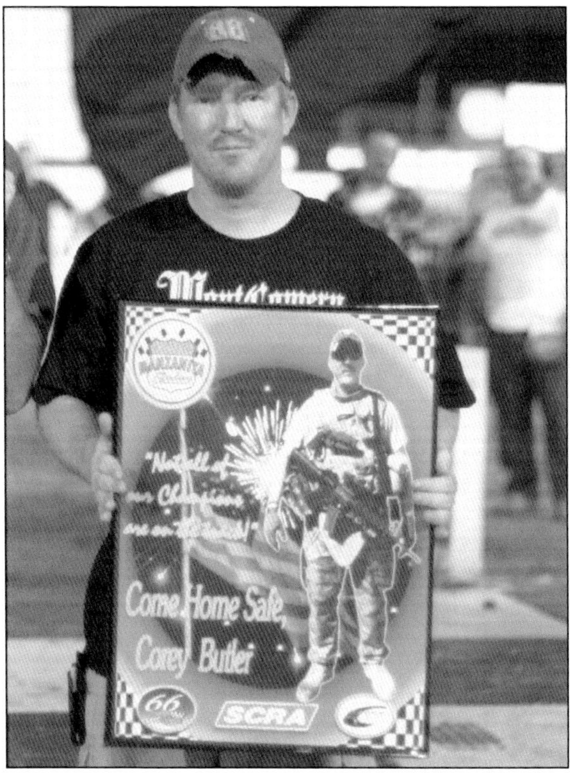

The aftermath of the Stock Car Nationals on July 9, 2004, shows SCRA driver Troy Mangano in a reflective mood. After winning a transfer position the previous night to the championship race, Mangano had high hopes, but this is what happens in racing. Mangano was racing hard in the outside groove when the inside driver ran too high and pushed Mangano into the wall on the front straightaway. Although the car was totaled, Mangano said, "I was not knocked out, but I did see stars!" (Courtesy of Troy Mangano.)

Corey Butler holds the award presented to him by the SCRA, which celebrates his service to his country in Afghanistan as a member of the US Air Force. Corey is a career serviceman stationed at Luke Air Force Base in Glendale, Arizona, racing in the SCRA Factory Stock Division as his military service permits. (Courtesy of Don Iverson.)

Five

One Way to Win a Championship

When Larry Upton was 10 years old, his father, Latt Upton, built a stock car and entered it into Beech Bend Park's inaugural season in 1951 in Bowling Green, Kentucky. Larry worshiped the young men who raced and dreamed of becoming a stock-car driver, but it was put on hold at age 13 when his parents sent him to live on a ranch in Luna, New Mexico, ultimately resulting in the family moving to Arizona.

With 51 years having passed, on Friday night, June 7, 2002, Upton saw an ad in the *Arizona Republic* for Manzanita Speedway, and went to the races, alone, and the dream was reborn. Upton went home and told his wife, "I'm going to buy a race car!"

Realizing that he knew little about cars, Upton convinced his son Justin to keep the car running in exchange for racing it every other week. They raced in the Bomber Division, cars with a $400 claim price. As a father and son adventure, it was great fun, but turned into an obsession to win. By the 2004 season, Upton realized that Justin had talent, so they put together a five-year plan to win the SCRA Factory Stock Division Championship, a daunting task since the division was one of the most competitive at Manzy, filled with good drivers and former champions. They were armed only with the knowledge that they could put together and follow a plan. Mentors, such as Larry Price and Jeremy Goetchius, filled in the gaps of know-how.

To win the championship, Justin had to develop the same skill-set as the top drivers, secure first-class equipment, and be lucky. Justin based his racing philosophy on that of Larry Graham, who drove Latt Upton's stock car to victory lane in 1951. Justin's goals were to earn the respect of the drivers at Manzy, obtain the best equipment, develop a routine that focused his mind on race day, and, perhaps most importantly, develop the patience to let the race come to him and be prepared to take advantage of opportunity even though it happened at high speeds.

The plan worked. Justin Upton won the SCRA Factory Stock Division Championship in 2007 with 16 top five finishes in 17 races, a phenomenal record of consistency, which is what it takes to win championships.

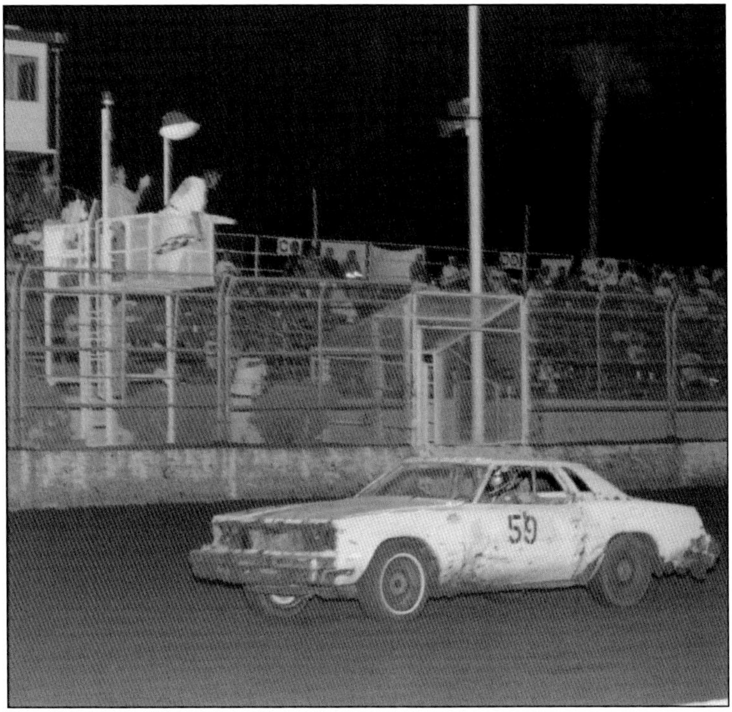

This is the bomber driven by Justin Upton in his first season of racing in 2002. Bombers were entry-level cars with a $400 claim price, which meant that any other bomber driver could buy any bomber car for $400 at the conclusion of the race. This was the method used by race officials to keep the entries equal and make the races competitive. The 1976 Oldsmobile Cutlass Supreme was purchased from a local used car lot for $450. Justin blew the old engine in the third race. (Courtesy of James A. Fargo.)

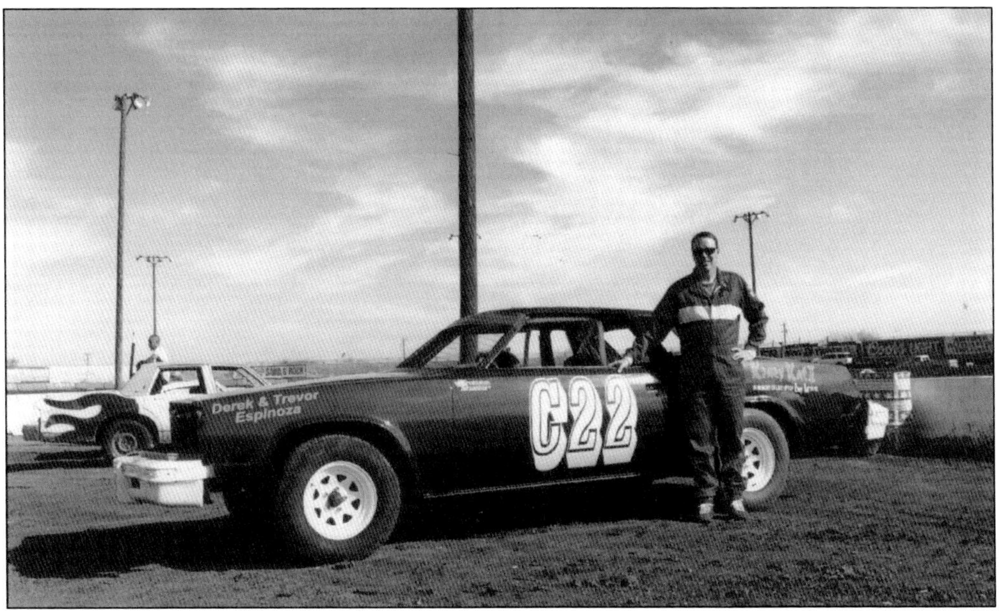

In 2003, Justin Upton rebuilt the 1976 Oldsmobile Cutlass Supreme and renamed it C22, moving from the bombers to the Claimer Division. This was a step up in competition and reflected his increasing confidence in his driving ability. By the end of the season, Upton had earned a fourth-place finish, which prompted him to move into the SCRA Factory Stock Division in 2004. (Courtesy of James A. Fargo.)

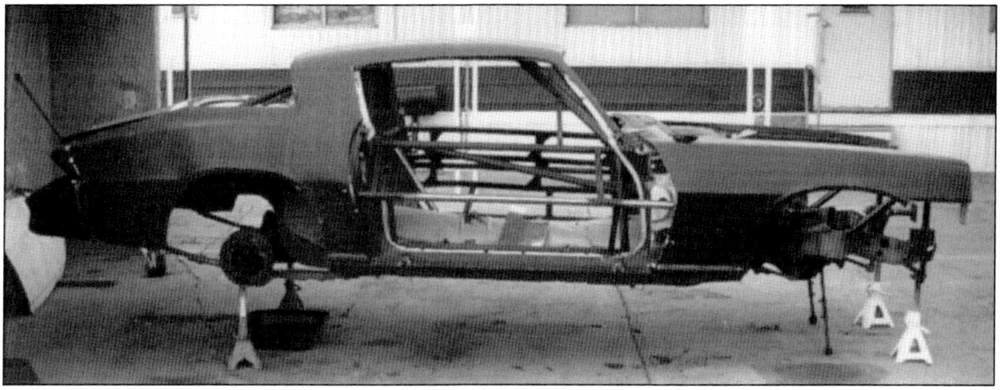

This is a 1976 Chevrolet Camaro. In the conversion to a race car, the only thing that matters is power and speed; comfort is jettisoned. The car is gutted, meaning the removal of the dash, the fender wells, the gas tank, carpet, glass, hinges, braces, latches, and everything under the hood except the engine. The doors are removed and stripped of all windows and locking mechanisms. Then, the roll cage is welded into the body-shell, and the door-skins are bolted onto the frame. This is a stock car. (Courtesy of Jane Upton.)

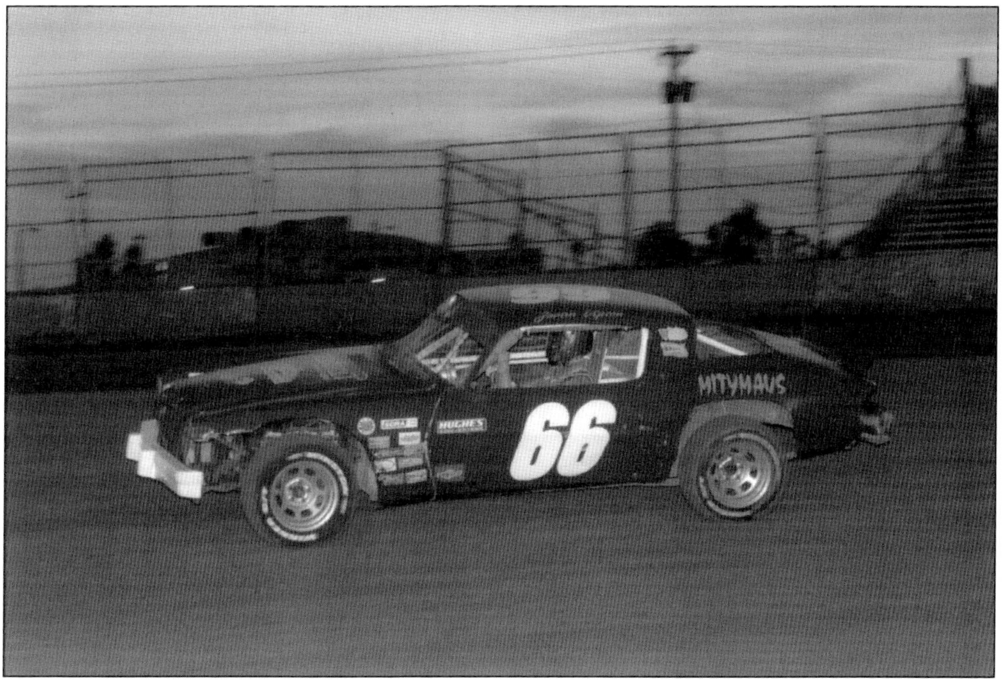

This is the product of a preseason of planning, building, and testing. Justin Upton was in the third year of a five-year plan to win the SCRA Factory Stock Division Championship at Manzy. Many observers identified this division as the toughest at Manzy; it was designed to provide drivers a racing experience at an affordable price. As a result, it attracted a large field of drivers, many of whom were seasoned competitors. (Courtesy of James A. Fargo.)

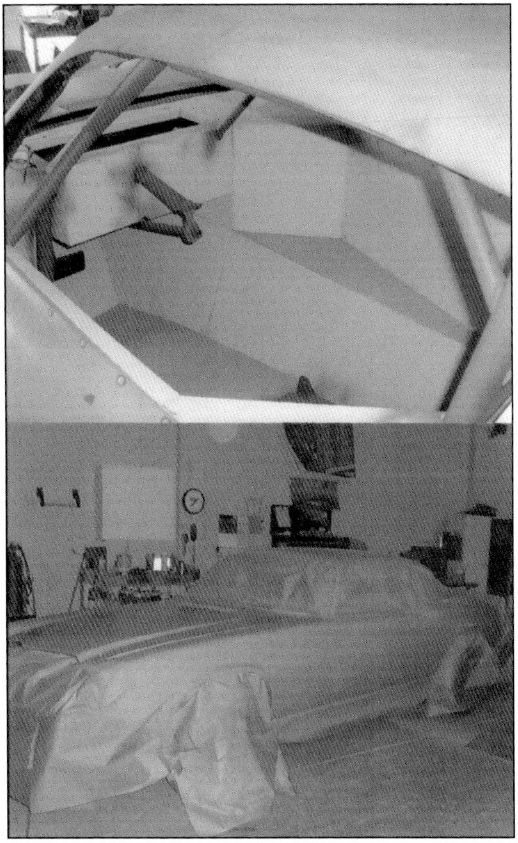

At left is the Justin Upton Racing LLC display car. This car never raced but was built as a replica of the No. 66 factory stock car and its identical twin, the backup race car. The display car was used for appearances at sponsor events and car shows, primarily in the Phoenix area. Through support of the sponsors' business objectives, Upton was able to obtain financing for his racing program. Pictured below are two complete, ready-to-race, 360-cubic-inch Chevrolet racing engines built by Five Star Engine & Exchange of Glendale, Arizona. Although many drivers suspected that Upton was using illegal equipment, these engines were built precisely to the SCRA's car-building rules. (Both, courtesy of Jane Upton.)

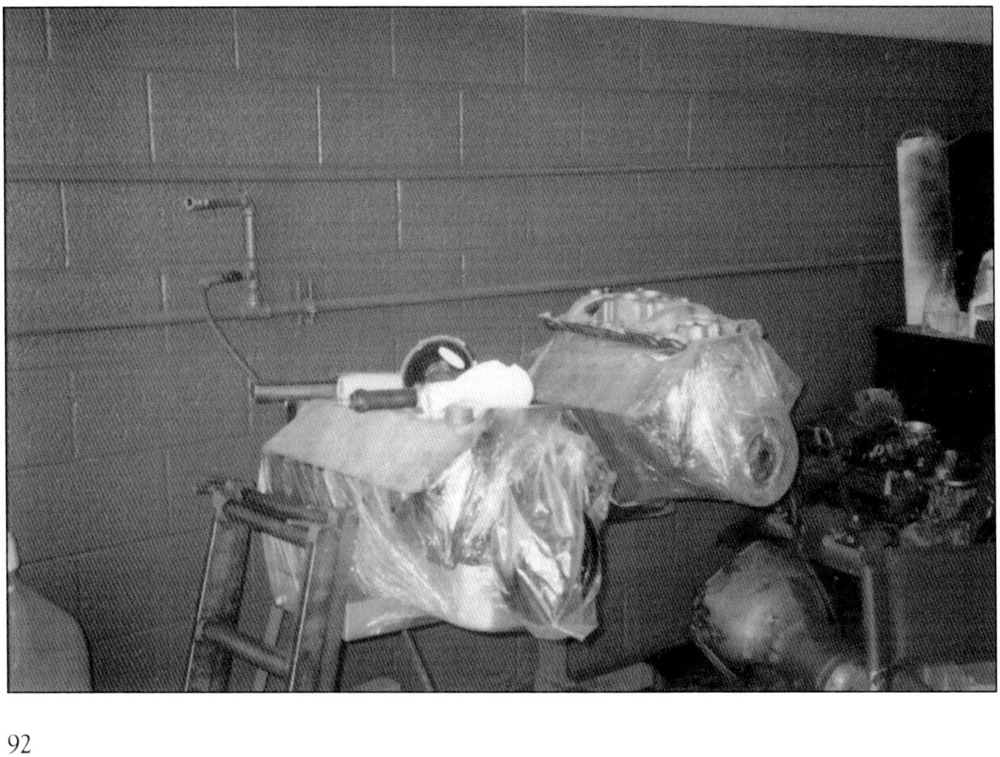

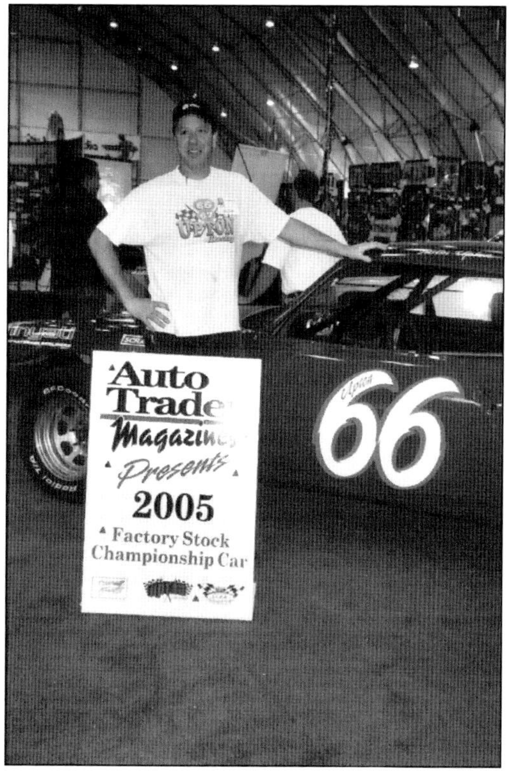

At right, Justin Upton is promoting *Auto Trader Magazines* at the Big Boys and Their Toys car show at WestWorld in Scottsdale. Shown below is the same display car at the University of Phoenix stadium in Glendale, home of the Arizona Cardinals. Many grassroots racers believe that sponsors hand out money to get their names on race cars, which is actually only a small part of their grand desire to have their businesses and products promoted by the drivers. To attract sponsor funding, a driver has to work on the sponsors' behalf when not racing. (Both, courtesy of Steve Alford.)

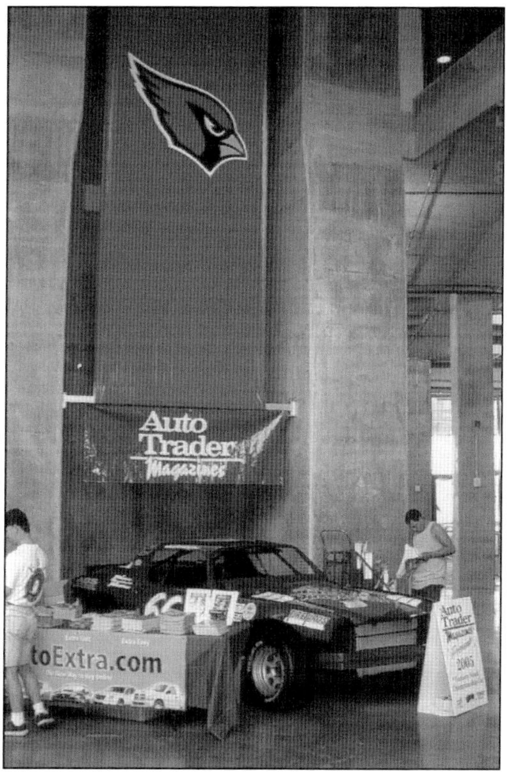

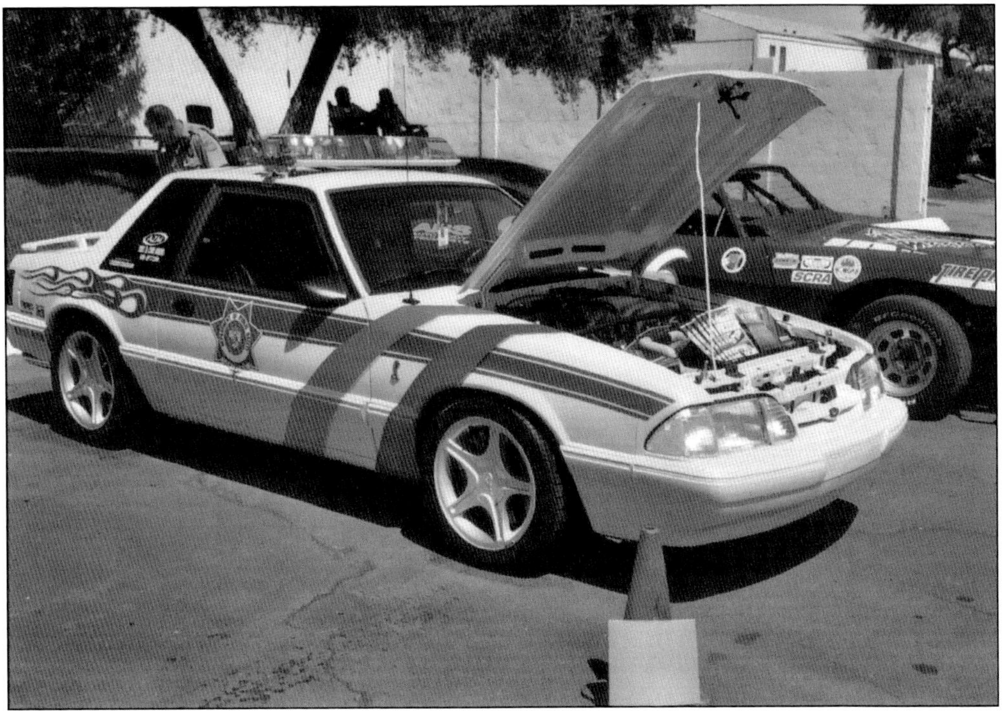

It seemed that everyone had a display car, including the Arizona Highway Patrol. This photograph shows the Ford Mustang used by the Arizona Department of Public Safety to promote automobile safety throughout the state of Arizona. This display was at Firebird Raceway in Chandler, Arizona. (Courtesy of Jane Upton.)

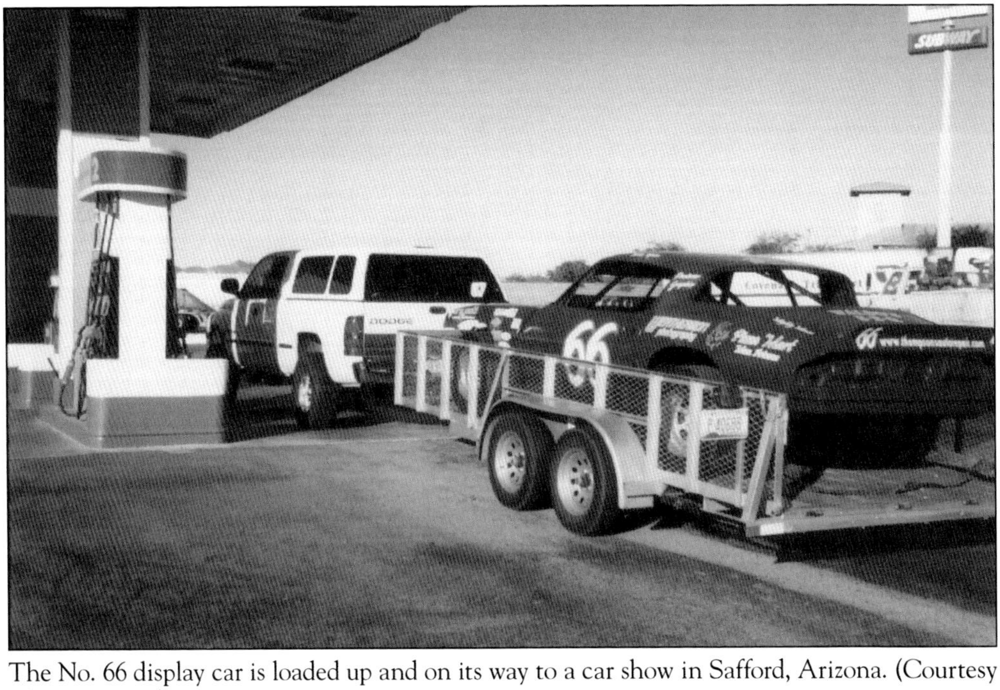

The No. 66 display car is loaded up and on its way to a car show in Safford, Arizona. (Courtesy of Jane Upton.)

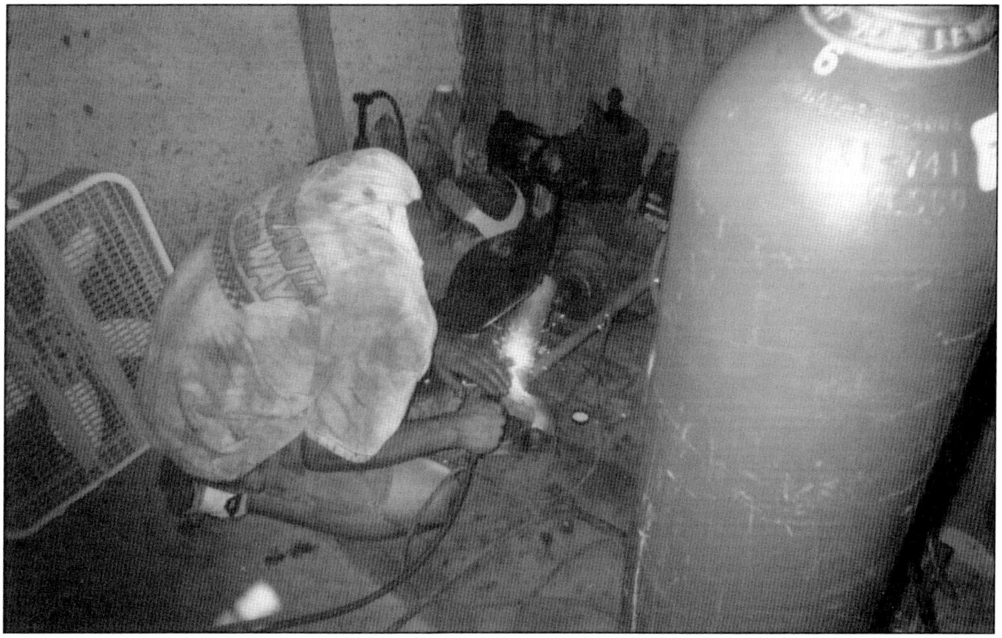

Above, Jeremy Goetchius is working on the Upton car during the preseason. When Larry and Justin Upton began racing in 2002, they knew next to nothing about the sport from an up-close perspective. It was with the help of people like Goetchius that the Uptons were able to learn the fundamentals of a racing program. Goetchius was also a driver in the SCRA Super Stock Division. Below, Jim Armstrong (left) and Richard Kirn work on a racing engine in the shop of Thompson Auto Service in Mesa, Arizona, a sponsor of Justin Upton Racing. (Both, courtesy of Jane Upton.)

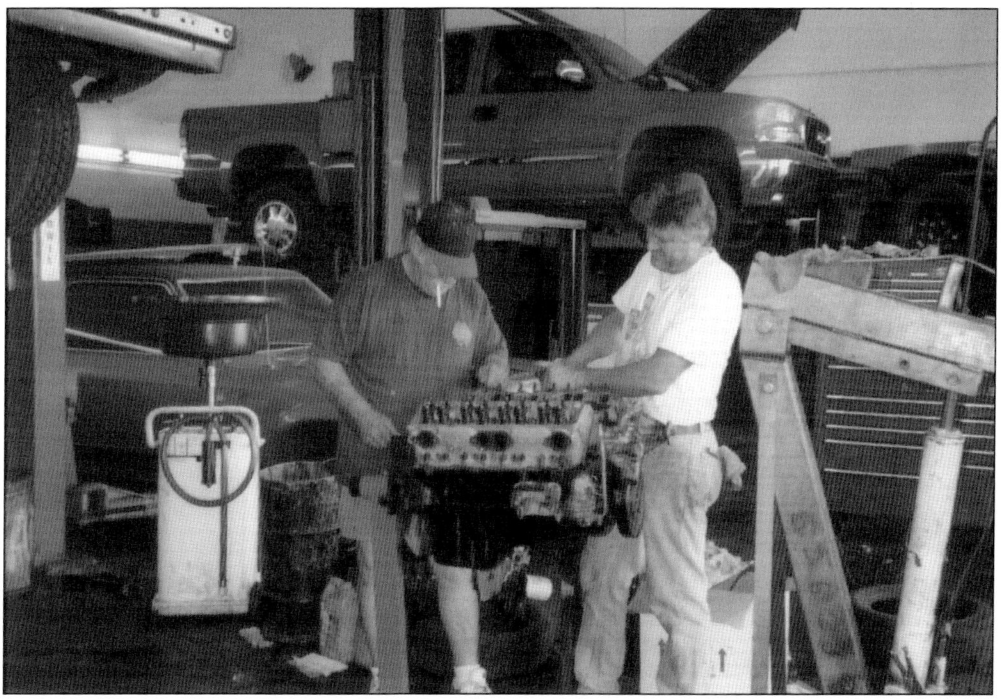

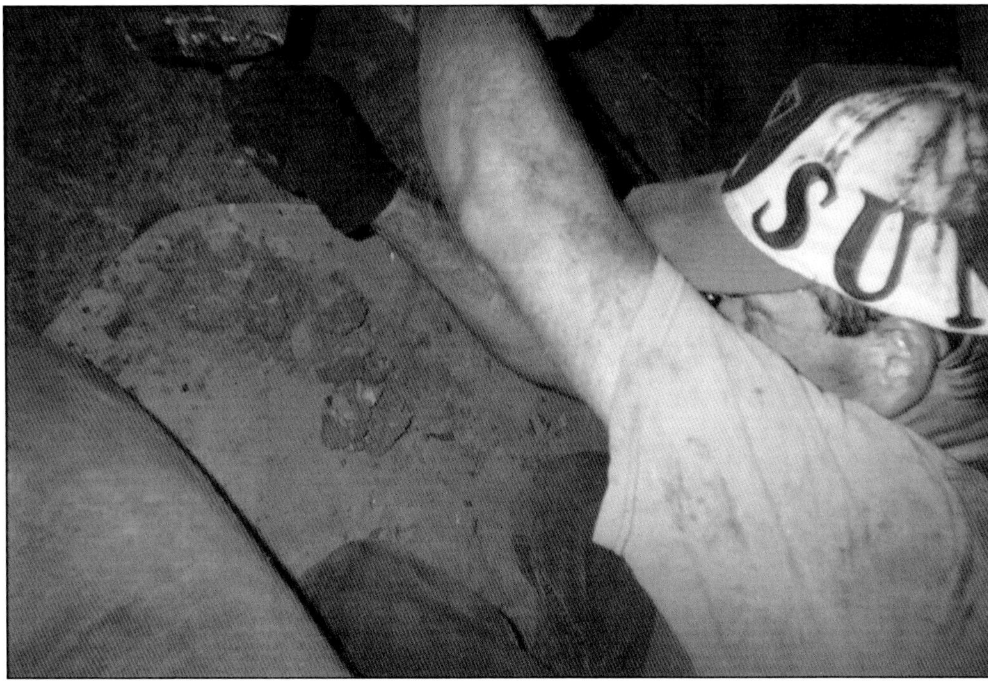

Both of these photographs illustrate to some degree the magnitude of a grassroots racer's constant contact with grease and grime in keeping the car on the track. Dirt-track racing is a contact sport, and each week's race invites door banging, bumps, and collisions between cars. The most skillful driver cannot avoid dings, scrapes, and crunches on a car driven in competition; therefore, this is what racers do after work each evening to prepare for next weekend's race. In these photographs, Justin Upton and Jim Armstrong are installing a new transmission. (Both, courtesy of Jane Upton.)

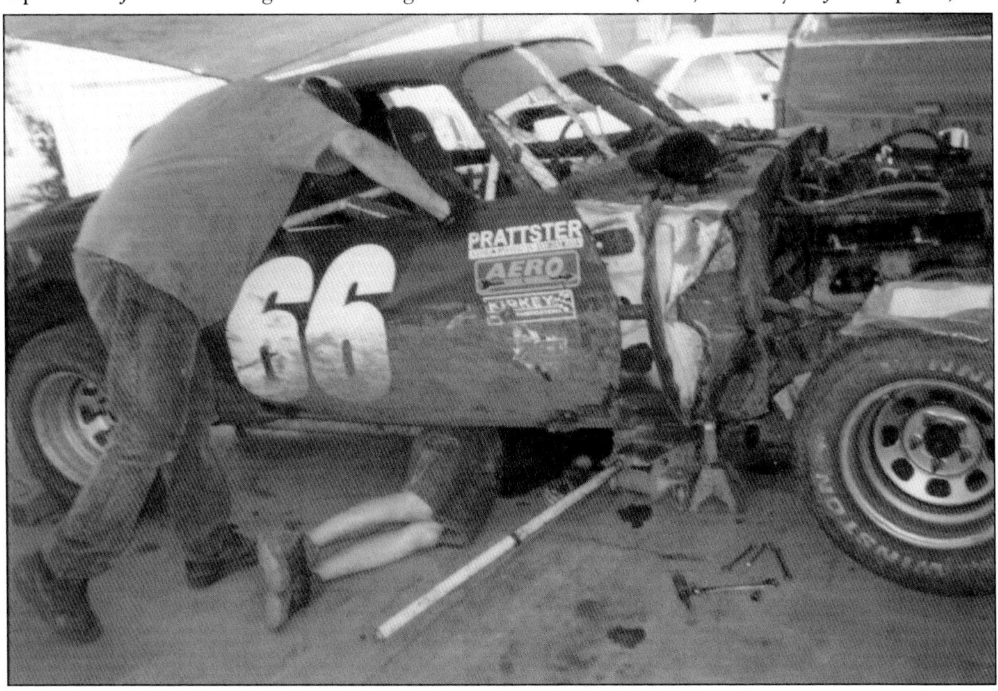

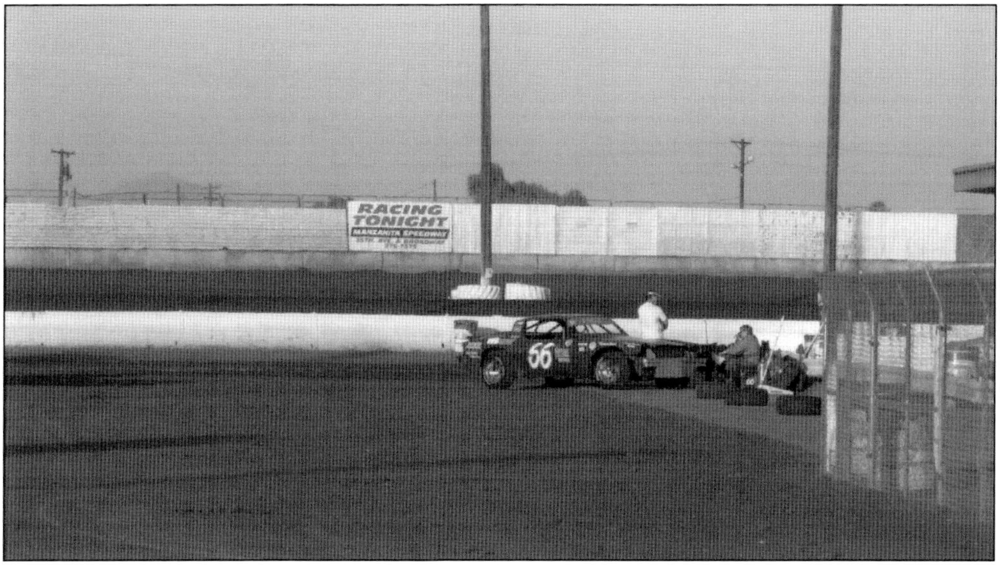

One can achieve something at the grassroots level of racing that is impossible to attain on the national stage where racing is all money and big business. This photograph captures the spirituality of the racer at Manzy where the desire to compete transcends victory on the track. The lone racer and his wife—Justin and Jane Upton—sit quietly in the sun, reviewing the pit setup, and meditating before the thunder of competition sets in. (Courtesy of Don Iverson.)

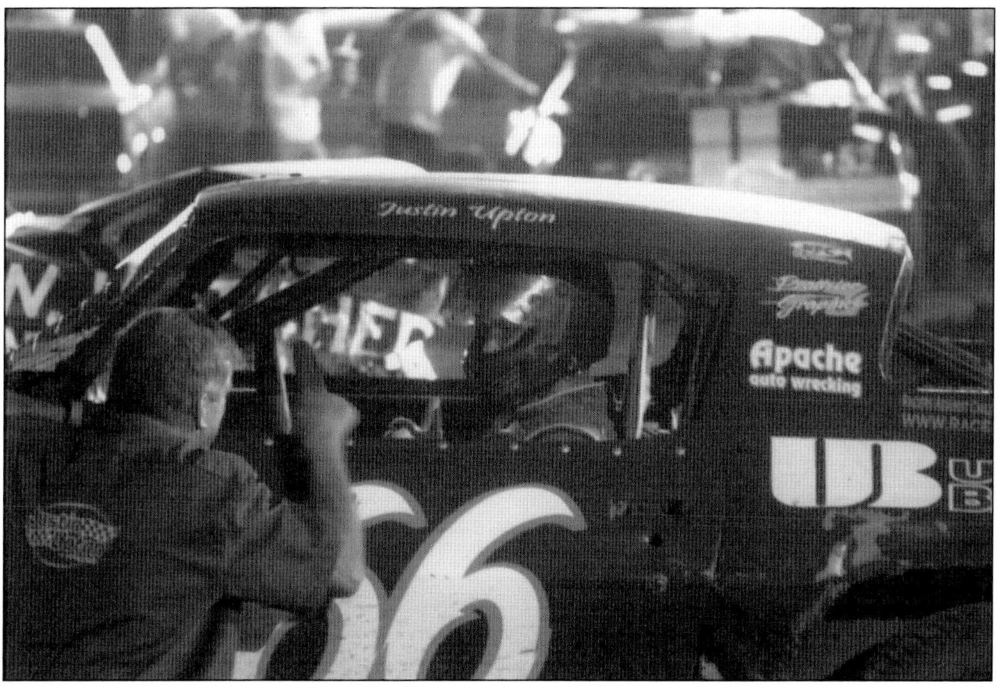

Richard Kirn, Justin Upton's crew chief during the 2007 championship run, points emphatically with last minute advice, as Upton listens intently. Although the SCRA's rules do not permit radios in factory stock cars, most drivers have someone who advises them on things to be aware of during on-track time. The action on short dirt tracks is so fast and furious that most drivers react rather than think about strategy. (Courtesy of Don Iverson.)

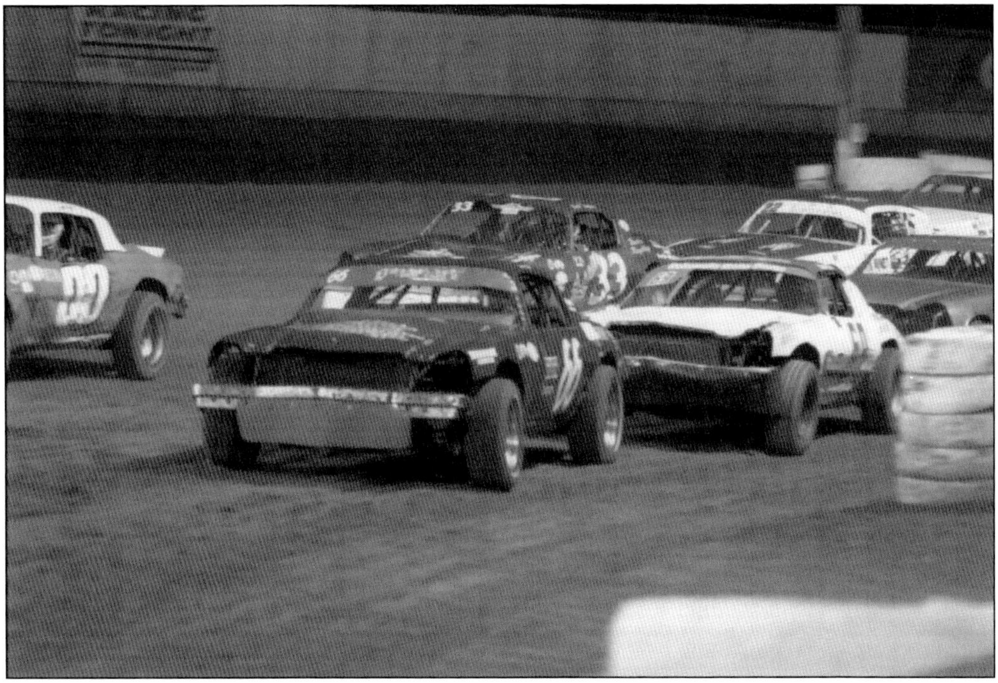

Action in the above photograph shows Justin Upton in No. 66 with a slight edge over SCRA Hall-of-Famer Larry Price in No. 00. Hot on the bumper of Upton is SCRA favorite Ron Poe in No. 69, with another SCRA Hall-of-Fame driver, Bobby Taylor, running outside of Poe in No. 33. Below, Upton in No. 66 runs behind No. 99 driven by Mike Lilly, with City of Mesa, Arizona, police officer Terry Mumaugh running outside in a 2006 race. (Above, courtesy of James A. Fargo; below, courtesy of Don Iverson.)

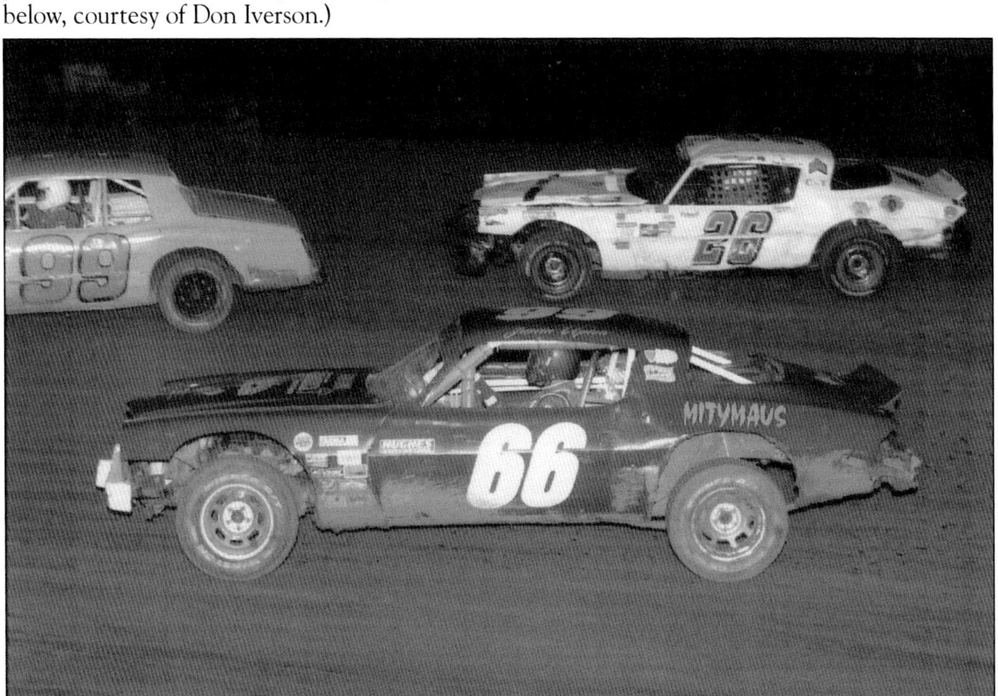

Shown at right are Justin Upton and his father, Larry Upton, an unlikely racing team. Justin was a 46-year-old optician with only 88 races under his belt when he won the SCRA Factory Stock Division Championship, and Larry was a 66-year-old lifelong banker. Taking the checkered flag in a final victory lap in 2007 was the culmination of a plan to win the championship. (Right, courtesy of Justin Upton; below, courtesy of Don Iverson.)

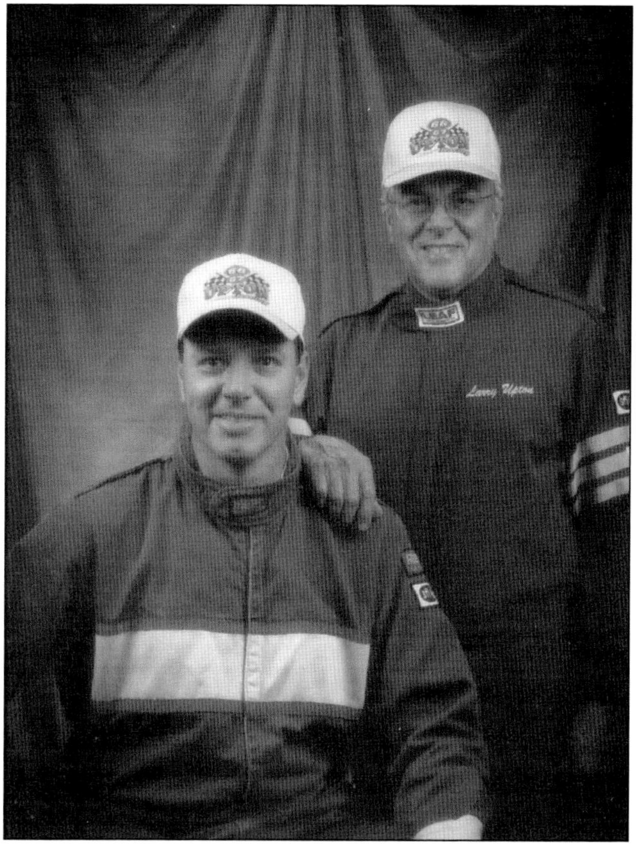

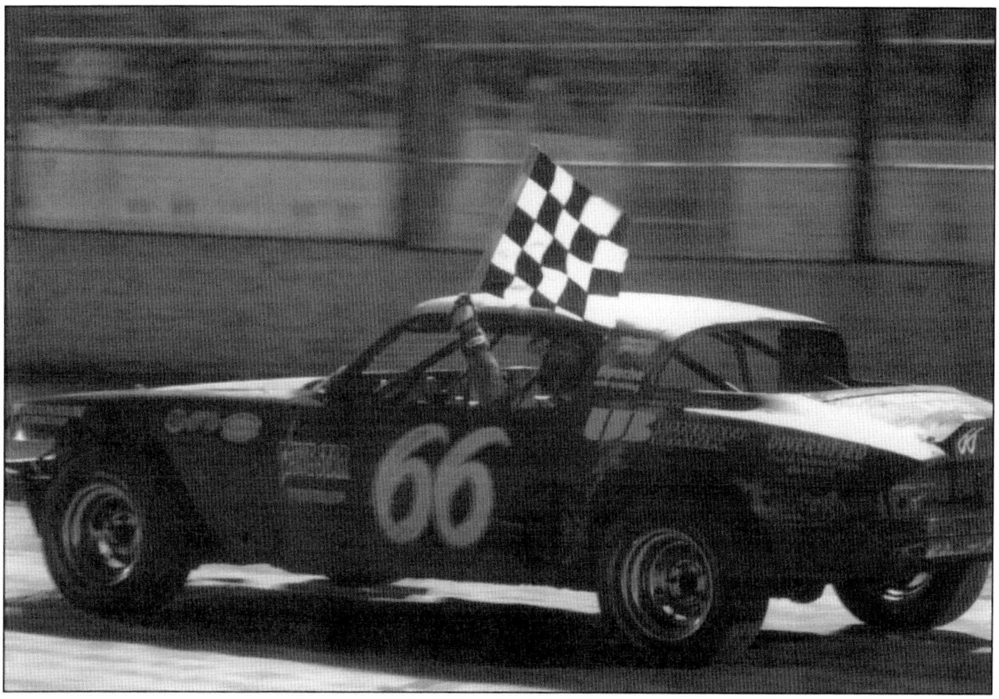

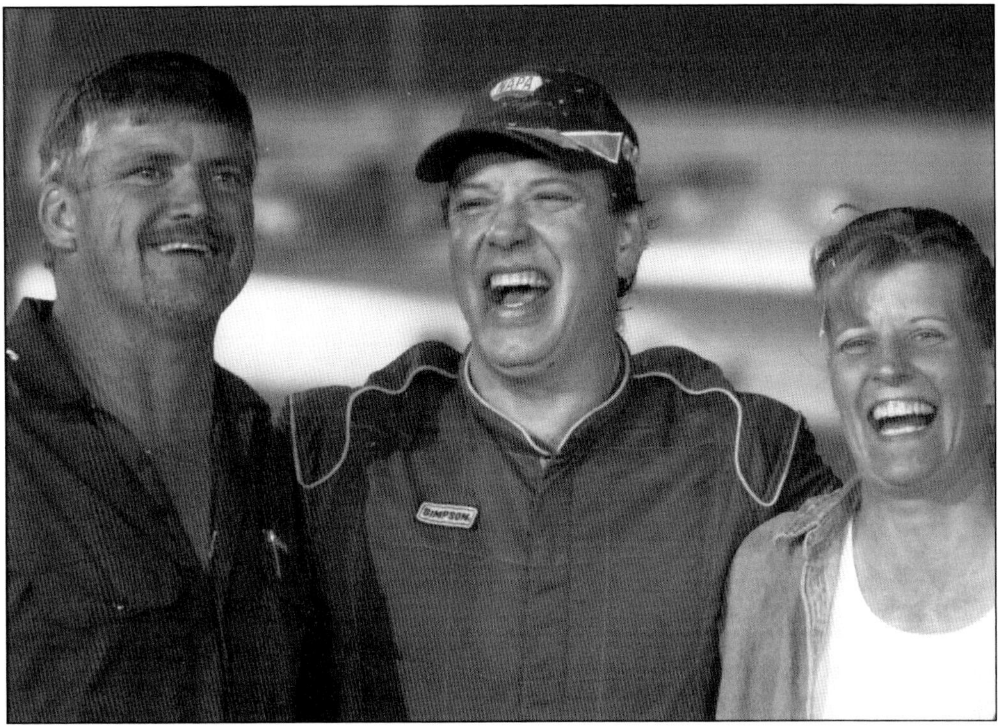

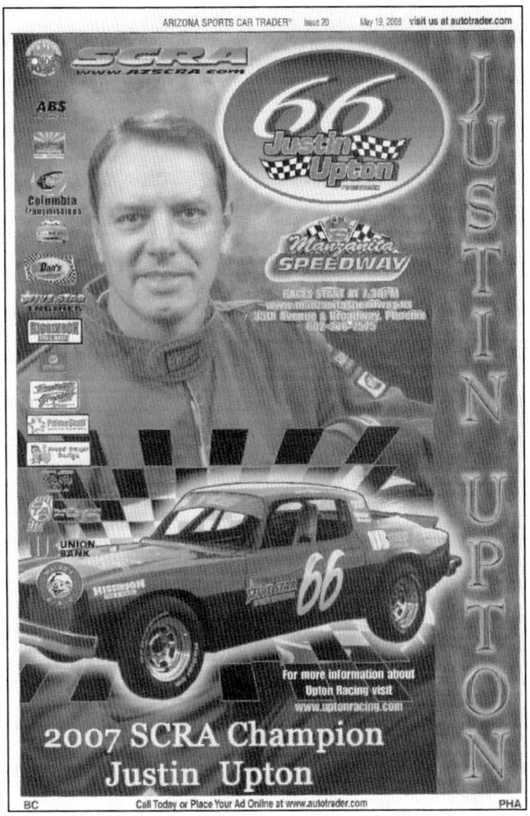

Above, Justin Upton, the champ, surrounded by his wife, Jane, and Richard Kirn, his crew chief, reacts enthusiastically after receiving the championship trophy for the 2007 season. Upton was champion in the SCRA Factory Stock Division, one of the toughest divisions at Manzy. Left, *Auto Trader Magazines*, a major sponsor of Justin Upton Racing LLC throughout his quest for a championship, ran this photograph of Upton, his race car No. 66, and the logos of all his sponsors on the back cover of its "Arizona Sports Car Trader," issue 20, on May 19, 2008. (Above, courtesy of Don Iverson; left, courtesy of *Auto Trader Magazines*.)

Six

Powder Puffs, Dirt Dolls, and Cupcakes

Jalopy racing was the sport, and Manzanita Park was the playground—for men only. Nevertheless, some of the women wanted to race, and the promoters thought it a novelty that might attract more fans, so Powder Puff racing was introduced on September 14, 1951—with conditions. Women were to remain in the grandstands until their race was announced and, upon completion, they were sent back to the grandstands. At first, that was fine; the women were only there to support their husbands. In due course, the women organized their own Powder Puff League, setting up rules and a points system so that they could crown a champion at the end of the season. Tina Hudson won the inaugural 1951 championship. The Powder Puffs worked well for a few seasons until one year, when so many of the women were pregnant that the league collapsed.

By the 1970s, women's place in American culture was changing. At Manzy, women were pushing for greater participation in racing, with some wanting to help in the pits and others wanting to compete against the men. At that time, the SCRA was the dominant racing association in Phoenix and had an agreement with Manzy that it would run its own show, including governing rules. In exchange, the SCRA brought a high car count to each race. A few SCRA wives wanted to race, but at first, Manzy would not permit it. History has a slow grind to it, and eventually, women here and there, names now lost to history, raced with the men. Most women drivers, however, continued to race with organizations such as the Mod Stock Mamas and Dirt Dolls. There was no purse, so Linda Price began baking cupcakes to raise funds for the women. However, Manzy wanted a cut of any funds connected to the track, so it demanded 15 percent of the sales; Manzy lost that fight to Price.

Linda Price had a successful career competing against other women and was ready to take on male competition. Price represented what all women want and deserve—the opportunity to compete in any endeavor in which they are qualified. With the support of Larry Price, her husband, and the SCRA, Linda raced in the Super Stock Division in 1999, winning Rookie of the Year honors. In 2002, 2003, and 2006, Price was honored with the SCRA Sportsman of the Year Award. In 2006, the SCRA awarded her a lifetime membership, and in 2008, she was inducted into the SCRA Hall of Fame. Today, women race with men in all divisions.

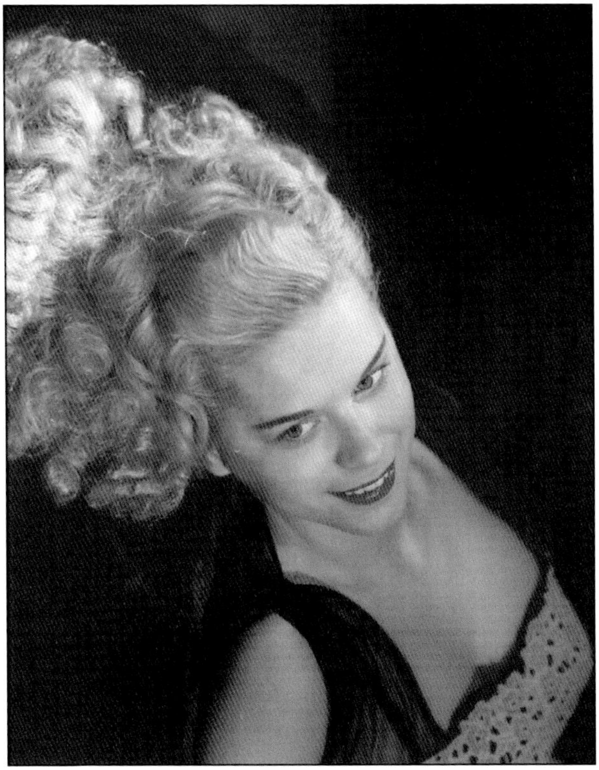

Bonnie Stevens was a model and movie star before she was a Powder Puff racer; however, it was her racing career that landed her on Herb Shriner's *Two for the Money* television show in New York City in 1954. New Yorkers could not get over the idea of a petite, beautiful woman driving a race car. Also, she was the only Arizona Powder Puffer to claim membership in the "Upside Down Club" by rolling her car going into turn one when a tire blew, bouncing off the wall and into a roll. At left is Bonnie at age 20 when she began her modeling career. Below, Bonnie sits poolside with William Bendix at the Camelback Inn. Bendix was the star of the television series *The Life of Riley*. Bonnie's movie credits include, among others, *Sound of Fury* with Lloyd Bridges and *Bus Stop* with Marilyn Monroe. (Both, courtesy of Bonnie Stevens.)

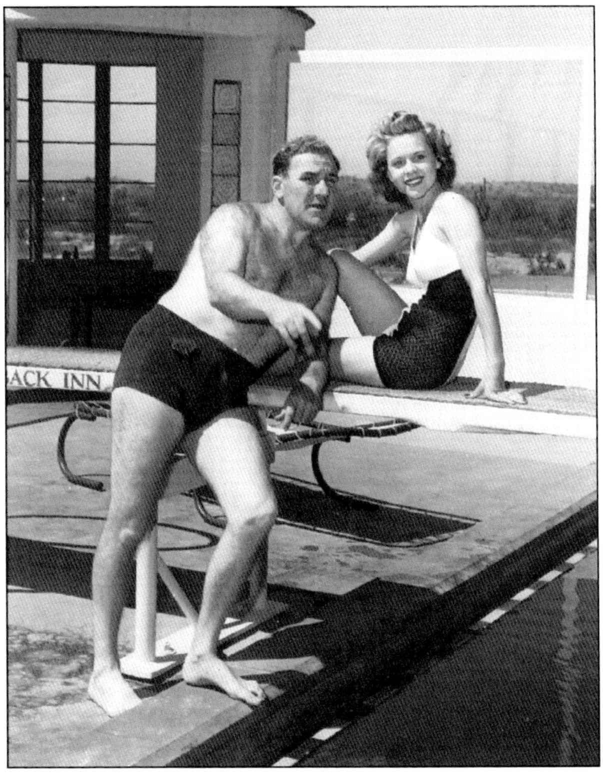

Vernie Haumont, the wife of Pete Haumont, drove his jalopy in the Powder Puff events. As it turned out, Vernie was an outstanding driver and won the Powder Puff Championship in 1952. Haumont was also raising a son and daughter and announced near the end of the 1952 season that she was giving up racing to concentrate on family affairs. (Courtesy of LaVerne Doyle.)

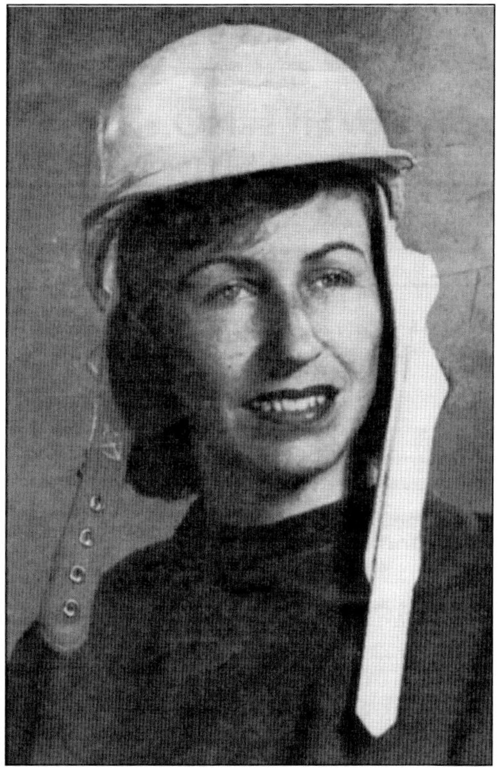

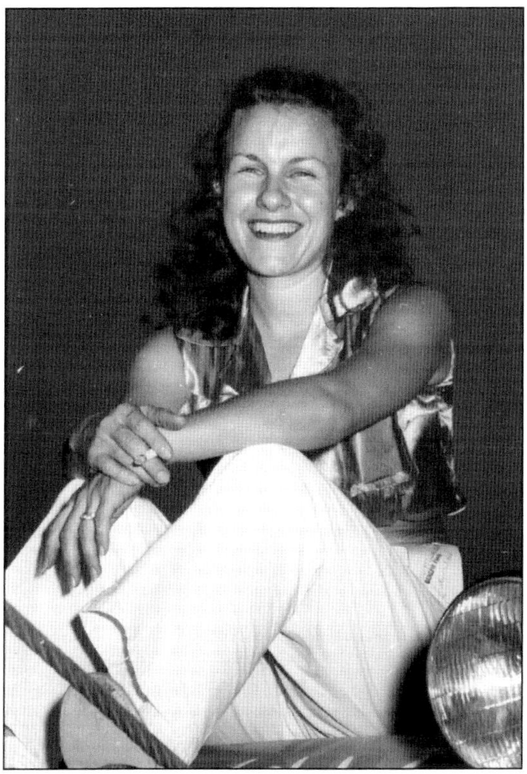

Esther Pritchard was a member of the racing Pritchard family from South Phoenix. Esther was the wife of Cecil Pritchard and raced his jalopy during Powder Puff races in the 1950s. (Courtesy of La Verne Doyle.)

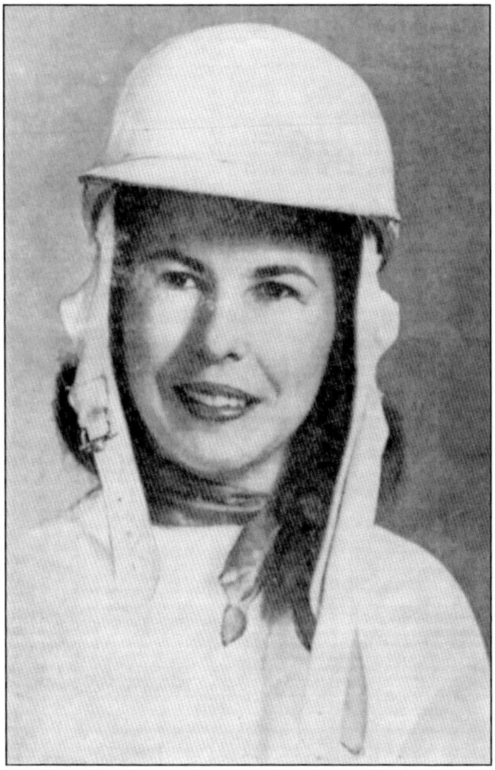

At left is Melba Pritchard, a talented high school athlete, later playing softball for the Double Cola Co. for two years, and the wife of Steve Pritchard, Manzy's first fatality. Below is Melba's sister-in-law Frances Pritchard, who was married to Leonard Pritchard, also a jalopy driver. Before her career in Powder Puffs, Frances was a professional softball player, playing for eight years with the PBSW Ramblers, a Phoenix women's softball team and a national powerhouse. She was the mother to a boy and girl during her Powder Puff days. (Both, courtesy of LaVerne Doyle.)

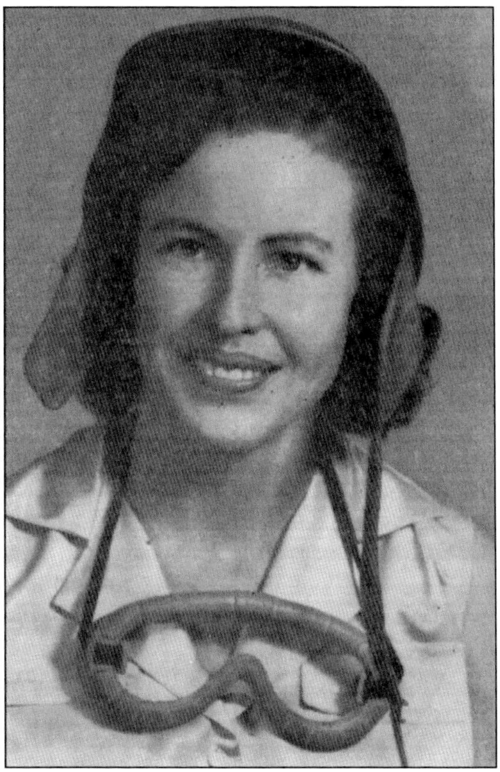

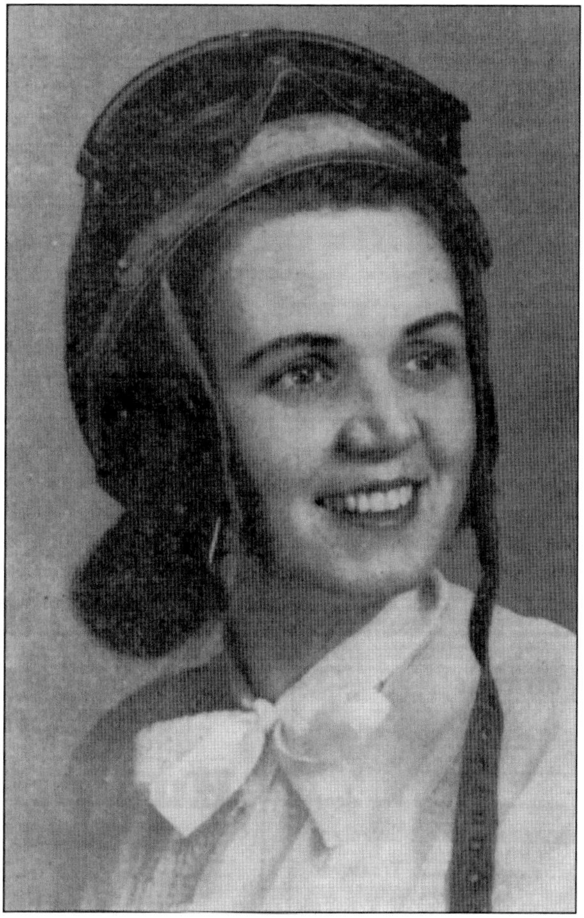

Shown at right is Gwen Tipton, mother to a seven-year-old son, who was most likely the first female driver at Manzy to build and own her own jalopy. Her husband, Hayden, and friend Jack Davis served as the pit crew. Below is No. 5, the Tipton jalopy. Occasionally, Tipton's car was driven in the men's events by Leonard Davenport. (Right, courtesy of LaVerne Doyle; below, courtesy of Don Appley.)

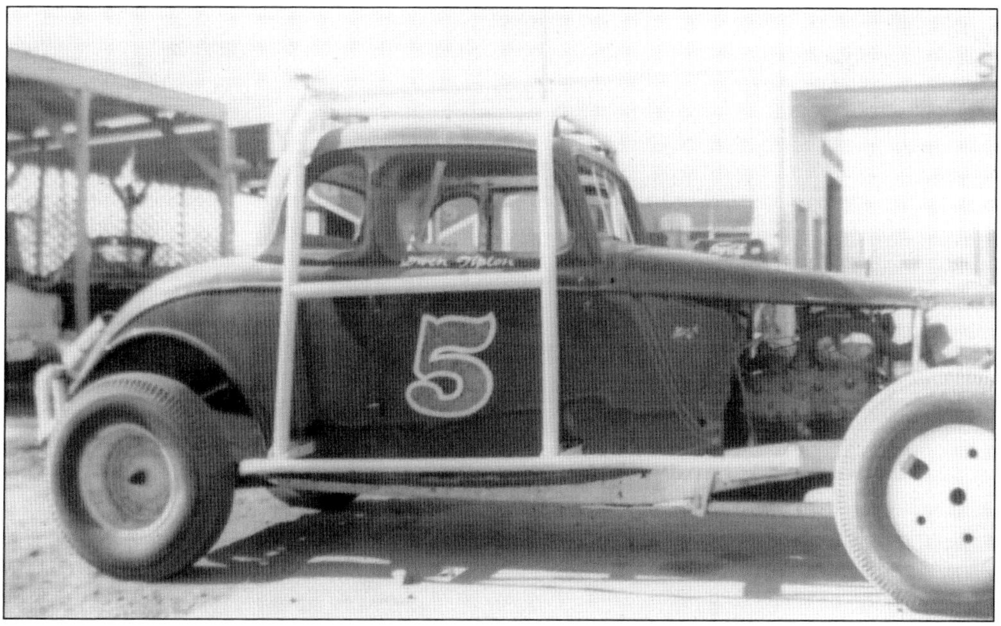

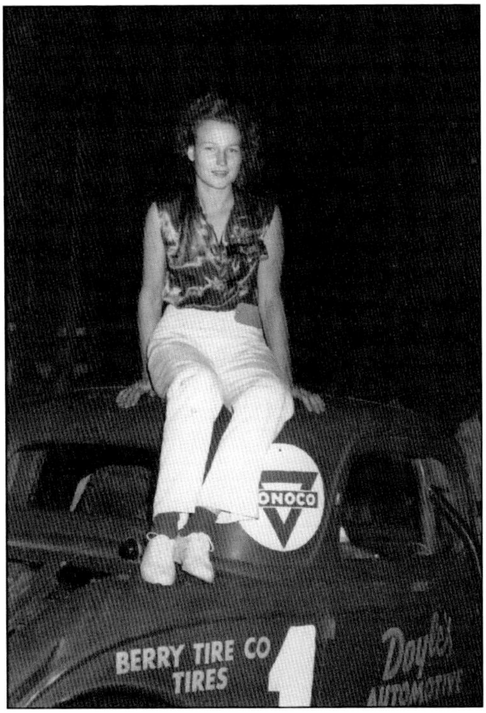

At left, LaVerne Doyle poses on her husband Avery's jalopy, which she drove in the Powder Puff races. LaVerne was the 1953 Powder Puff champion. She could do it all. Below, she is shown gassing up before a race. She set the three-lap record for women at an average speed of 52 miles per hour on the quarter-mile oval, which also beat the existing men's record. Bonnie Stevens said, "LaVerne was such a good driver that the other women suspected she must secretly be practicing during the week. She could have raced against the men." (Both, courtesy of LaVerne Doyle.)

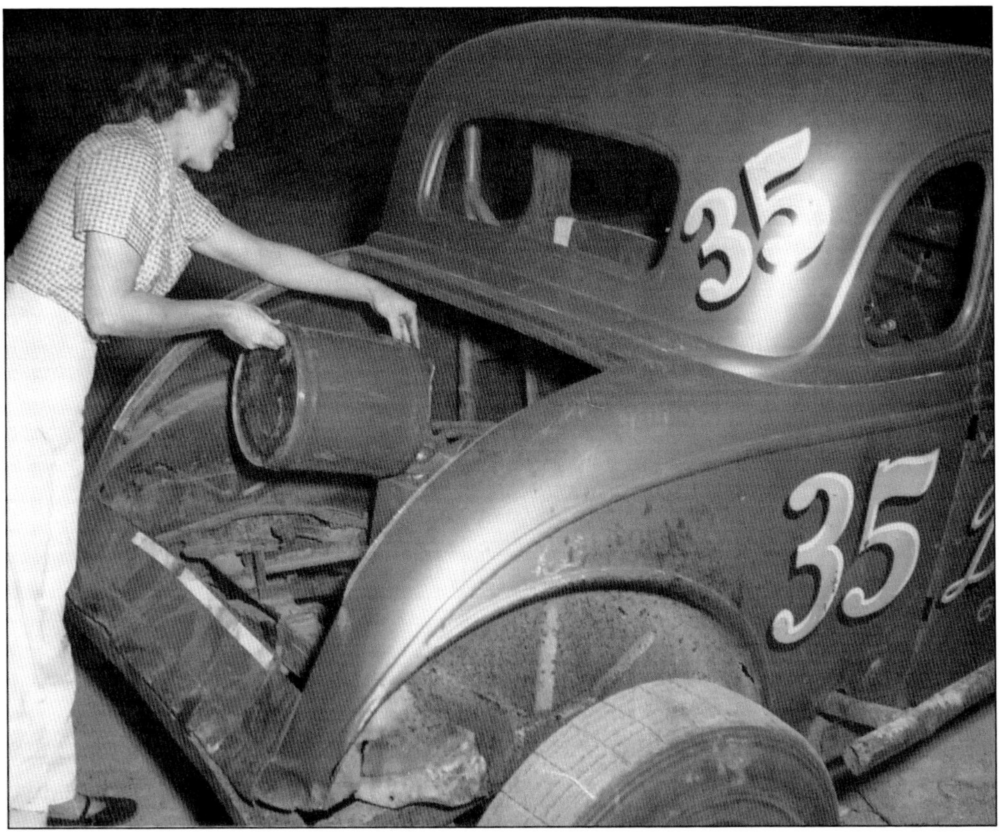

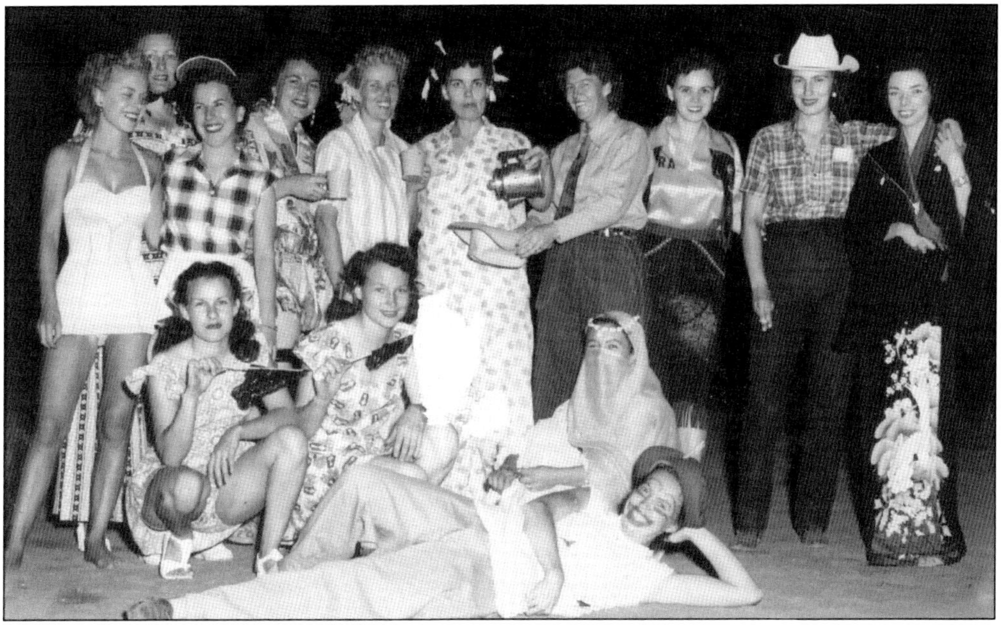

The Powder Puffers celebrate Halloween. Pictured are, from left to right, (standing) Bonnie Stevens, Ruth Cromer, Melba Pritchard, Josie Creach, Norma Buchan, Tina Hudson, Norma Jackson, Gwyn Tipton, Jodie Gunn, and Dorothy Milner; (kneeling) Esther Pritchard, LaVerne Doyle, and Pat Hubbard. Joyce Stump is stretched out on the ground. (Courtesy of LaVerne Doyle.)

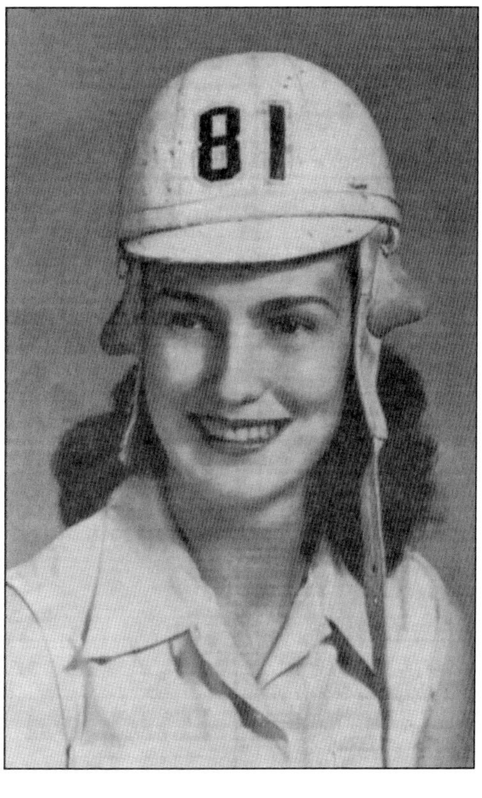

Jody Gunn was the wife of Gene Gunn, who was instrumental in the organization of Manzanita Park as a jalopy track. Jody was only 21 when this photograph was taken in 1952. She was a young mother of two sons, ages four and six, when she began racing in 1951. (Courtesy of LaVerne Doyle.)

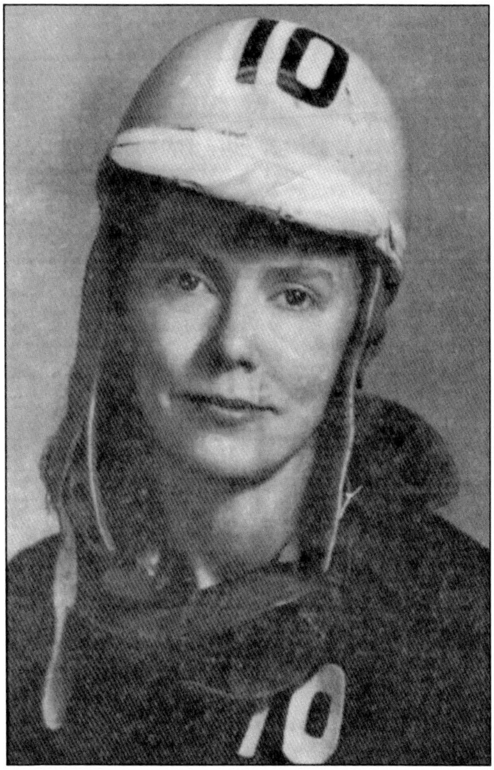

Joyce Stump was married to Frank Stump, a former P-38 fighter pilot. When she began racing in 1951, Joyce was 25 years old and a mother of two sons. She was the first woman to hold office in the AJRA. Joyce said that her "biggest ambition is to be half as good a driver as my husband, Frank, my favorite driver." (Courtesy of LaVerne Doyle.)

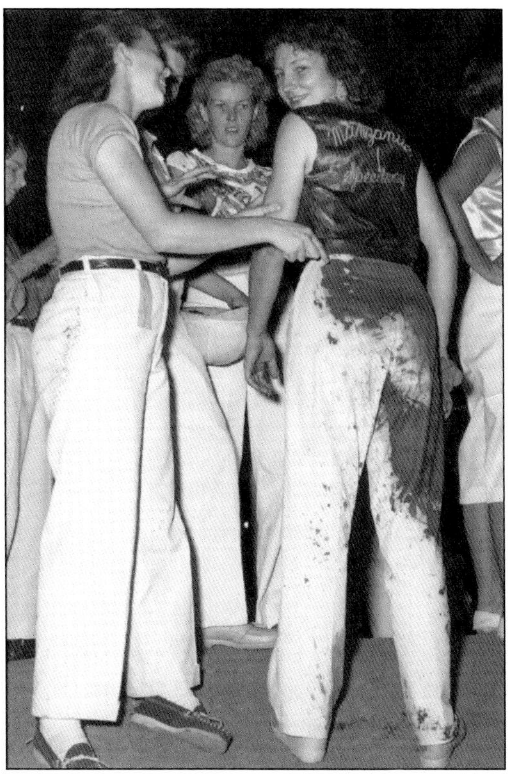

Men and women jalopy drivers in the 1950s were required to wear white pants. LaVerne Doyle laughs off a spill in the mud after she hit the wall and was stunned. Her husband, Avery, ran up and, instead of helping her, yelled, "Get out, get out, so I can fix the car before the next race!" Winning is everything. (Courtesy of LaVerne Doyle.)

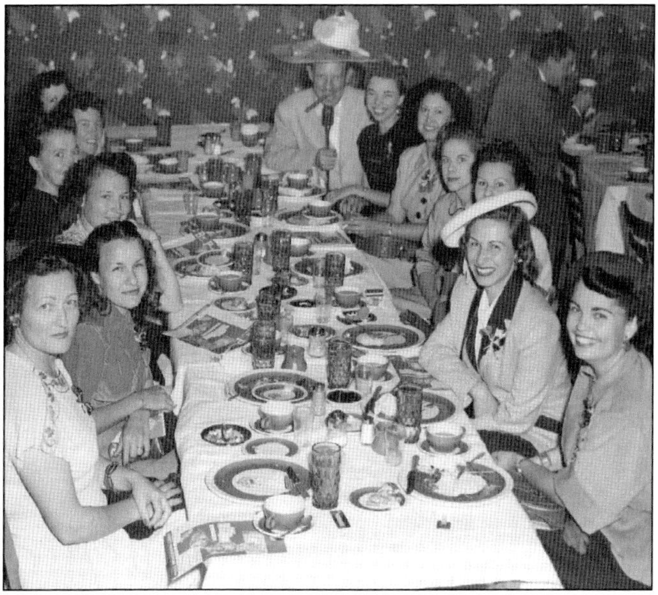

The Powder Puff racers organized elegant dinners to celebrate their jalopy racing, which separated them from the men's organizations. Here, women are shown at a 1952 event at the Hotel Westward Ho in Phoenix. Seated on the left are, from front to back, Ruth Cromer, Esther Pritchard, LaVerne Doyle, unidentified, and Norma Jackson. Seated on the right are, from front to back, Josie Creach, Vernie Haumont, Dorothy Peacock, Bonnie Stevens, unidentified, and Dorothy Milner. The man is unidentified. (Courtesy of LaVerne Doyle.)

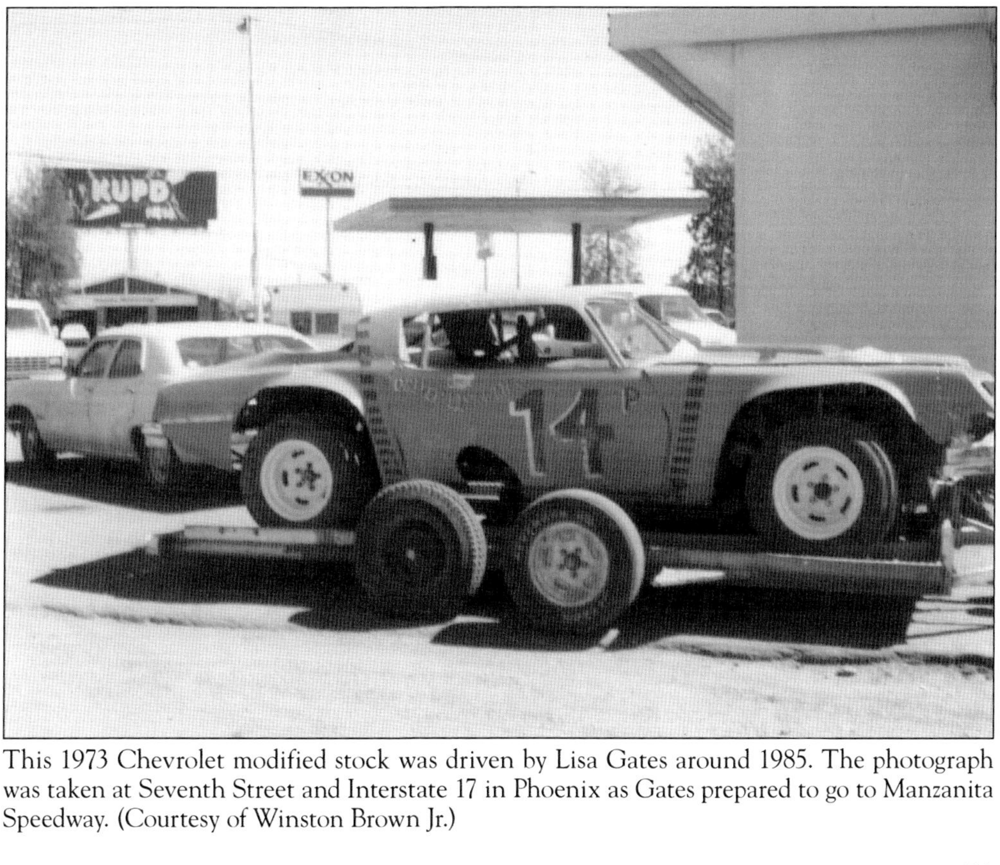

This 1973 Chevrolet modified stock was driven by Lisa Gates around 1985. The photograph was taken at Seventh Street and Interstate 17 in Phoenix as Gates prepared to go to Manzanita Speedway. (Courtesy of Winston Brown Jr.)

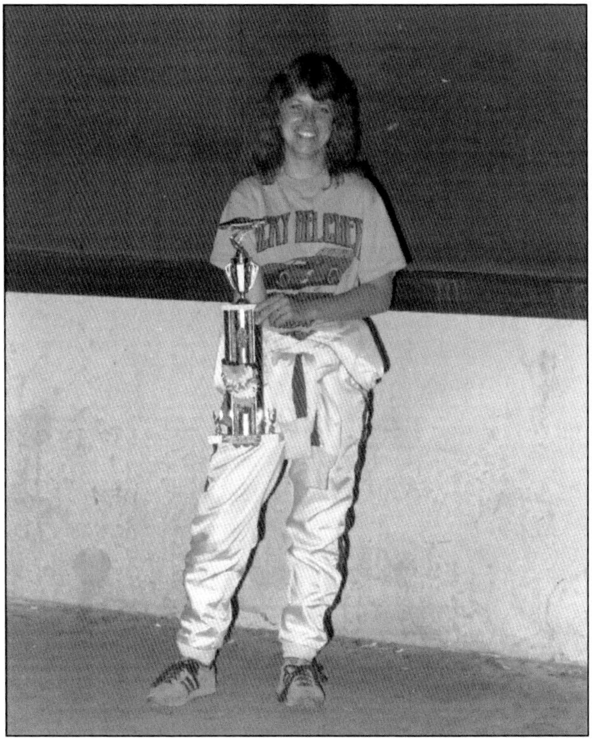

Terri Horton Belcher was the daughter of Ollie Horton, a three-time SCRA stock-car champion. Terri raced street stocks, now known as super stocks. This photograph was taken around 1987. (Courtesy of Winston Brown Jr.)

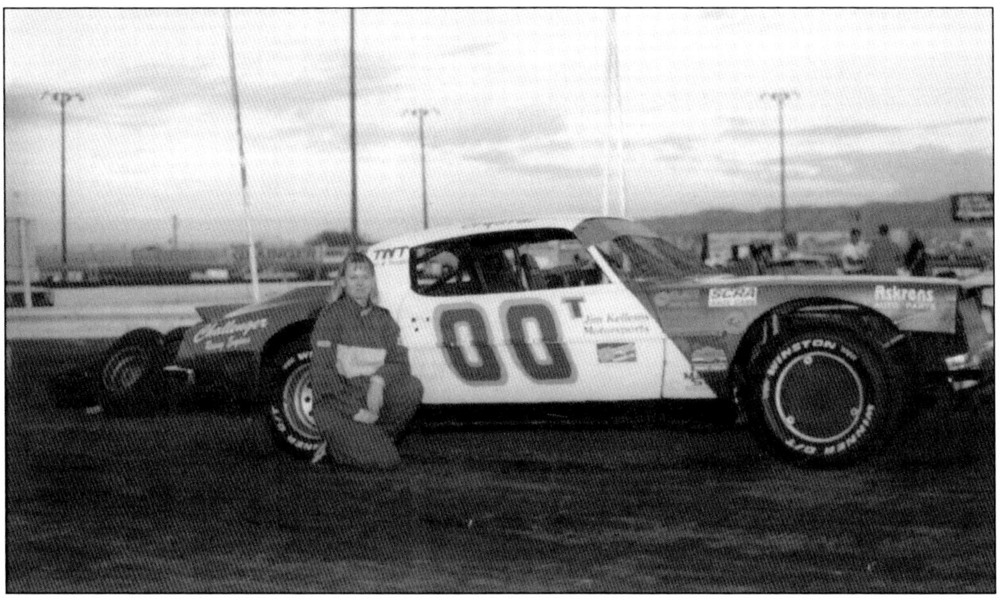

Crystal Price Hemphill is the daughter of Linda and Larry Price, both of whom are members of the SCRA Hall of Fame. Hemphill has raced since age 16, beginning with the Dirt Dolls; however, her goal was to race against men in the Super Stock Division, which she entered in 2002 and won Rookie of the Year honors, earning more top five finishes than any other driver. Her first super stock race was protested when another driver claimed that her father actually drove the car; he lost the protest. "When I get in the car, I'm a driver, not a man or woman," says Hemphill. (Courtesy of Crystal Hemphill.)

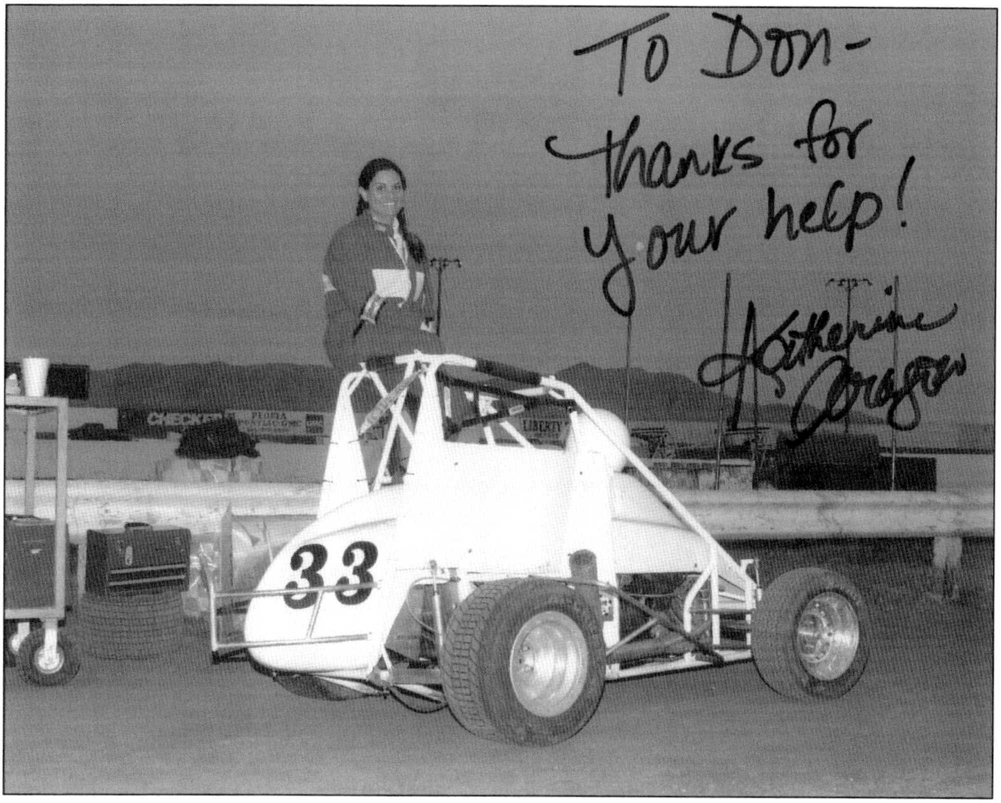

Katherine Aragon has raced mini sprints since 2005. She says, "Coming from a racing family, you don't have a choice. You race!" Katherine is the niece of Arizona Motorsports Hall-of-Famer Warren Wampole; her father, Jim Aragon, and brother James also race. Early on, guys tried to push her around on the track, but she said, "When you put the helmet on, everyone is the same." Aragon's career almost ended in her second season when she crashed, flipping nine times, which caused serious injuries, but she was back in 2007! (Courtesy of Don Appley.)

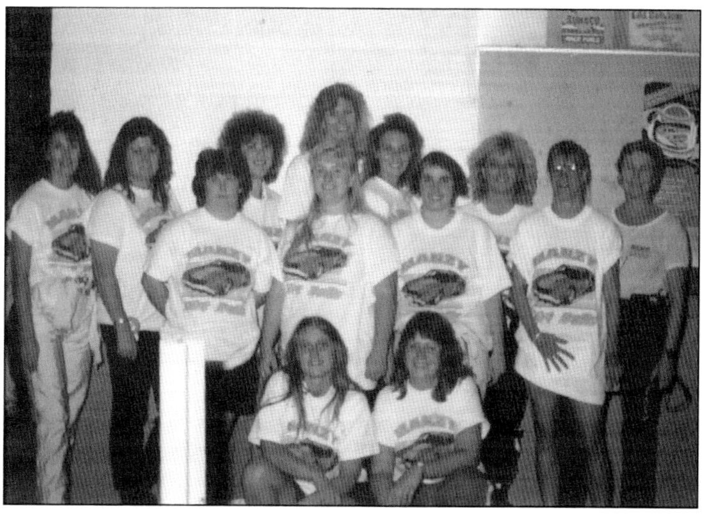

This is a group photograph of the Manzy Dirt Dolls in 1994. From left to right are, (first row) Mindy Powers and Sue McCartney; (second row) Tammy Odom, Lisa Way, Kathy Metzler, and unidentified; (third row) Rosann Young, Linda Price, Denice Woody, Cindy Meredith, Dawn Klein, Mary Kay ?, and Jean Gilbert. (Courtesy of Linda Price.)

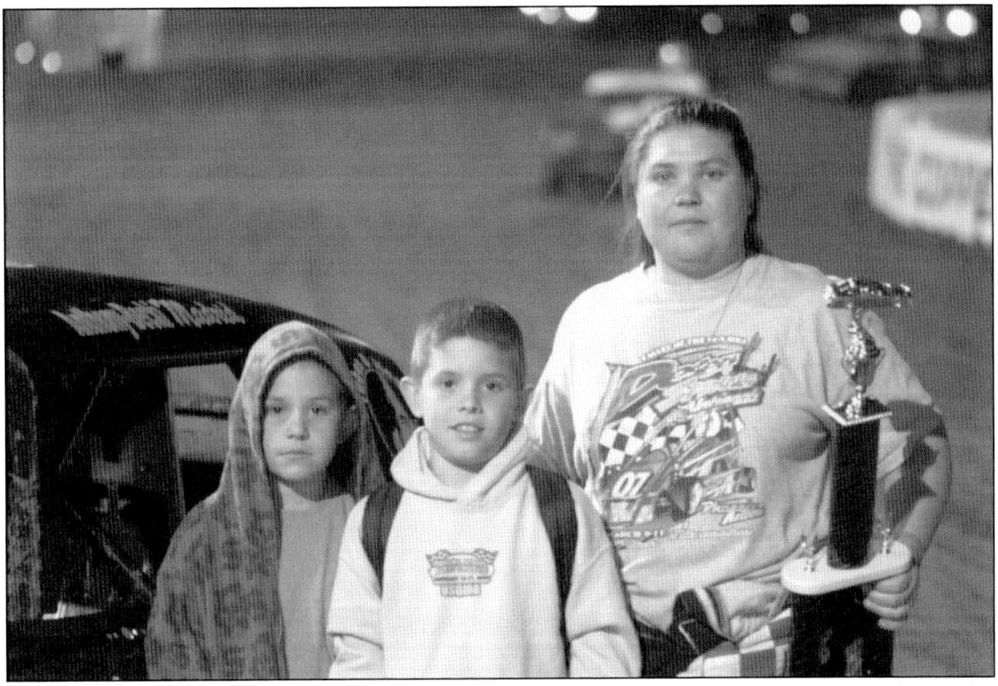

Becky Madrid, wife of perennial champion Anthony Madrid, poses with young copilots, who had chosen her to win the SCRA women's race. Becky was a lead-foot in her own right, winning often in husband Anthony's race car. (Courtesy of Don Iverson.)

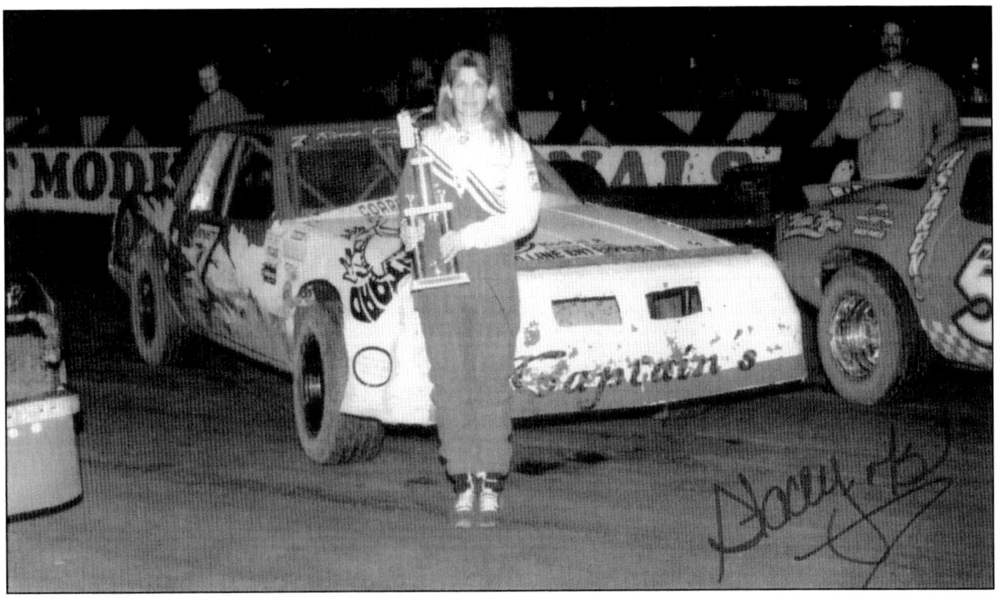

Stacy Bennett won a raffle for a bomber in 1998. She decided to race it, winning 13 trophies over the next two years. She moved up to factory stocks in 2002, winning two main events. Bennett moved to super stocks in 2007 and has two wins. Stacy says that "racing against men is tough, and men put women through the 'respect' test. Something mentally happens when men are passed by a woman." Further, she says, "The reward for the effort is phenomenal." (Courtesy of James A Fargo.)

Racing on the inside is Crystal Price Hemphill in No. 00. Her mother, Linda, is on the outside. Crystal later transferred into super stocks, racing solely against the male drivers, winning Rookie of the Year honors in 2002. Linda Price was one of the women who helped open Manzy racing to women, earning her own Rookie of the Year award in the Super Stock Division in 1999. (Courtesy of Linda Price.)

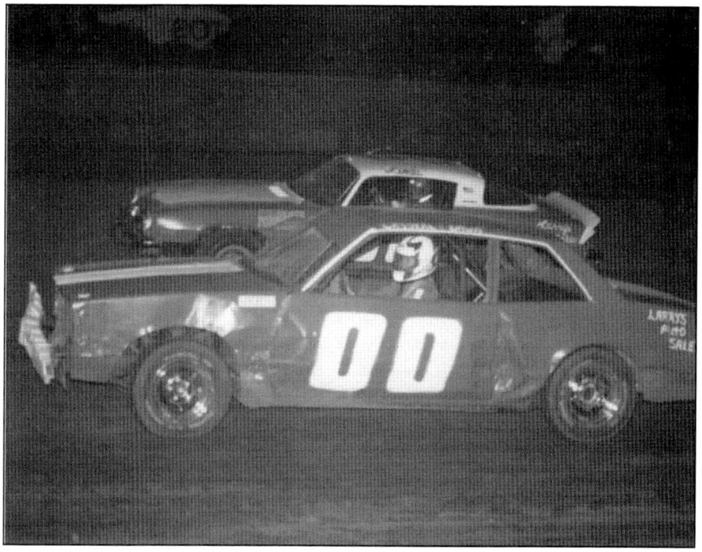

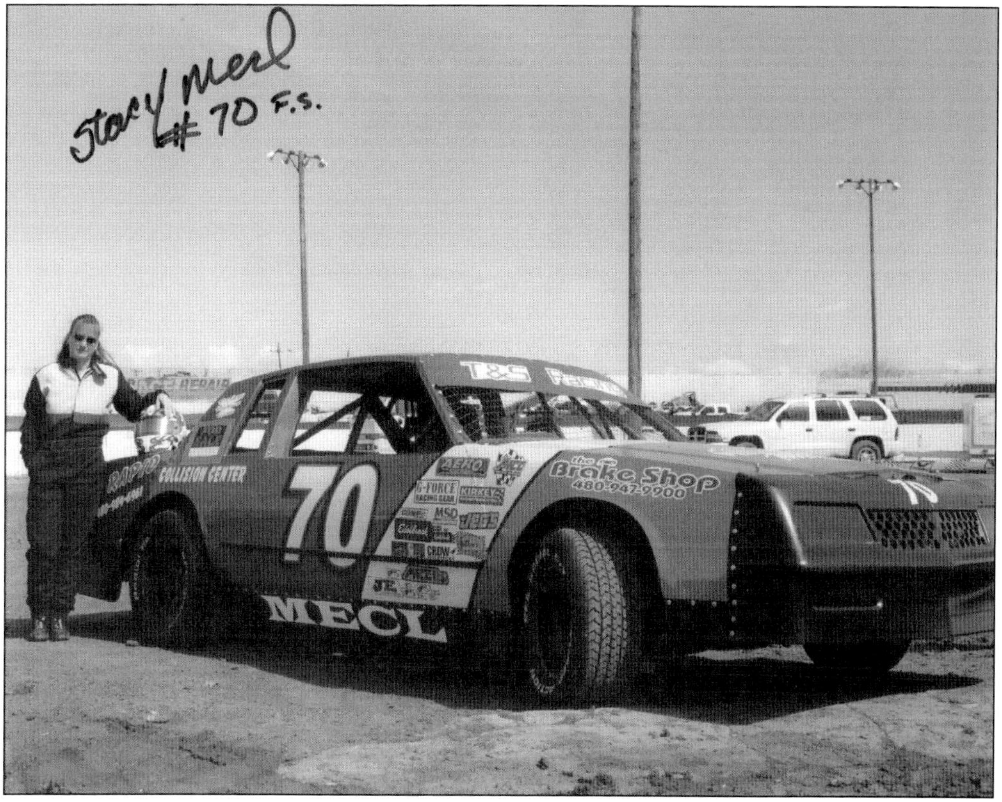

Stacy Mecl comes from a racing family. Four of her five siblings race. Her father, Frank Sosovoski, raced; her husband, Tim, is a top super stock driver; and her son and daughter race. Although Stacy's focus is currently on her children, she still gets on the track occasionally. On June 25, 2011, Stacy finished third in a super stock race, which was her best finish against male competition. She has three Dirt Doll Championships under her belt, but Stacy likes the more aggressive racing style of the men. (Courtesy of James A. Fargo.)

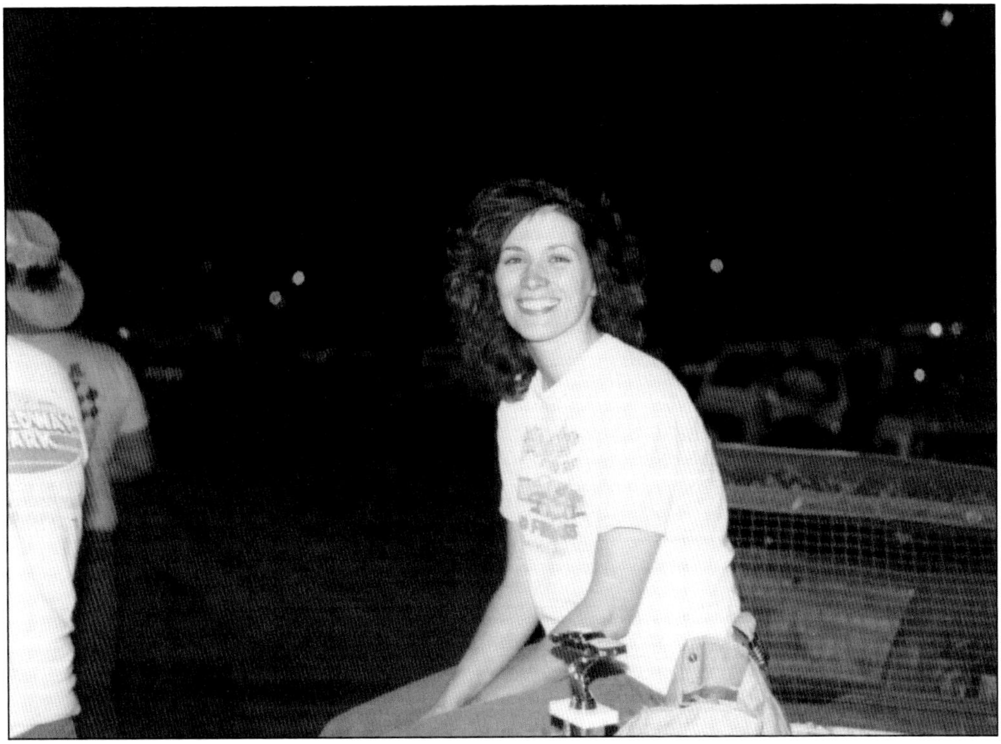

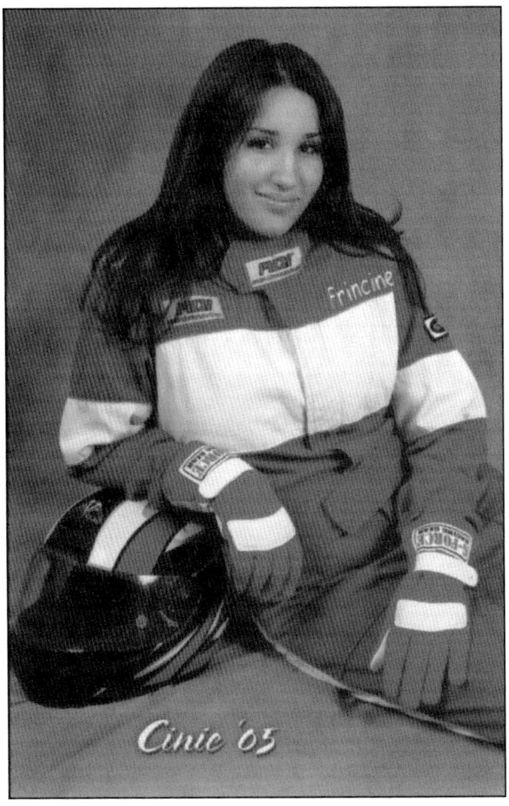

Above, ? Sherrill, a young stock-car driver from the 1980s, smiles cheerfully after winning a trophy for the night's event. At left, 16-year-old Frincine Pino poses in a more relaxed setting than the racetrack. 'Cine, as she is called, developed an interest in stock-car racing by helping her father, Joe Pino, work on his stock car. By the age of 16, 'Cine was determined to join the SCRA and race. During a local television interview soon after making her entry at Manzy, she told the interviewer "I just like to go fast!" (Above, courtesy of Winston Brown Jr.; left, courtesy of Frincine Pino.)

Seven

The Last Days of Manzanita Speedway

For the past decade, many people associated with Manzanita Speedway speculated and worried that its days were numbered. The reasons were obvious. There was an ongoing lawsuit between Joe and Millie Kimbro and Keith Hall over who really owned the track, the track facilities were showing signs of deferred maintenance, there was increasing competition for the spectators' dollars as major-league sports continued to expand in Arizona, and finally, the crowds that attended racing events at the track were dwindling.

In 2004, the lawsuit was decided in favor of Joe and Millie Kimbro, which resolved what appeared to be the most significant problem facing the track. Immediately, the Kimbros turned to Dennis Wood, a man with a long history at Manzy and, more importantly, the man credited with saving Phoenix International Raceway and the open-wheel racing that it brought to Phoenix, ultimately paving the way for the introduction of NASCAR to Phoenix. Wood's accomplishments eventually led to his selection to the Arizona Motorsports Hall of Fame. With Wood as the track manager, there was tremendous hope among the fans and drivers that Manzy might be restored to its glory days. But it was not to be, simply because the track had declined to the point that the cash flow needed for the restoration was not available. Enter father and son Mel and Bobby Martin.

Most Manzy regulars were acquainted with Mel Martin. He had been a promoter of numerous events at the track and a major supporter of sprint-car racing. Furthermore, his reputation was that he was well-heeled and had an enduring passion for sprint-car racing. The Martins seemed to be the solution.

The Martins invested heavily during their first year of operation, remodeling the dilapidated concession facilities, grandstands, and fencing. Excitement was back in the air, but one essential was missing, the crowds.

As the final race approached on April 11, 2009, most fans and drivers could not accept that after 58 years Manzanita Speedway would be gone, replaced by a 33-acre storage yard for heavy equipment. While the track was a commercial enterprise, fans and drivers had come to view it as if it belonged to them. How could anyone possibly exchange this sacred ground, this icon of Phoenix history, for cash? There was no reasonable answer in the minds of the devoted. Their outrage was real and remains an open wound to many fans and drivers to this day.

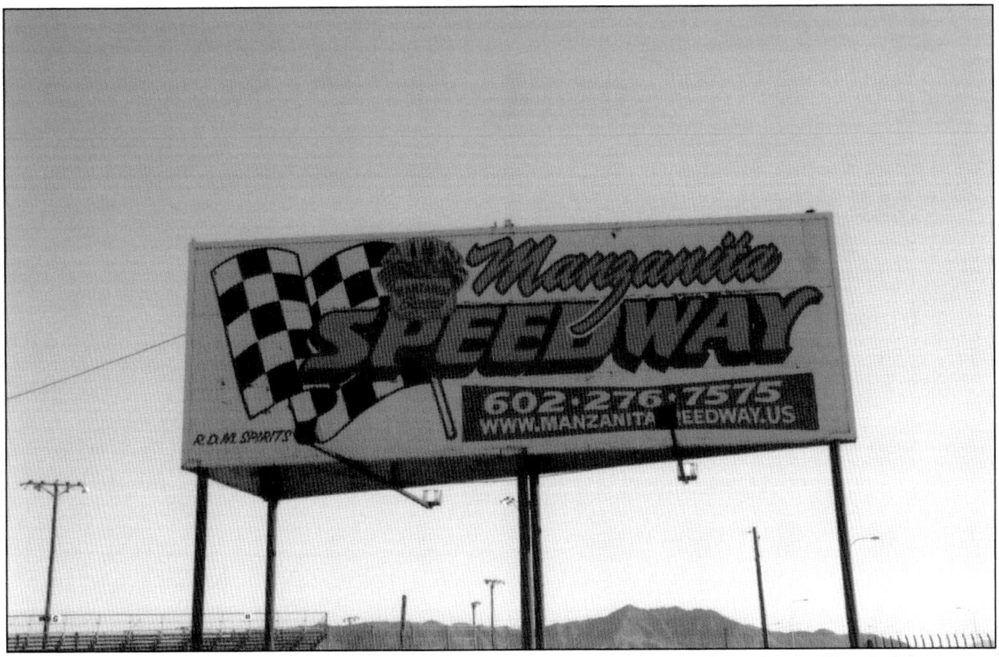

This sign marked the Thirty-fifth Avenue entrance to Manzanita Speedway. South Mountain is in the background. Just beyond the sign to the south is the entrance to the pits. An identical sign stood on Broadway Road marking the entrance on that side of the intersection. (Courtesy of James A. Fargo.)

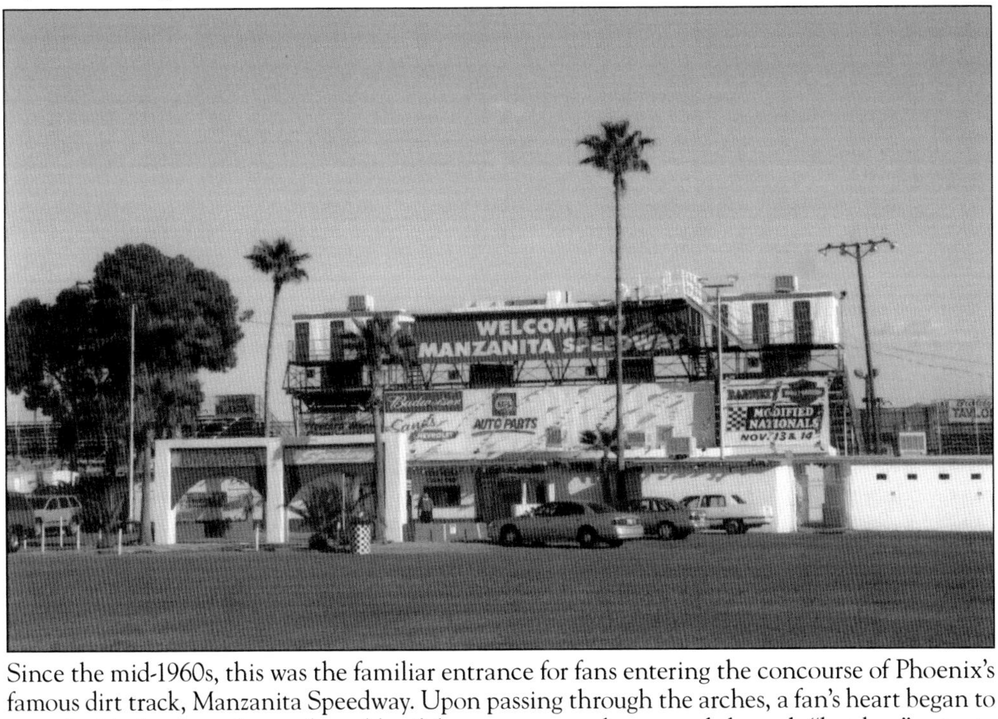

Since the mid-1960s, this was the familiar entrance for fans entering the concourse of Phoenix's famous dirt track, Manzanita Speedway. Upon passing through the arches, a fan's heart began to pound with the deep-throated rumble of the race cars as they roared through "hot laps" prior to the races. (Courtesy of James A. Fargo.)

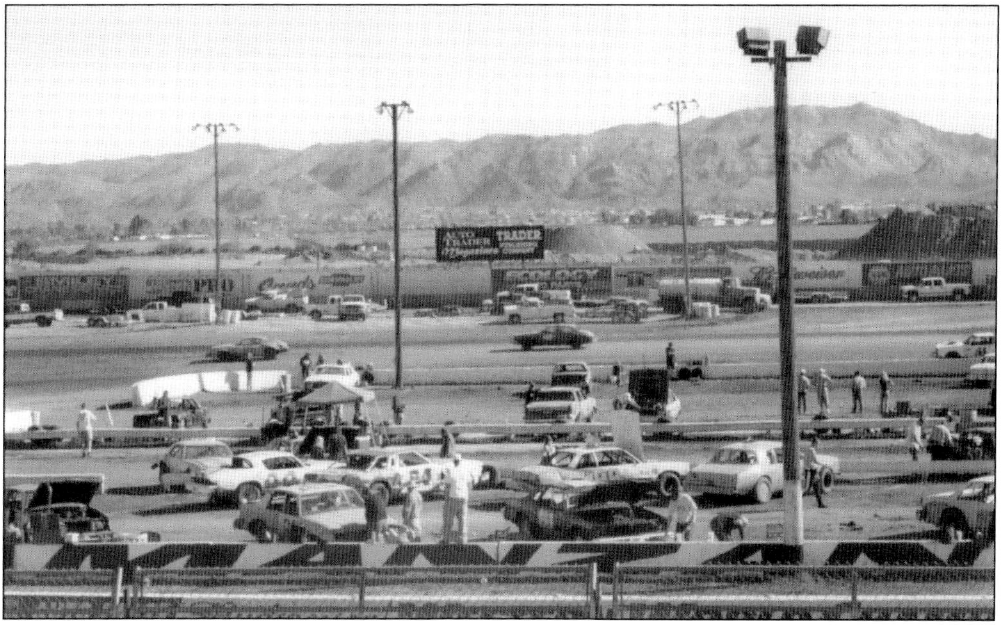

Upon entering the grandstands, the fans faced the infield, which was where all the race cars were parked. Circling the pits was a third-mile banked track, and encompassing that was the half-mile track. Both the short track and the half-mile track were considered very fast tracks by race-car drivers, with drivers hitting top speeds of about 85 miles per hour on the short track and 125 miles per hour on the half mile. (Courtesy of James A. Fargo.)

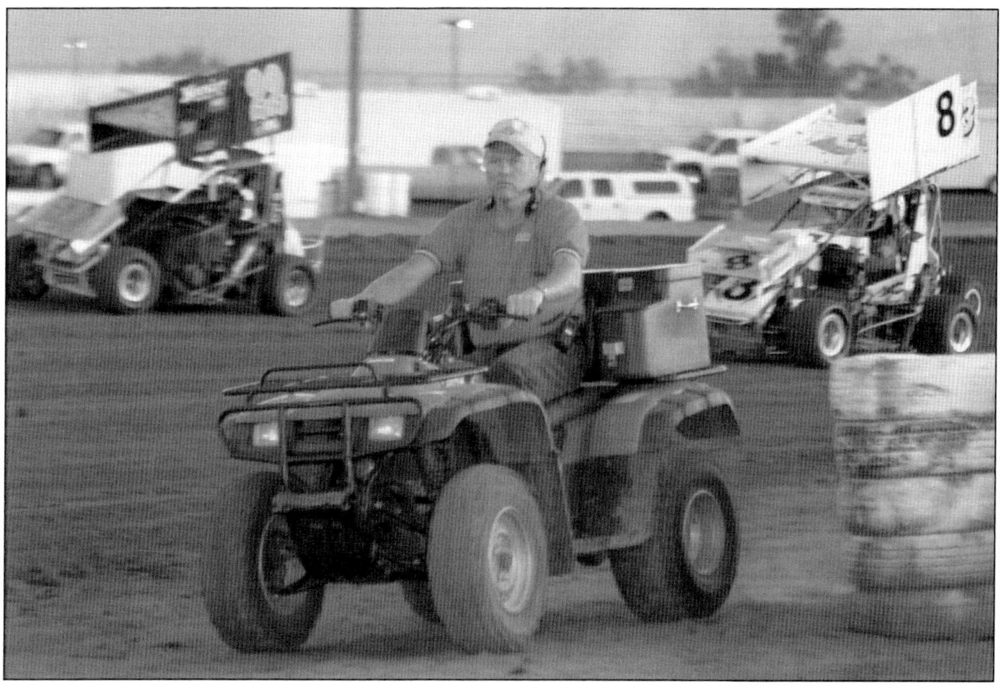

As the winged mini sprints prepare for a parade lap before a race on June 9, 2007, pit steward Rick Setser races off the track on his four-wheeler, a familiar sight during the last days of Manzy. (Courtesy of Don Iverson.)

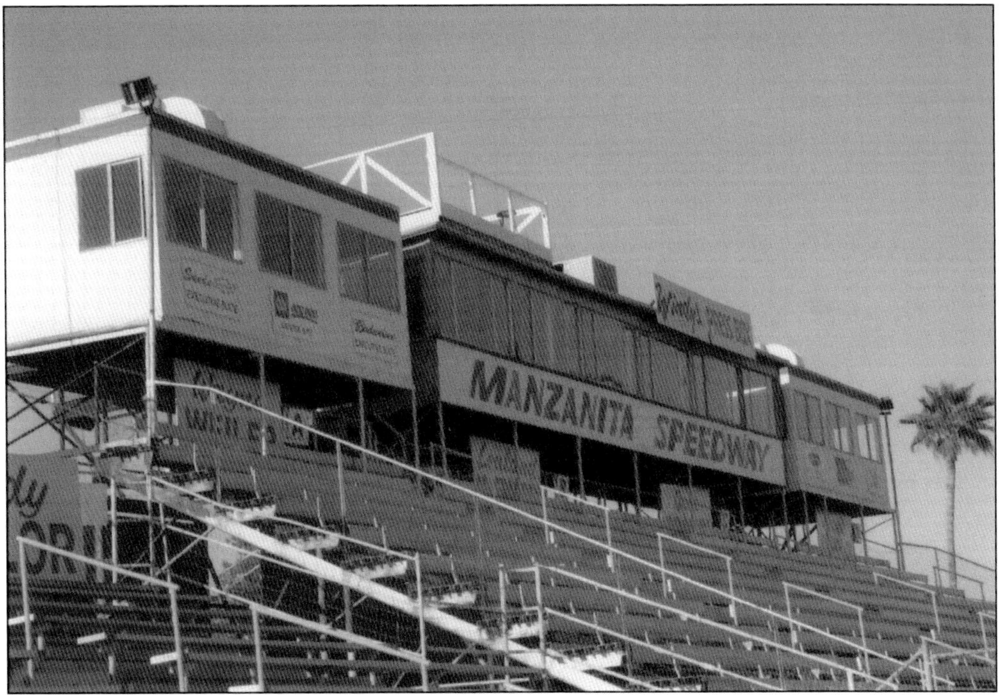

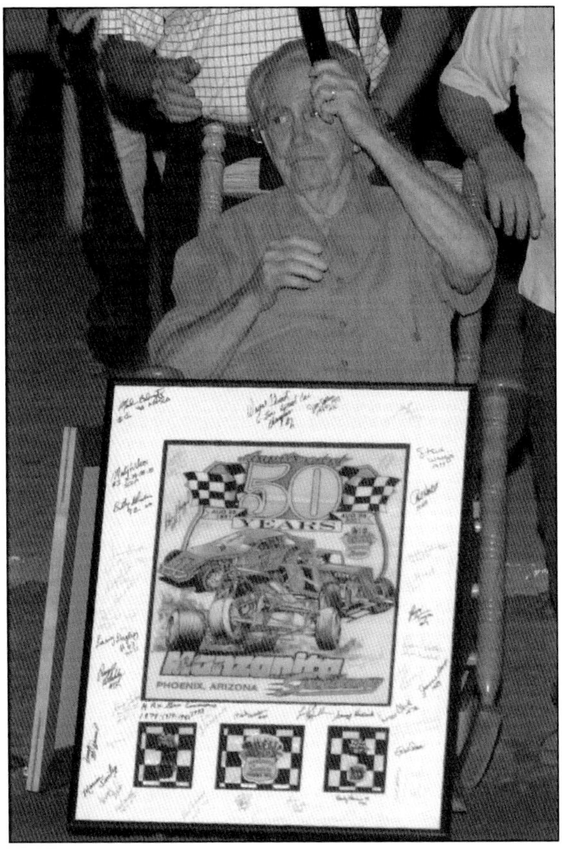

Sitting atop the grandstands was the press box and VIP boxes, shown above. At left, announcer Windy McDonald, Manzanita Speedway's Hall of Famer, ruled the press box for over 50 years and was the "voice" known to all dirt-track fans in Phoenix and the surrounding Valley of the Sun. In recognition of his service to Manzy and the racing community, McDonald was honored prior to the track's closing with the award of the old rocking chair and his own special night at the races. (Above, courtesy of James A. Fargo; left, courtesy of Don Iverson.)

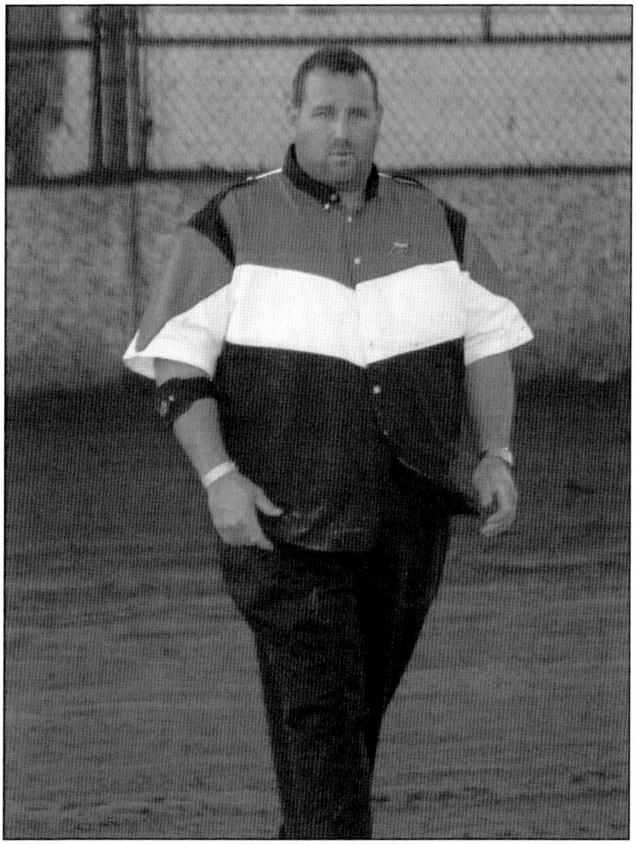

At right, Chris Odom, one of the flagmen at Manzy since 1987, strolls across the main straightaway from the flag stand toward the pits. Odom was associated with Manzy from his youth, selling programs and concessions and working with the fire safety crew. The photograph below is of Odom in his super stock. Chris began in the Bomber Division in 1988, moving to factory stocks, and, later, super stocks. At times during his career, Odom and his wife, Tammy, have shared driving duties. (Both, courtesy of Don Iverson.)

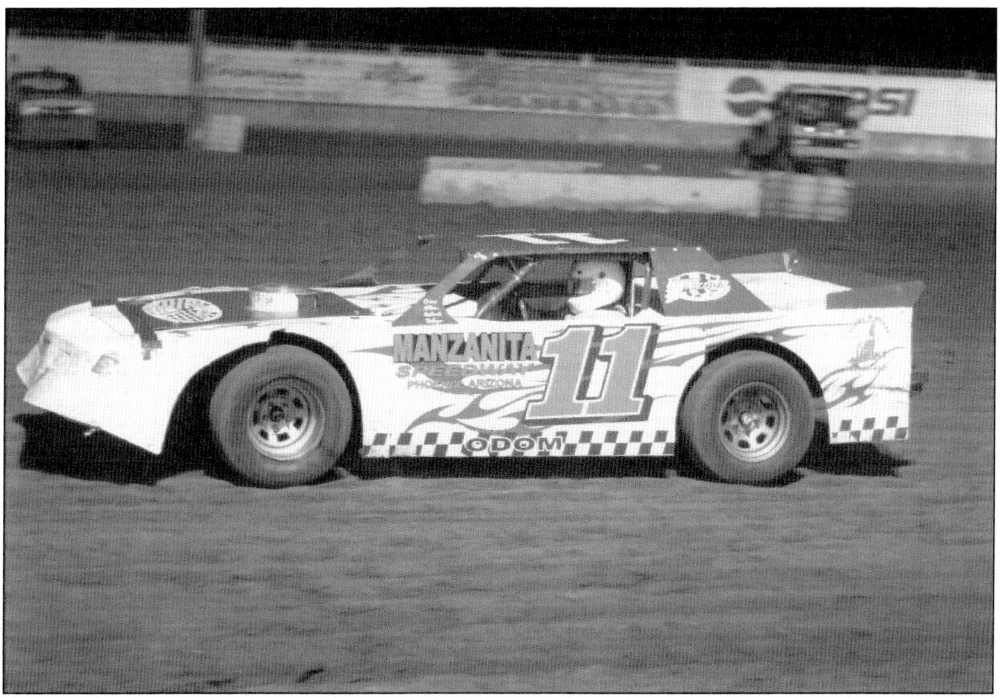

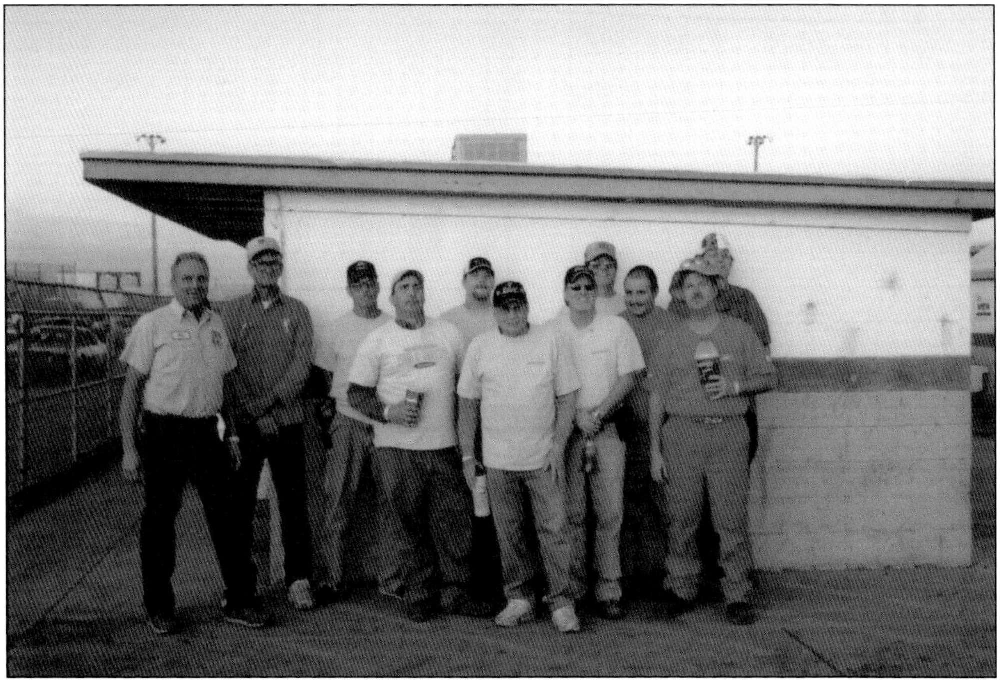

Pictured here from left to right are the employees who made Manzy safe for the racers: Phil Hertel and Don Appley, both of Sunoco Race Fuels; Bobby Dodd, Randy Allen, Steve Dunn, Gerald Tuscano, Steve Grant, Don Case, and Bubba Dodd, the fire and safety team; Geoff Kozel, tow truck; and Peter Blanchard, fire and safety. (Courtesy of James A. Fargo.)

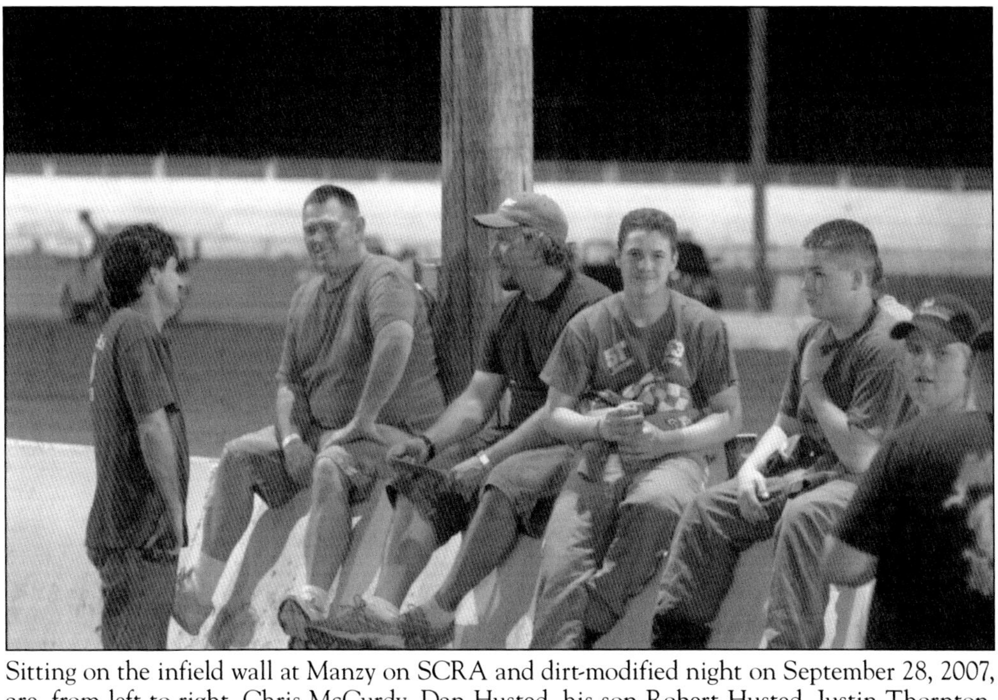

Sitting on the infield wall at Manzy on SCRA and dirt-modified night on September 28, 2007, are, from left to right, Chris McCurdy, Dan Husted, his son Robert Husted, Justin Thornton, Chris McCurdy Jr., and Josh Crabtree. (Courtesy of Don Iverson.)

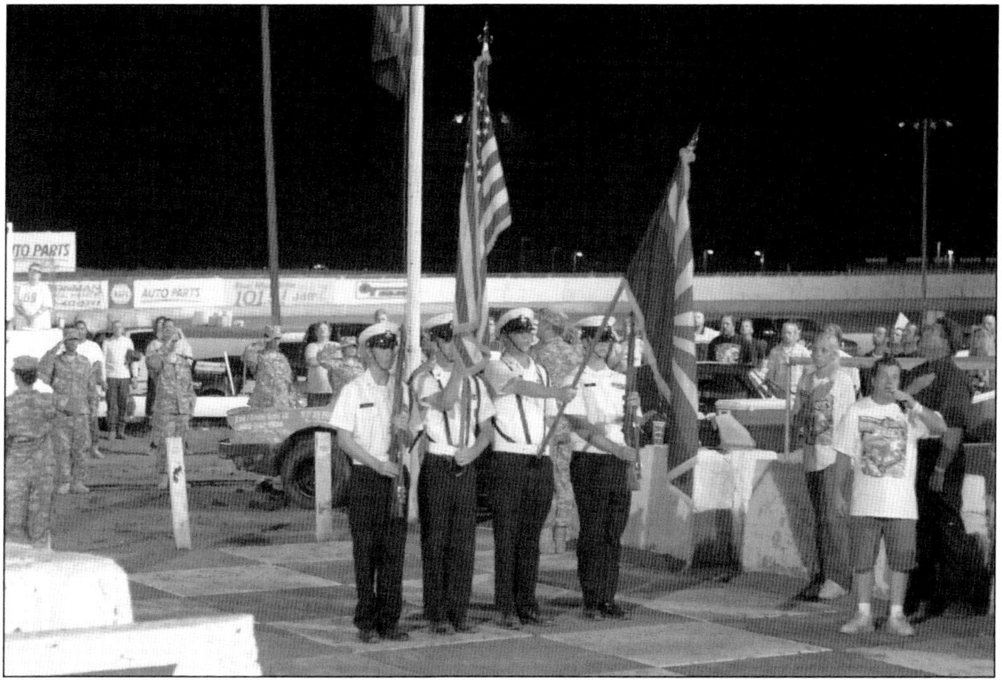

The Manzy racing community always stands up for the troops; actually, many race-car drivers are themselves military veterans. This photograph depicts a special ceremony to honor the US armed forces on October 4, 2008. (Courtesy of Don Iverson.)

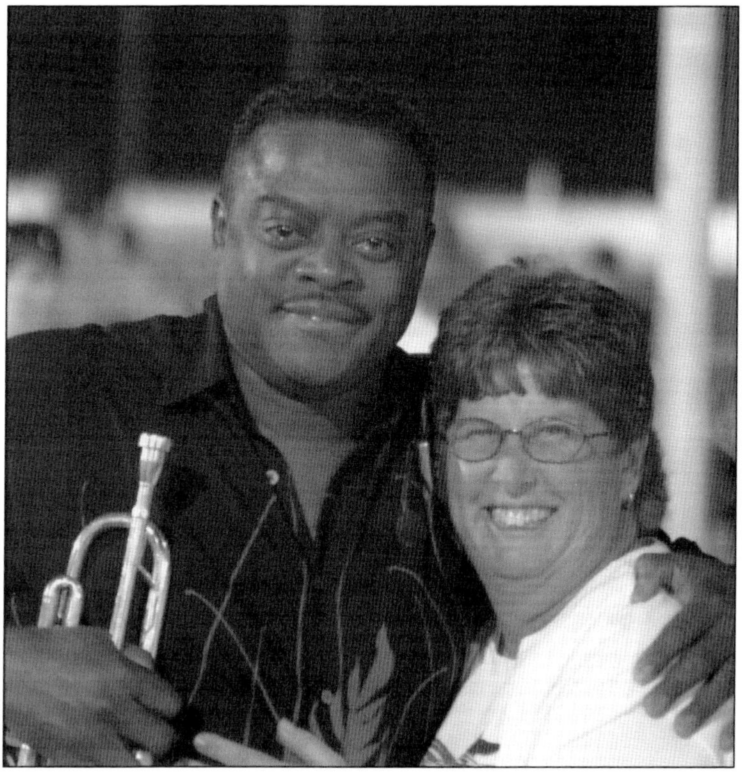

Dr. Jesse McGuire and Tammy Odom are seen at the Western World Championships on November 11, 2007. Odom is a fixture at the Manzy scoreboard, while Dr. McGuire, a Phoenix resident, is a world-renowned trumpet player, composer, minister, and author. (Courtesy of Don Iverson.)

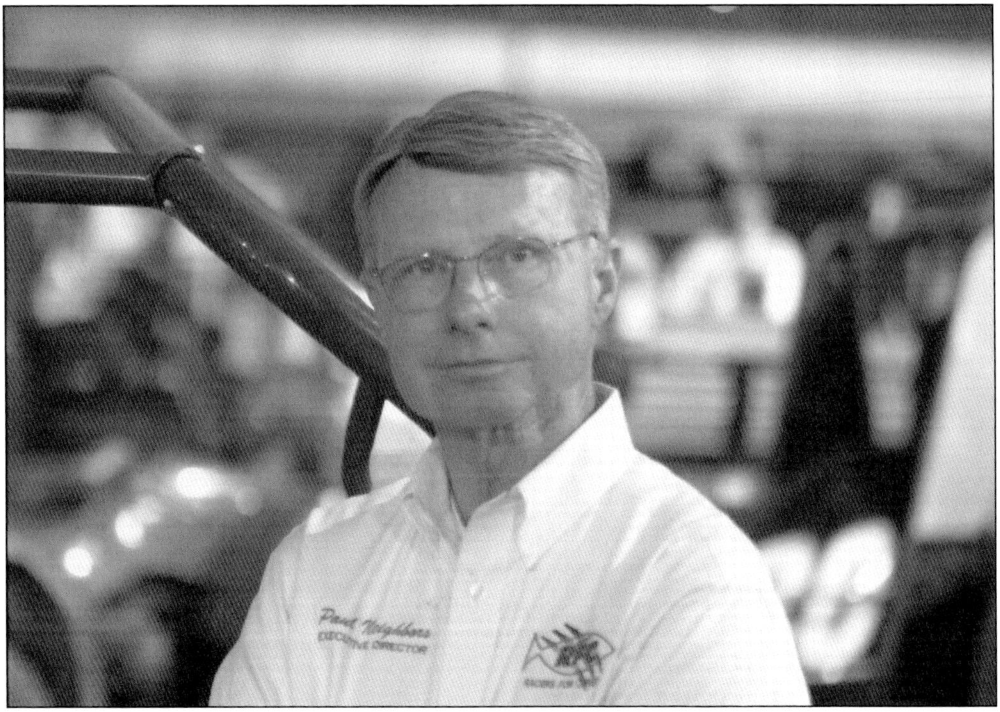

All of Manzy's racing events were preceded by an invocation by Racers for Christ, a nationwide nonprofit religious organization that serves the racing community. Phoenix-area executive director Paul Neighbors is shown here presiding over a Manzy event. Neighbors was special to the local racing community as he was a racer himself, competing in the Bomber Division at Manzy. (Courtesy of Don Iverson.)

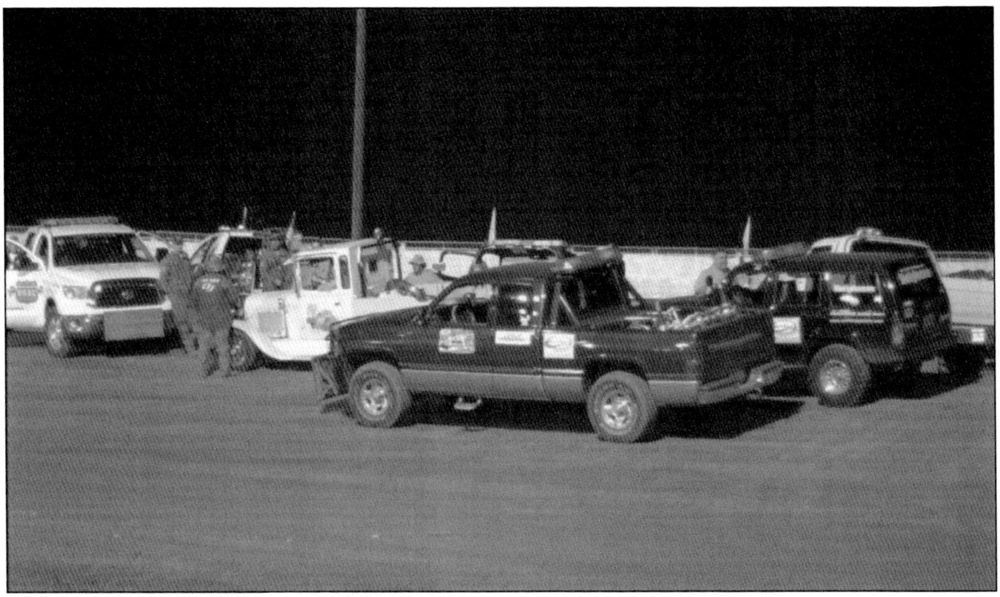

No racing event can be held without the services of a trained and certified safety crew. These team members volunteer their efforts to ensure a safe event. Shown here is the safety crew at the last Copper on Dirt race in 2009. (Courtesy of Don Iverson.)

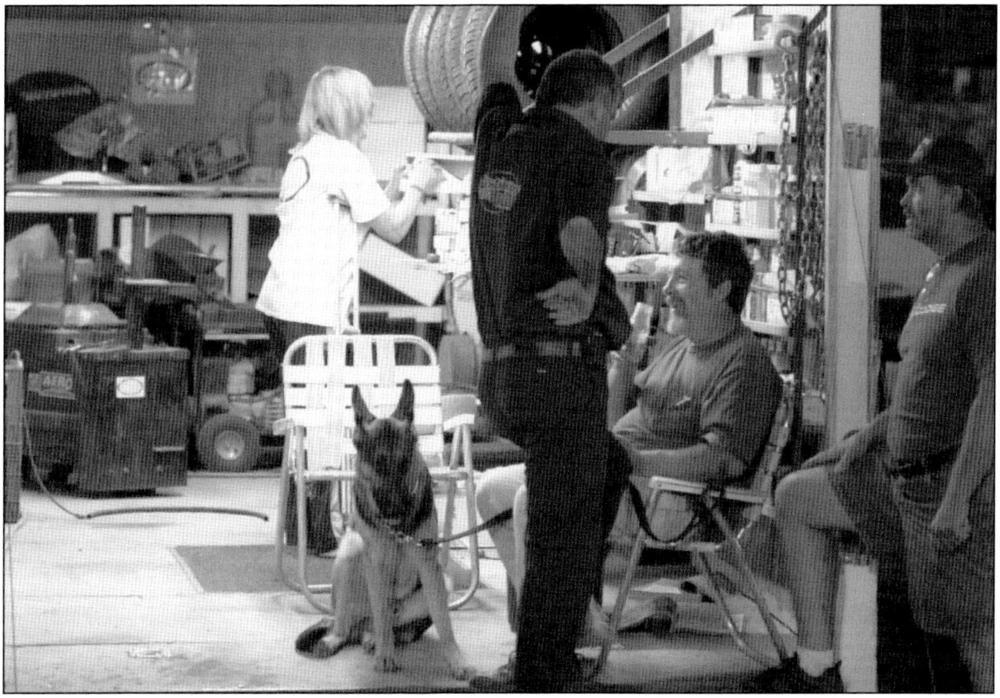

Kathy and Joe Sarginger operated the mobile racing parts store at all Manzy events. Regardless of how many tools and supplies the pit crews bring to the track, something is always missing, and Joe and Kathy are there to bridge the gap. In addition, Joe Sarginger is a hard-charger in the Super Stock Division. Those pictured are, from left to right, Kathy Sarginger, Richard Kirn, Joe Sarginger, and Joe Atkinson, president of the SCRA. (Courtesy of Don Iverson.)

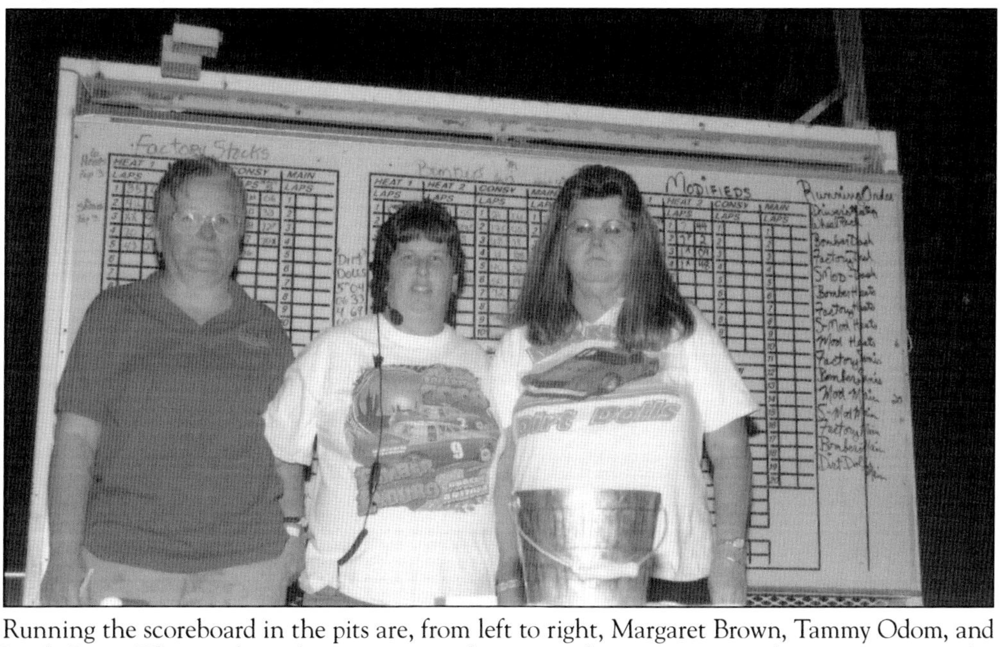

Running the scoreboard in the pits are, from left to right, Margaret Brown, Tammy Odom, and Linda Price. This is where the racers go to determine their positions in the race events as the evening unfolds. (Courtesy of James A. Fargo.)

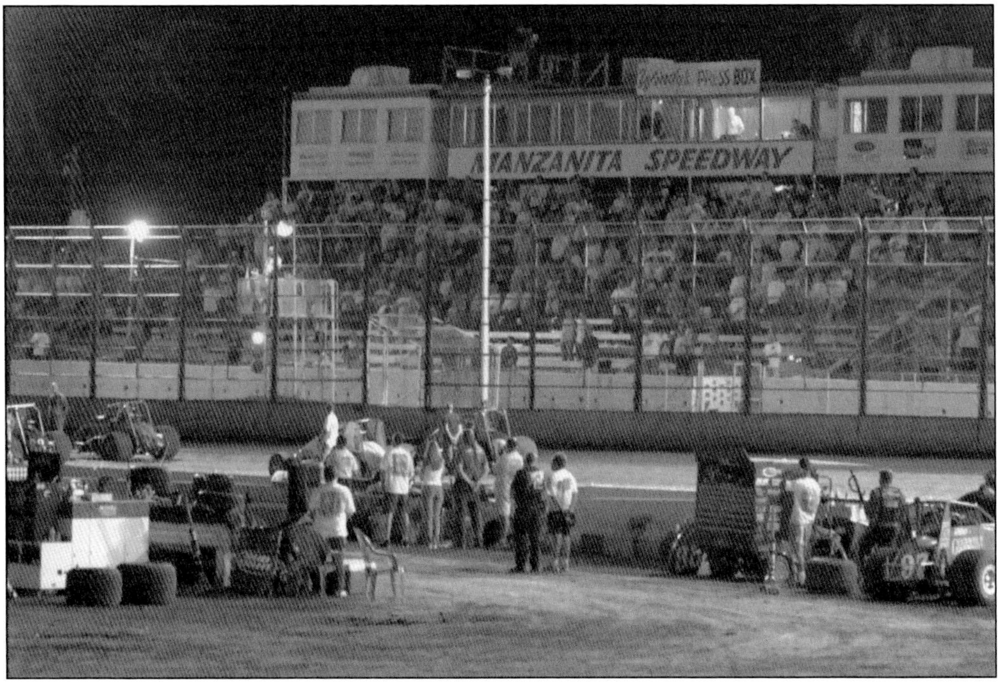

This view from the pits shows the race cars lined up on the front straightaway at a USAC race on September 22, 2007. The fans and teams in the pits stand in preparation for the national anthem. (Courtesy of Don Iverson.)

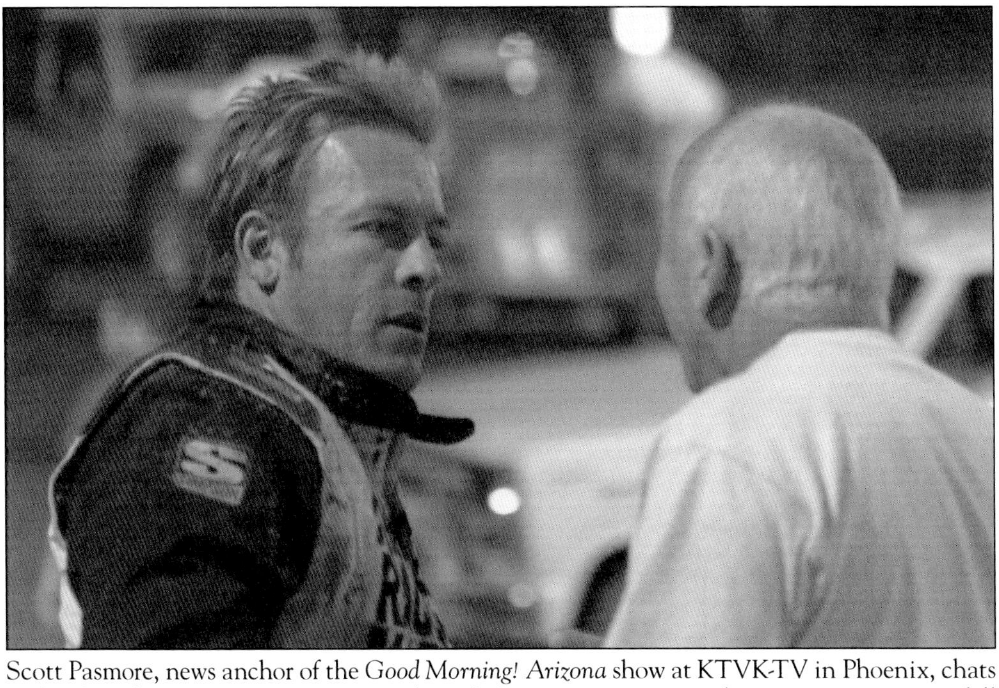

Scott Pasmore, news anchor of the *Good Morning! Arizona* show at KTVK-TV in Phoenix, chats with a fan after a race. Pasmore, somewhat of a Renaissance man with many interests, is in full race regalia. In addition to being an award-winning journalist, he is into sprint cars, motorcycles, airplanes, and boats. (Courtesy of Don Iverson.)

"I'm really a frustrated chef, but I'm pretty good at it," says Don Iverson, who finished up as Manzy's official photographer in 2009. His father, Carl Iverson's, career was the US Air Force, but he was also an amateur photographer, and his sister Carlyn Iverson was a professional illustrator and photographer. "I guess the arts are in my genes," said Iverson, who now runs www.classickmotorart.com. (Courtesy of Don Iverson.)

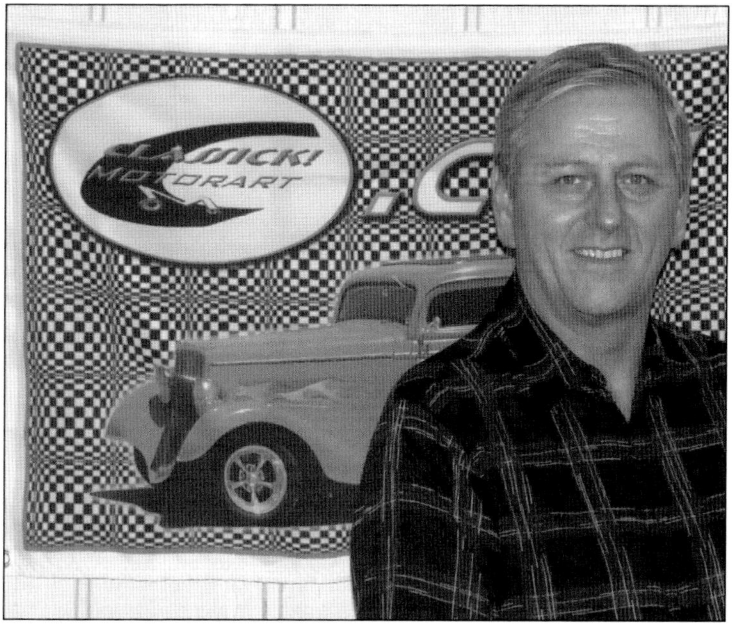

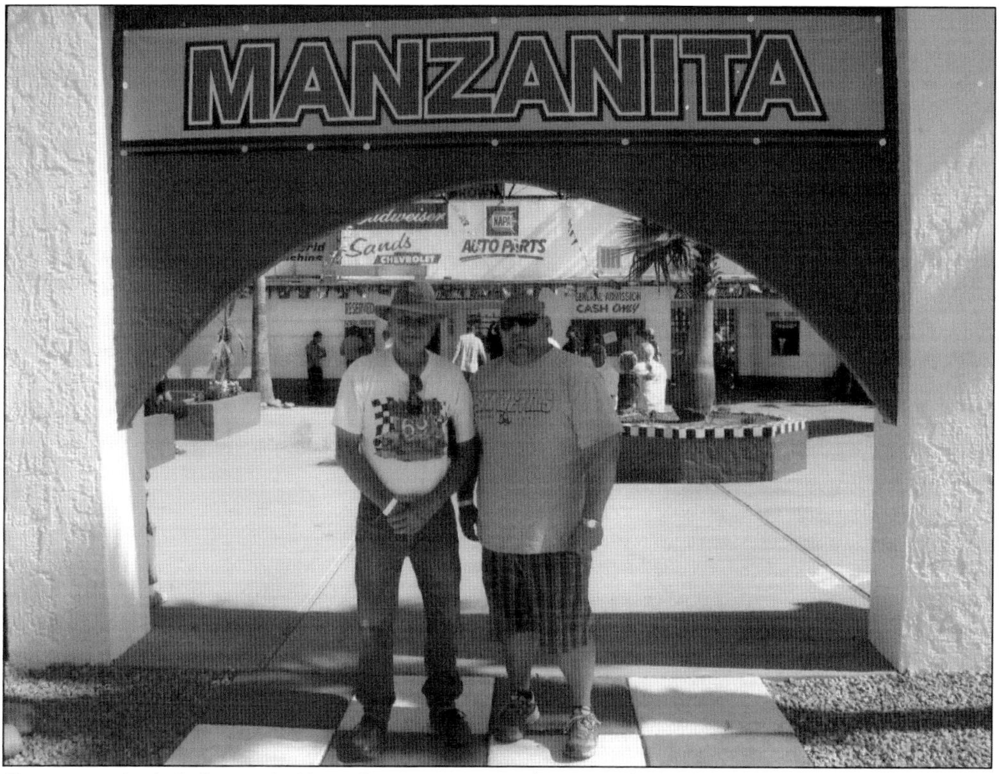

Shown on the left, James A. Fargo began racing go-karts in the mid-1960s, winning the Arizona Karting Association Championship two years running in 1966 and 1967. Later, he raced late models in Tucson. Fargo became a photographer in the 1960s after receiving a camera as a birthday gift. He shot at Phoenix International Raceway from 1988 to 2000 before moving to Manzy as official track photographer from 2001 to 2006. (Courtesy of James A. Fargo.)

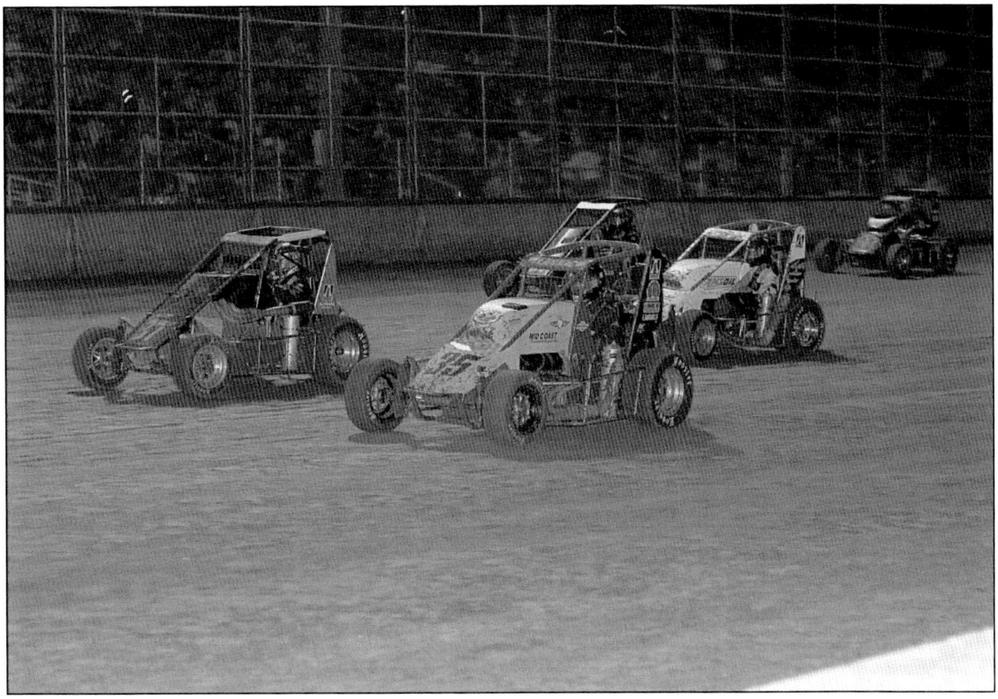

Shown above are midget cars on parade at the final 2009 Copper on Dirt race. Below, 24-year-old Brad Sweet of Grass Valley, California, celebrates his win in the final Copper on Dirt midget race in 2009. Sweet made it two in a row by winning the transported Copper on Dirt at USA Raceway in Tucson in 2010. Sweet drives for NASCAR star Kasey Kahne Racing. (Both, courtesy of Don Iverson.)

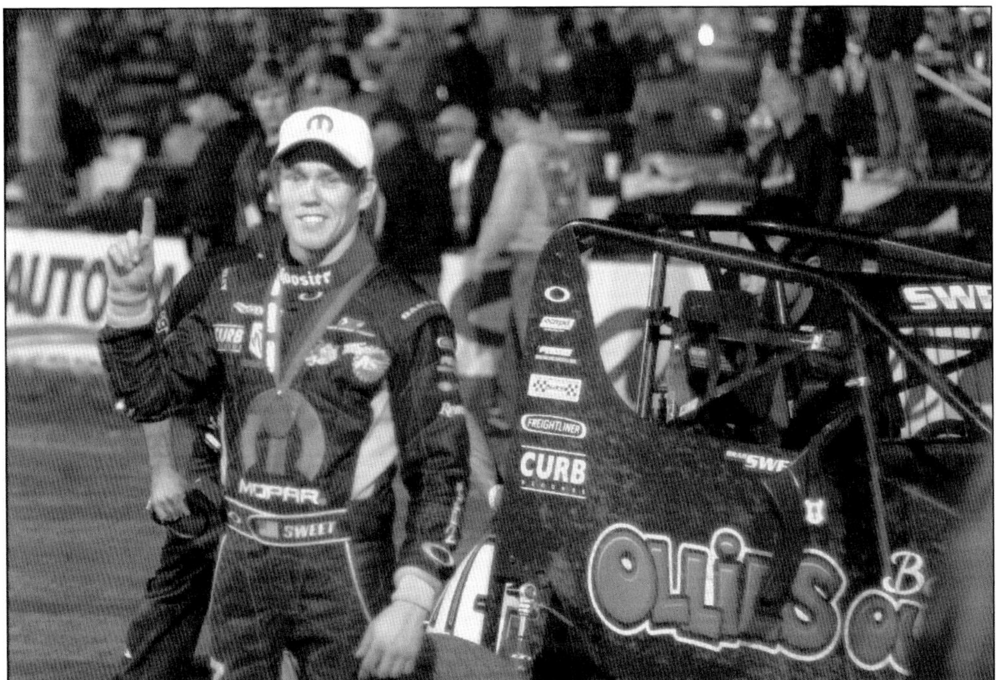

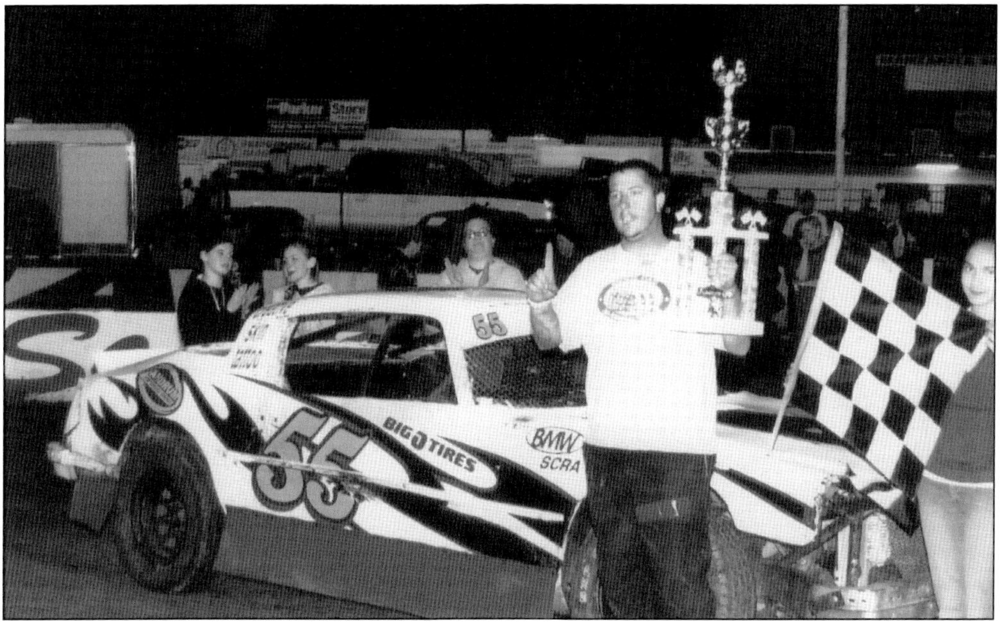

Every racer in Arizona wanted to win the last stock-car race at Manzy on April 9, 2009. The honor went to Joey McCullough, shown standing next to his 1979 Chevrolet Camaro and hoisting up the last stock-car trophy at the end of Manzy's 58-year run. Although McCullough was a long shot to win the last race against the best competition in Arizona, his credentials included the 2006 SCRA Rookie of the Year award. (Courtesy of Mary McCullough.)

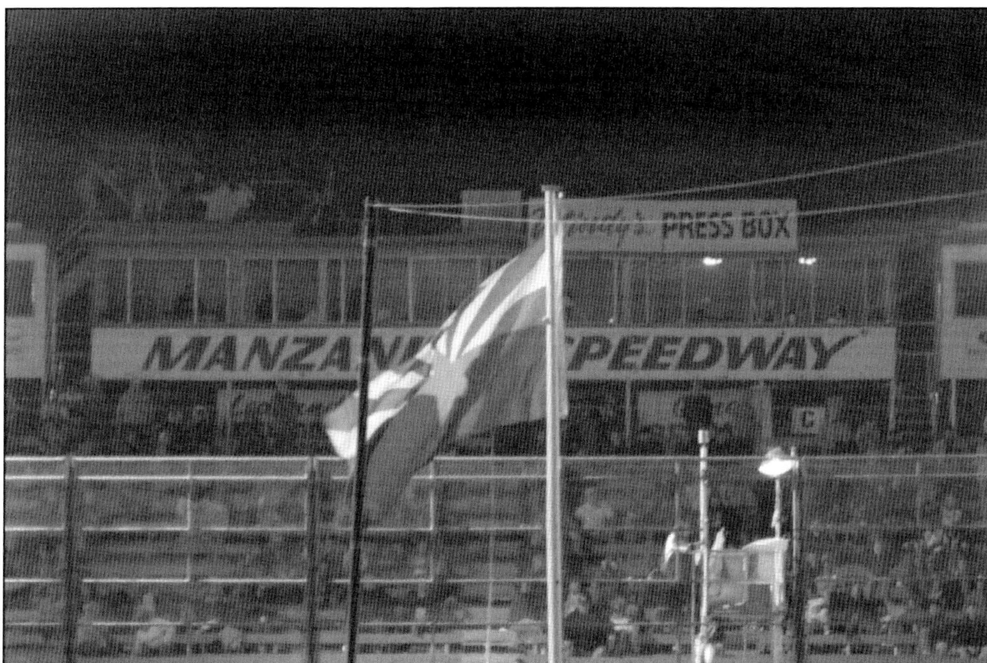

As the lights go out on Manzanita Speedway on April 12, 2009, for the last time, one thinks of Phil Hertel, a part-time announcer at the track, who always closed with, "I want to thank all of you for being a part of the legend that is . . . Manzanita Speedway." (Courtesy of Don Iverson.)